HOW TO GO TO HEAVEN 3

According to the Mind, Body & Spirit

Compiled and Edited by
Craig L. Kelley

On-Demand Publishing, LLC
CreateSpace.com
Charleston, SC

How to Go to Heaven 3: According to the Mind, Body & Spirit

Compiled and Edited by Craig L Kelley

Copyright 2014 Craig L Kelley

ISBN-13:9781499708455
ISBN-10:1499708459
Library of Congress Control Number (LCCN):

http://CraigLKelley.com

CreateSpace Independent Publishing Platform
North Charleston, South Carolina, USA

Preface

This book is a compilation of fifteen years of research into many diverse areas that I think and feel are important to know if one wants to spiritually evolve and ascend to heaven in the afterlife. Some of my areas of study include the following: theology; comparative religions; metaphysics, physics, and quantum physics; psychology, parapsychology, and transpersonal psychology; mind, body, and spirit; consciousness, cosmic consciousness, and cosmology; philosophy; the esoteric, mysteries and mystical teachings of antiquity; energy, vibrations, and matter; our creation and the Creator; our evolution and spiritual evolution; non-locality, parallel worlds, the universe, and multiverses; the afterlife, the spiritual central universe, superuniverses, heaven and Paradise. This book is a dictionary of words, terms, phrases and some important subject areas related to God's world that I think are important to understand if one wants to acquire a cosmic consciousness and go to heaven more knowledgeably.

Explaining how you can go to heaven is a little complicated and very difficult for me to explain and foretell: What happens in the afterlife and how we go to heaven has pretty much always been a mystery; most aspects and definitions of God, the afterlife and theology have been left up to speculations. It would be a little presumptuous for me to profess that I know how each and every person on planet Earth can go to heaven, since your path to heaven may be affected by your consciousness, current belief system, faith in God and willingness to do thy Father's will, your spiritual evolutionary plan and path, your knowledge of cosmic consciousness, and a number of other complex and difficult to understand factors. But I have compiled, from numerous sources, definitions of a number of words, terms and concepts that may *help* you go to heaven more expediently, knowledge that may help you spiritually ascend to the heavens and Paradise in the most expeditious manner.

The following words, terms, phrases and concepts are intended for the purpose of expanding one's knowledge of our potential consciousness of the mind, body and spirit in our ascent to Heaven.

Craig L. Kelley

Notes to the Reader

The Urantia Book (1955) was authored by spiritual beings and commissions of spiritual beings, and was channeled through a sleeping subject living in Chicago in the early 1900s.

Each citation or reference to *The Urantia Book* (1955), in the following work, will note the page and paragraph number, i.e., the first reference of a subject or term will use the style (*The Urantia Book*, 1955, 1008:2), indicating the source, page number 1008, and paragraph 2. Secondary references of *The Urantia Book* will only cite the page and paragraph number, i.e. (1008:3).

Some words are italicized, in the following work, per this editor, for emphasis to the subject at hand. Words italicized in the original *The Urantia Book* have been retained in the below work.

Some of the abbreviations used in the following work include the following:

<u>Languages</u>
Arab. - Arabic
Lat. or L. - Latin
Chin. - Chinese
Gk. - Greek
Heb. - Hebrew
Jap. - Japanese
Skt. - Sanskrit
<u>Other Abbreviations</u>
B. - *Babli* (Babylonian Talmud)
P. or J. - Palestinian or Jerusalem Talmud
R. - Rabbi
eccles. - ecclesiastical
e.g. - for example
i.e. - that is to say
s.v. - "(Origin from L. *sub voce* or *sub verbo*, lit. 'under the word or voice'). (in textual reference) under the word or heading given." (*The Concise Oxford Dictionary*, 1999).

Disclaimer and Advance Apology

I have tried to follow the writing style suggested in Kate L. Turabian's *A Manual for Writers of Research Papers, Theses, and Dissertations*, 8th edition, Chicago, IL: The University of Chicago Press, 2013.

It has always been my intention to quote material exactly as published in the source material, except as noted above with *The*

Urantia Book material (utilizing a slightly different reference style).

Most of the below material was written in WordPerfect 12 (WP) and then translated into Microsoft Word 2010 before uploading to CreateSpace for publication in PDF format. Some characters in WP (most notably quotation marks, apostrophes, and some dictionary symbols) have not translated well in the process of publishing. I've tried to correct all errors before publication but some may have slipped through, un-noticed until printing, even though multiple proof reading and editing passes have transpired. So I'm apologizing ahead of time for any errors you may notice in the below work.

Introduction

Heaven, and the idea of going to heaven or ascending to heaven in the afterlife can be viewed from many perspectives: 1. Going to heaven can be viewed from one's faith and beliefs under the umbrella of theology; 2. from the viewpoint of various religions; and 3. from the mind, body and spirit, in our ascent to Heaven.

Everyone has a soul, while living their physical life on planet Earth, regardless of whether or not they believe in God or have a religious faith.

I believe one can ascend to the heavens without any religious beliefs or faith. All you need is your soul and hang on for the ride, for the journey to heaven may be a long path into eternity.

I believe our mind, intellect, personality and degree of cosmic consciousness can affect how fast we journey through the heavens, and hopefully to Paradise.

I believe we should improve our level of consciousness in matters of the mind, body and spirit in this lifetime so we can ascend to Heaven and Paradise quicker than ever imagined. Read on brothers and sisters in the spirit of love.

A

a priori "based on theoretical deduction rather than empirical observation." (*The Concise Oxford Dictionary*, 1999).

Absolute space "Newton's view of space; envisions space as unchanging and independent of its contents." (Greene, 2004, 537).

Absolute spacetime "View of space emerging from special relativity; envisions space through the entirety of time, from any perspective, as unchanging and independent of its contents." (Greene 2004, 537).

Afterlife "1 (in some religions) life after death. 2 later life." (*The Concise Oxford Dictionary*, 1999).

"The condition awaiting humans and the cosmos after death or at the end of time. Beliefs vary greatly between religions, though in origin the major continuing religious traditions, both East and West, had no belief that there would be a worthwhile existence after death. They could not deny that in some sense there is a trace of the dead, in memory or dreams, or in the resemblance of offspring to ancestors; but whatever state the dead may be in, it is a condition of extreme weakness, in which all connection with God and with the living is cut off, and certainly to be avoided or postponed as long as possible: it is, in Sophocles' words, *ton apotropon Haidan*, Hades to be shunned. The most militant reaction to this occurred in China, in the quest for immortality; and gradually both traditions came to realize that there may be [something] about us that does endure through the process of time and therefore perhaps through the event of death." (*The Oxford Dictionary of World Religions*, 1997).

"The Jewish tradition has come to believe that the life of human beings continues through death, and that there will be a consummation of the purposes of God in the messianic age. But in the biblical period, there was no such belief until the very latest time. Then it seemed incoherent to have experienced the faithfulness (*hesed*) of God in creation and history, and to suppose that God was incapable of continuing it beyond death. The dead had been thought to maintain nothing but a shadowy existence beneath the earth in Sheol, with all relations with God severed. For that reason, the Sadducees, relying on the absence of such teaching in Torah, could deny resurrection. In the later biblical books and in the apocryphal literature, the doctrine of the resurrection of the dead emerges, and the 1st cent. CE philosopher Philo taught that the individual soul was immortal. In the Talmudic period, the rabbis had many opinions, but in general it was believed that after the messianic redemption, the person would be reconstituted before judgment and the righteous would enjoy God's presence forever. The wicked, however, would be punished. In the Middle Ages, Maimonides taught that the belief in the resurrection of the dead was a fundamental principle of the Jewish faith, but some philosophers understood immortality in terms of the intellectual contemplation of God while others claimed it was the love of God which was all important. Today, Orthodox Jews still maintain a belief in bodily resurrection, but most Reform Jews are only concerned with spiritual survival. The Jewish equivalent of hell is derived from the mundane 'valley of Hinnom', Gehinnom, Gk., Gehenna." (Ibid).

"Christian beliefs were formed in the context of acute Jewish debates, in the period of the second Temple, about the likelihood and nature of the afterlife, and are controlled by the astonished and grateful acceptance of the resurrection of Jesus Christ. Jesus himself had affirmed belief in life after death, arguing against the Sadducees, but not going into detail. Early Christianity put together the two Jewish forms of speculation, thereby talking of the resurrection of the body, but also of the continuing life of the soul in the interval before the resurrection body is restored to it--a 'gap' which eventually allowed the doctrine of purgatory. The New Testament is not detailed in its descriptions of the afterlife, apart from the visionary poetry of the Book of Revelations. Heaven and hell are filled out somewhat in later Christian imagination, but there remains a necessary agnosticism as regards detail in Christian accounts. It has become an issue (of universalism) in Christianity whether hell is an eternal condition, or whether the objectivity of Christ's atonement will eventually bring all to salvation." (Ibid).

"The afterlife in Islam is known as *al-akhira*. The Muslim understanding of the afterlife is based on vivid and literal pictures in the Quran. After an interval in the grave (barzakh), the dead will be raised by the summoning angels, Munkar and Nakir, and, with souls and bodies reunited, will be taken to the day of judgment (*yaum al-din*). Deeds will be weighed so exactly that nothing will be overlooked, even to the weight of the thread on a date-stone. The intercession of Muhammad will help those who are on an exact balance. Those for whom the judgment is adverse will burn in fire (*jahannam*: see Hell, Islam) with new skins beings prepared for them when the old are scorched. The fire may not be eternal (the issue is disputed). Those for whom the judgment is favorable will enter the Garden, with cool streams and beautiful maidens (*hur*); how far

8

these are to be understood metaphorically is again an issue." (Ibid).

"The early understanding in India of human nature and its destiny much resemble in attitude those of the Jewish Bible. The Vedic imagination could conceive only of this life as a place of guaranteed worth, though they recognized that the gods worked hard (with the help of sacrifices) at maintaining their own (limited) immortality; and that death had been handed over to Yama as a part of this process. According to *Taittiriya Brahmana* 3.9.15.53-56, 'through special sacrifices, the gods became immortal. Death was apprehensive: What shall be my portion? They said, None shall be immortal in the body...Those who do not know or do not perform this sacrificial action will come to life again and again after death, and become food for Death.' This revolutionary passage introduces a hint of an immortal soul and of recurrent rebirth (*samsara*). Neither samsara nor atman as immortal soul are present in the Vedas. The advance to atman was made in the Brahmanas and Aranyakas via prana, breath--the recognition that prana is the support of life. Prana is like the logos in the W., since it not only supports life, but is the creator of sound..., and becomes equated with Brahman as creator. Thus the life-principle in humans (and other manifestations) is eventually believed to be not other than the undying Brahman--so that atman is Brahman. A transitional passage in the *Sankhayana Aranyaka* (3.1-7) describes the soul's reception in heaven, coming in the end before Brahman who says, 'That which you are, that I am'--an anticipation of the mahavakyas of the Upanisads. In these early texts, Brahman oscillates between the masculine and neuter (i.e. between being understood personally and impersonally, e.g. *Aitareya Aranyaka* 2.6.1; 3.2.2-4), a division which was formalized and never reconciled in subsequent faith. On the one side (advaita), the afterlife is a final realization that there is no other than Brahman, so that the afterlife is as a drop merged with the entire ocean; on the other side (e.g. the theistic religion of the Saivites and the Vaisnavites, and indeed virtually the whole of Hinduism as lived), the afterlife is a personal relation with the object of devotion in this life; the 'heaven' thus attained is variously described. For both positions, rebirth has become an evil to be brought to an end. The many hells belong firmly within the process of rebirth, not to any eternal destiny--an understanding which is true of Eastern religions in general." (Ibid).

"For Jain, the afterlife is mapped onto a cosmography in which the Middle World includes the part inhabited by humans. Below are a series of hells of increasing unpleasantness; above are a

9

series of heavens of increasing brightness, including the abode of the gods. But those heavens are not the desirable state: this is the Isatpragbhara, the slightly curved (shaped somewhat like curved space in a parabola), where the jivas which have ceased to be encumbered by bodies abide." (Ibid).

"Buddhists pressed further in resisting the Hindu move toward an eternal atman. While there is continuity of consequence through samsara, there is no eternal and undying subject of this process (anatman). The process may move through heavens and hells, but these are no 'abiding city'. They are, nevertheless, vividly described, and are often the goals (or avoidances) in practice of the majority of Buddhists, for whom the ultimate goal of nirvana is too remote. It was this observation which led M. Spiro to describe Buddhism as a religion of proximate and ultimate salvation (*Buddhism and Society*). The afterlife may involve being reborn as an animal or attaining the condition of arhat: between the two, many Theravadin Buddhist aim for a better outcome in the next birth without aiming too far. In Mahayana, the realization of the ultimate goal was brought closer within reach, particularly through devotion to bodhisattvas, whose role it is to save all sentient beings. This is dramatically illustrated in devotion to Amida/Amithaba. The heavens described in devotional Buddhism (e.g. Sukhavati) are as attractive as the Garden of Islam. While sharing Hindus' presuppositions about rebirth, Sikh teaching emphasizes the possibility of attaining mukti during one's present life." (Ibid).

"In the case of the religious traditions, both East and West, the development of beliefs in an afterlife was tentative and extremely reluctant to advance beyond the evidence of experience in this life. Once those beliefs had become established, attempts were often then made to use them as coercive instruments in the control of human behavior. Even humans have remained robustly resistant to the misuse of the largely unknown, continuing to behave in ways that are scarcely consistent with the knowledge of hell and heaven." (Ibid).

Age "1 the length of time that a person or thing has existed; a particular stage in someone's life; old age. 2 a distinct period of history; a division of geological time that is a subdivision of an epoch. (archaic) a lifetime taken as a measure of time..." (*The Concise Oxford Dictionary*, 1999).

Air "One of the four alchemical elements, the others being Fire, Water, and Earth. The spirits of Air were known as sylphs. The three astrological signs linked to Air are Gemini, Libra, and

Aquarius." (Drury, 2002, 6).

Ajna "To know, to perceive, and to command. The name of the sixth chakra." (Judith, 1999, 413).

Akasha "(Origin from Skt. *akasa*). (chiefly in Hinduism) a supposed all-pervading field in the ether in which a record of past events is imprinted." (*The Concise Oxford Dictionary*, 1999).

"Ether, space, vacuity; the place where traces of all existence and events remain." (Judith, 1999, 414).

"Akasha...is the Sanskrit word meaning 'aether' in both its elemental and metaphysical senses." ("Akasha," *Wikipedia*).

"In Hinduism, Akasha means the basis and essence of all things in the material world; the first material element created from the astral world (Air, Fire, Water, Earth are the other four in sequence). It is one of the *Panchamahabhuta*, or 'five elements'... In Sanskrit the word means 'space', the very first element in creation..." (Ibid).

In Jainism, "Akasha is space in the Jain conception of the cosmos. It falls into the *Ajiva* category, divided into two parts: *Loakasa* (the part occupied by the material world) and *Aloakasa* (the space beyond it which is absolutely void and empty). In *Loakasa* the universe forms only a part. Akasha is that which gives space and makes room for the existence of all extended substances." (Ibid).

"In Buddhist phenomenology Akasha is divided into limited space (*akasa-dhatu*) and endless space (*ajatakasa*)." (Ibid).

"The Western religious philosophy called Theosophy has popularized the word Akasha as an adjective, through the use of the term 'Akashic records' or 'Akashic library', referring to an ethereal compendium of all knowledge and history." (Ibid).

"From a Sanskrit word meaning 'luminous', but referring to 'essence' or 'space', *Akasha* is one of the five Hindu elements: the black egg of Spirit." (Drury, 2004, 7).

"*Akasha* (akasa), Skt.; the all-pervasive, space (Pali, akasa); in Buddhism understood not as in Hinduism as a substantial 'ether' but as space. Two kinds of space are distinguished: (1) space limited by corporeality and (2) unlimited space. The former belongs to the corporeality aggregate (*skandha*); the latter is one of the six elements (*dhatu*), possesses no substance whatsoever, yet is the basic condition for any corporeal extension and is the container for all materiality manifesting through the four elements--earth, water, fire, air. It is emptiness, free from admixture with material things; unchangeable, imperishable, and beyond all description." (*The*

Shambhala Dictionary of Buddhism and Zen, 1991).

"*Akasha* (a-ka-sha) is a Sanskrit word meaning 'ether': all-pervasive space. Originally signifying 'radiation' or 'brilliance,' in Indian philosophy *akasha* was considered the first and most fundamental of the five elements--the others being *vata* (air), *agni* (fire), *ap* (water), and *prithivi* (earth). *Akasha* embraces the properties of all five elements: it is the womb from which everything we perceive with our senses has emerged and into which everything will ultimately re-descend..." (Laszlo, 2004, xi).

"*Akasha*...is so subtle that in itself it's beyond ordinary perception. But when it has taken form, we can perceive it..." (Ibid, 4).

"The unified field is a space-filled medium that underlies the manifest things and processes of the universe. It is a complex and fundamental medium. It carries the universal fields: the electromagnetic, the gravitational, and the strong and weak nuclear fields. It carries the ZPF (zero point field), the field of zero-point energies. And it is also the element of the cosmos that records, conserves, and conveys information. In the latter guise it is the Akashic field, the rediscovered ancient concept of *Akasha*. A lived connection to this field is the hallmark of the Akashic experience." (Ibid, 5).

Akashic Chronicle "...The Akashic Record (also called *The Akashic Chronicle*) is the enduring record of all that happens, and has ever happened, in space and time." (Laszlo, 2004, xi).

Akashic Experience "...a real, lived experience that conveys a thought, an image, or an intuition that was not, and very likely could not have bee, transmitted by our senses either at the time it happened or at any time beforehand--at least not in our current lifetime. In a popular, though overused and misused formulation, the *Akashic experience* is a lived experience in the extra- or non-sensory mode." (Laszlo, 2009, 1).

"The *Akashic experience* comes in many sizes, forms, and flavors, to all kinds of people, and all its varieties convey information on the real world--the world beyond the brain and body. The experience ranges from artistic visualizations and creative insights to nonlocal healings, near-death experiences, after-death communications, and personal past life recollections. Notwithstanding the great variety in which it occurs, the *Akashic experience* has strikingly uniform features. Whatever else it may contain, the *Akashic experience* conveys the sense that the experiencing subject is not separate from the objects of his or her experience--the sense that 'I, the experiencing subject, am linked in subtle but real ways to other people and to nature.' In deeper experiences of this kind there is a sense that 'the cosmos and I are one'." (Ibid, 1-2).

"In its many variations, the kind of experience reported...suggests that it comes from somewhere beyond our brain and body, and that the information on which it is based is conserved somewhere beyond our brain and body. The *Akashic experience* gives clear testimony that we are connected to an information and memory field objectively present in nature..." (Ibid, 2).

"The Akashic field--the information and memory components of the unified field--is not mere theory: it's a part of the real world. And...it's an *experienceable* part of the real world. Access to the Akashic field--the *Akashic experience*--is a genuine and indeed fundamental element of human experience..." (Ibid, 7).

"The recognition that the *Akashic experience* is a real and fundamental part of human experience has unparalleled importance for our time. When more people grasp the fact that they can have, and are perhaps already having Akashic experiences, they will open their mind to them, and the experiences will occur more and more frequently, and to more and more people. A more evolved consciousness will spread in the world. People will shift from the ego-centered skin-enclosed consciousness of the modern age to the interconnected transpersonal consciousness foretold by thinkers such as Sri Aurobindo, Jean Gebser, Richard Bucke, Rudolf Steiner, Stanislav Grof, Don Beck, Ken Wilber, and Eckhart Tolle, among a growing number of others." (Ibid).

"Phase-conjugate quantum resonance between the human brain and the information stored in the unified field offers a promising foundation for a scientific explanation of the standard varieties of the *Akashic experience*. Ordinarily we can access quantum holograms in the field because our brain can function in the quantum mode..." (Ibid, 254).

Akashic Field "...at the roots of reality there is an interconnecting, information-conserving and information-conveying cosmic field. For thousands of years, mystics and seers, sages and philosophers maintained that there is such a field; in the East they called it the *Akashic Field*...The effects of the Akashic Field are not limited to the physical world: the A-field (as we shall call it) informs all living things--the entire web of life. It also informs our consciousness." (Laszlo, 2004, 3).

"...a new concept of the universe is emerging. The established concept is transcended; in its place comes a new/old concept: the informed universe, rooted in the rediscovery of ancient tradition's Akashic Field as the vacuum-based holofield. In this concept the universe is a highly integrated, coherent system, much like a living organism. Its crucial feature is information that is generated, conserved, and conveyed by and among all its parts. This feature is entirely fundamental. It transforms a universe that is blindly groping its way from one phase of its evolution to the next into a strongly interconnected system that builds on the information it has already generated." (Ibid, 112).

A-Field (Akashic Field) "...The effects of the Akashic Field are not limited to the physical world: The A-field (as we shall call it) informs all living things--the entire web of life. It also informs our consciousness." (Laszlo, 2004, 3).

"...The zero-point field of the quantum vacuum is not only a super-dense energy field; it is also a super-rich information field-- the holographic memory of the universe. This finding recalls Indian philosophy's concept of the Akashic Chronicle, the record of everything that happens in the world traced in the Akashic Field. It makes sense to name the newly (re)discovered information field of the universe the '*A-field*', after ancient tradition's Akashic Field. The *A-field* takes its place among the fundamental fields of the universe, joining science's G-field (the gravitational field), EM-field (electromagnetic field), and the various nuclear and quantum fields." (Ibid, 56).

"The evidence for a cosmic information field--like the evidence for all fundamental laws and processes in nature--is not direct; it must be reconstructed by reasoning. Like the G-field and the EM-field, the *A-field* cannot be seen heard, touched, tasted, or smelled. It is indicated, however, by many things that we can and do perceive." (Ibid, 56-57).

"Recognition that there is a bona fide scientific explanation for the observed nonlocality of consciousness would give legitimacy to research on psi phenomena and open the way to a better understanding of the as yet mysterious dimensions of the human mind. Such explanation is now at hand. The information field that links quanta and galaxies in the physical universe and cells and organisms in the biosphere also links the brains and minds of humans in the sociosphere. This *A-field* creates the human information pool that Carl Jung called the collective unconscious, Teilhard de Chardin the noosphere, and the scientists such as

14

Erwin Schrodinger, David Bohm, William James, and Henry Stapp have not hesitated to discuss and to affirm." (Ibid, 103).

"The *A-field* conveys information, and this information, subtle as it is, has a notable effect: it makes correlation and creates coherence...*A-field* information is carried by superposed vacuum wave-interference patterns that are equivalent to holograms. We know that in a hologram every element meshes with isomorphic elements: with those that are similar to it. Scientists call such meshing 'conjugation'--a holographic pattern is *conjugate* with similar patterns in an assortment of patterns, however vast." (Ibid, 107).

"...through torsion waves in the vacuum the *A-field* links thing and events in the universe at staggering speeds...The interference patterns of torsion waves create cosmic-scale holograms, the holograms of stars and entire stellar systems. These extend throughout our universe and correlate its galaxies and other macro structures." (Ibid).

"Information through the *A-field* accounts not only for the quasi-instant coherence of all parts of an organism, but also for the subtle but effective correlation between organisms and environments. The hologram of entire colonies, groups, and communities of organisms are conjugate with the hologram of the ecology of which they are a part. The hologram of the ecology in which organisms are embedded correlates all organisms in that ecology, down to the structure of their genome. Thereby, the ongoing variation of the genome is subtly informed, increasing the probabilities that when the environment changes, the genome comes up with mutations that are viable in the new milieu." (Ibid, 110-111).

"The informed universe is a universe where the *A-field* is a real and significant element. Thanks to this field, this universe is of mind-boggling coherence. All that happens in one place happens also in other places; all that happened at one time happens also at all times after that. Nothing is 'local,' limited to where and when it is happening. All things are global, indeed cosmic, for the memory of all things extends to all places and all times. This is the concept of the informed universe..." (Ibid, 116).

"...In this theory (the *A-field* theory) the underlying physical reality is a holographic field in which everything--be it a particle, an atom, a molecule, an amoeba, a mouse, or a human being--is connected with every other thing. And everything affects every other thing through wave pressures that literally shape the things

15

around them." (Ibid, 118).

"...In the *A-field*, the waves carry information without carrying force, meaning that you can't feel them...In the *A-field*, the waves never attenuate because they are moving through a frictionless medium, with nothing to slow their progress...You cannot see or feel waves in the *A-field*. Energy moves through super conductive material without ever slowing down or diminishing..." (Ibid).

"...In the *A-field*, waves can travel faster than the speed of light--faster than 186,000 miles per second. This very high speed of information transmission accounts for events that appear to be synchronized over great distances--a kind of instant correlation, known as nonlocality, that scientists are discovering in a number of disciplines..." (Ibid, 119)

Akashic Records "Theosophical concept for an astral memory of all events, thoughts, and emotions that have arisen since the world began. Psychics are said to be able to tune into this dimension and receive authentic impressions of past ages. Some theosophical descriptions of Atlantis derive from apparent Akashic memories." (Drury, 2004, 7).

"Chronicles of all that occurs in one's life. Everything is inscribed in the akasha, which is etheric energy vibrating at a frequency that records all of the impressions of life, whether created in or out of embodiment. Any individual can learn to access these records by developing inner sight." (Milanovich and McCune, 1997, 367).

"...The *Akashic Record* (also called The Akashic Chronicle) is the enduring record of all that happens, and has ever happened, in space and time." (Laszlo, 2004, xi).

"In the Infinite One manifest we note the attributes of Force, Intelligence and Love, and a person may be in full accord with one of these attributes and not with the others...Knowledge is not gained through the spirit of either Force or Love. It is only from Universal Mind, which is Supreme Intelligence, called by Oriental scholars the *Akashic Records*, and by Hebrew masters, the Book of Remembrance, that knowledge of any kind can be obtained." (Levi, 1907, 10).

"...The imperishable records of life, known as the *Akasha Records*, are wholly in the domain of Supreme Intelligence, or Universal Mind, and the Akashic Record reader must be in such close touch with the Holy Spirit, or the Holy Breath, as the ancient masters call this spirit of Supreme Intelligence, that every thought vibration is instantly felt in every fiber of his being." (Ibid, 11).

The *Akashic Records* are records, located somewhere in the heavens, somewhere in the infinite dimensions of God's world, records which contain all the memories of our previous thoughts, emotions, and events of all mortals; records of our past lives, records of our present life, and even records of future potential events that may occur in our present life. (Kelley, 2013).

"The *Akashic Records* might seem to be some heavenly office room filled with file cabinets. *Akasha*, however, means 'space.' The 'records' implied are intrinsic to the oneness of infinite consciousness. They are called so because it's possible to access any specific part of omniscience you wish..." (Laszlo, 2009, 22).

"The *Akashic Records* are a dimension of consciousness that contains a vibrational record of every soul and its journey. This vibrational body of consciousness exists everywhere in its entirety and is completely available at all times and in all places. As such, the Records are an experiential body of knowledge that contains everything that every soul has ever thought, said, and done over the course of its existence, as well as all its future possibilities." (Howe and Looye, 2009, 3).

"In the process of accessing, or 'opening,' the Akashic Records, we transition from a state of ordinary human consciousness to a state of Divine universal consciousness in which we recognize our Oneness with the Divine at all levels. This state of consciousness allows us to perceive the impressions and vibrations of the Records. In this way, the Records have served humanity throughout its unfolding by being an extraordinary state through which we can receive Divine illumination at a manageable rate and integrate it into our human experience. Because of this integration, we can quite literally say that accessing the Akasha allows us glimpses of heaven on earth!" (Ibid, 4).

"The Akashic Records are the Light Body of universal self-awareness. As such, they contain the universal consciousness, with its three main components of mind, heart, and will. The Records also contain the radiant vibrations of Light that all things generate. Every time we access the Records, our awareness is affected by this quality of Light, and we become 'en-Lightened' by it. When this happens, the effects of the light become evident in our thoughts and emotions (and in those of our clients), and we begin to experience an increased sense of peace and well-being." (Ibid, 6).

"...working in the Akashic Records requires an understanding and acceptance of the concept of reincarnation. From the perspective of the Records, all souls are eternal. At this level of understanding, the Records hold the archive of each soul as it has existed from lifetime to lifetime as different human beings on the earth plane while evolving throughout time and space. A human incarnation occurs as a specific manifestation of the perfect blueprint of the soul. The idea of the human experience is to become in the physical the perfect self that already exists in the Akasha at the soul level. Growing into the awareness of one's spiritual nature and being able to anchor that awareness in the physical and become that optimal self on the earth plane takes time--many lifetimes, in fact. In the Records, we are able to see and register our various incarnations. So in essence, the Akashic Records are both the perfect soul-level blueprint and the catalogue of experience of an individual soul as it grows into awareness of itself as a spiritual being, Divine in nature and manifesting in the physical earth-arena." (Ibid, 7-8).

"The Akashic Records are always changing and expanding. As our souls evolve over time, our Records adjust to reflect our growth and are in a continual state of refinement as we align with our perfection and manifest that perfection in our earthly lives. Therefore, we can look at the Records as an intermediary body of all past, present, and future possibility, probability, and eventuality. Through them we can derive understanding and direction as we open up within ourselves on our journey to becoming our optimal selves in the physical world." (Ibid).

"In the mid-twentieth century, Edgar Cayce (1877-1945) was the only person reading the Akashic Records publically. He was known as 'the sleeping prophet' because his method of accessing the Records was to put himself into a sleep state that allowed him to shift his consciousness and access the Akasha. While in this state, Cayce relayed information while someone else took notes. Upon awakening, he shifted back to his ordinary state of consciousness and remembered nothing of what had transpired." (Ibid, 11).

"For forty-three years, Cayce gave daily Akashic Records readings. Today those readings--more than fourteen thousand of them--are available to the public and provide a wealth of information about the Akashic Records themselves, as well as answers to thousands of questions related to health and spirituality. What is significant for us today about Cayce's work is that he popularized the Akashic Records. Though theosophist H. P. Blavatsky (1831-1891) and anthroposophist Rudolf Steiner (1861-1925) referred to the Akashic Records in their writings, it was not until Cayce's work in the early to mid-twentieth century that Akashic Records readings became a familiar practice in the movement of consciousness development." (Ibid).

Alchemy "The ancient science of transmuting base metals into gold and silver. The etymology of the word is uncertain, but it may derive from the Arabic *al kimiya*, meaning 'the magical craft of the Black Country', a reference to northern Egypt and the Nile Delta (southern Egypt, by way of contrast, had red, sandy soil). The ancient Egyptians were master metalworkers and believed that magical powers existed in certain fluxes and alloys. When the Arabs conquered Egypt in the seventh century, they brought alchemy back with them to Morocco and Spain. From the ninth to the eleventh centuries, Seville, Cordova, and Granada were leading centers for alchemy; later, this esoteric science spread to France, England, and Germany." (Drury, 2002, 8).

"The three main aims of alchemy were to attempt to make gold from base metals with the aid of the Philosopher's Stone; to search for an elixir that could prolong life indefinitely; and to acquire methods of creating life artificially. In the Middle Ages considerable fortunes were lost by wealthy patrons who financed alchemical experiments that came to nothing. Nicholas Flamel (1330-1418) claimed to have transformed mercury into silver and gold, but it is more likely that he acquired his wealth as the result of his moneylending business." (Ibid).

"In some degree at least, alchemy was also a metaphor for spiritual transformation, a process quite divorced from laboratory experimentation. The imperfect person, leaden and dark, could become pure and golden through gradual processes leading to spiritual illumination. Basil Valentine, a celebrated alchemist and Benedictine monk, described alchemy as 'the investigation of those natural secrets by which God has shadowed out eternal things' and Jacob Boehme regarded the Philosopher's Stone as the spirit of Christ, which would 'tincture' the individual soul. In this sense, alchemy was both a precursor of modern chemistry and also a complex spiritual philosophy--one of the major sources of medieval esoteric thought." (Ibid).

Alpha Brain-Wave State "A specific brain-rhythm pattern associated with relaxation and meditation. Measured as amplitudes of 8-13 cycles per second in an electroencephalograph (EEG) pattern." (Drury, 2002, 9).

"An altered state of consciousness characterized by relaxation, creativity, and expanded awareness; brain-wave activity of 8-13 Hz." (Backman, 2009, 229).

Altered states of consciousness "A state of consciousness different from normal, everyday consciousness, the latter sometimes being referred to as the 'consensus reality' on which normal patterns of communication are based. Altered states exclude or minimize the external world, allowing subconscious imagery to rise into consciousness. Altered states include some types of dreams, trance states, out-of-body experiences, dissociation experiences, mystical states, and hallucinations associated with psychedelic drugs." (Drury, 2002, 10).

"The brain-wave states of alpha, theta, and delta, as opposed to the general waking-state brain wave termed beta." (Backman, 2009, 229).

Amorphous "1 without a clearly defined shape or form. 2 (Mineralogy & Chemistry) not crystalline, or not apparently crystalline." (*The Concise Oxford Dictionary*, 1999).

Anahata "Sound that is made without any two things striking; the name of the heart (fourth) chakra." (Judith, 1999, 414).

Anima "Psychoanalysis 1 (in Jungian psychology) the feminine part of a man's personality. Compare with Animus. 2 the part of the psyche which is directed inwards, in touch with the subconscious. Compare with Persona." (*The Concise Oxford Dictionary*, 1999).

Animus "1 hostility or ill feeling. 2 motivation to do something. 3 Psychoanalysis (in Jungian psychology) the masculine part of a woman's personality. Compare with Anima." (*The Concise Oxford Dictionary*, 1999).

Anomalous cognition (AC) "A form of information transfer in which all known sensory stimuli are absent; that is, some individuals are able to gain access to information by an as yet unknown process; also known as 'remote viewing (RV)' and clairvoyance." (Tart, 1997, 221).

Anthropic principle "The cosmological principle that theories of the universe are constrained by the necessity to allow human existence." (*The Concise Oxford Dictionary*, 1999).

"The idea that we see the universe the way it is because if it were any different, we wouldn't be here to see it." (Hawking, 2001, 203).

"The principle that the constants of nature are tuned to allow for life and intelligence. The strong anthropic principle concludes

20

that an intelligence of some sort was required to tune the physical constants to allow for intelligence. The weak anthropic principle merely states that the constants of nature must be tuned to allow for intelligence (otherwise we would not be here), but it leaves open the question of what or who did the tuning. Experimentally, we find that, indeed, the constants of nature seem to be finely tuned to allow for life and even consciousness. Some believe that this is the sign of a cosmic creator. Others believe that this is a sign of the multiverse." (Kaku, 2005, 381).

Apparition "A remarkable thing making a sudden appearance." (*The Concise Oxford Dictionary*, 1999).

"The appearance of someone living or dead in conditions that cannot be accounted for by a physical cause. Although apparitions are often thought of as ghosts, the term is also used in occult literature to describe human forms that appear to another person as the result of astral projection or clairvoyance. Here one person is willing his or her consciousness to appear to another person, for purposes either of observation or direct communication. Many accounts exist in parapsychological literature of a person appearing in spirit form at the time of death, as if wishing to communicate this fact to a friend or loved one some distance away." (Drury, 2002, 15).

Applied kinesiology (AK) "is the technique in alternative medicine to be able to diagnose illness or choose treatment by testing muscles for strength and weakness..." ("Applied kinesiology," *Wikipedia*).

"Meridians are pathways for many different types of physical and subtle energies. While invisible to the naked eye, they are circuits of positive and negative energies, as well as bodily fluids, and have been measured using various methods...Electromagnetic in nature, acupuncture points can be found by hand, through testing with micro-electrical voltage meters, and through the use of *applied kinesiology* or 'muscle testing,' which tests the body's reactions to concepts or substances..." (Dale, 2009, 169).

"Applied kinesiology analyzes the chemical, structural, and mental aspects of the body's current state. It takes into account the following key functions of the body: Nervous system health (N); Neurolymphatic system (NL); Neurovascular system (NV); Cerebral-spinal fluid (CSF); and Acupuncture meridians (AMC)." (Ibid, 369).

Please also see Kinesiology.

Archetype "(Origin C16: via L. from Gk. *arkhetupon*

21

'something molded first as a model', from *arkhe*- 'primitive' + *tupos* 'a model'). 1 a very typical example. 2 an original model. 3 Psychoanalysis (in Jungian theory) a primitive mental image inherited from the earliest human ancestors and supposed to be present in the collective unconscious. 4 a recurrent motif in literature or art." (*The Concise Oxford Dictionary*, 1999).

Archetypes "...are elementary ideas, what could be called 'ground' ideas. These ideas Jung spoke of as archetypes of the unconscious. 'Archetype' is the better term because 'elementary idea' suggests headwork. Archetype of the unconscious means it comes from below. The difference between the Jungian archetypes of the unconscious and Freud's complexes is that the archetypes of the unconscious are manifestations of the organs of the body and their powers. Archetypes are biologically grounded, whereas the Freudian unconscious is a collection of repressed traumatic experiences from the individual's lifetime. The Freudian unconscious is a personal unconscious, it is biographical. The Jungian archetypes of the unconscious are biological. The biographical is secondary to that." (Campbell and Moyers, 1988, 60-61).

"All over the world and at different times of human history, these archetypes, or elementary ideas, have appeared in different costumes. The differences in the costumes are the results of environmental and historical conditions..." (Ibid, 61).

"Jung coins the term 'archetypes' for the building blocks of the collective psyche. The archetypes are dominant motifs, formative patterns, prototypical images, primordial symbols, or predispositions. Jung see the archetypes as 'thought forms' that have been created through common repetitive thoughts and actions through the millennia by our ancestors. These archetypes (inborn behavior patterns and images) are charged with energy and drive us to action." (Seifer, 2011, 173).

"In the psychology of Carl Jung, a primordial image found in the collective unconscious. According to Jung, archetypes appear in mystical visions as sacred or mythic beings and have the power to 'seize hold of the psyche with a kind of primeval force'. Archetypes are often personifications of processes or events in Nature (e.g. the sum--hero or lunar goddess), or universal expression of family roles (e.g. the Great Father and Great Mother)." (Drury, 2002, 17).

"Jung believed that mythic images have an 'autonomous' existence in the psyche. This concept is important for religious and mystical thought because, historically, archetypal visions have often been regarded by mystics as personal revelations from an external divine source. For Jung, however, such experiences could be regarded as an expression of the most profound depths of the psyche." (Ibid).

Asanas "Pose or posture comfortably held; refers to the various hatha yoga positions." (Judith, 1999, 414).

"Yogic postures associated with the practice of meditation. There are many different asanas, the most famous being the lotus, in which the meditator sits upright with the legs crossed, with the foot resting on the opposite thigh, and the hands resting palm upwards on the knees. Asanas are supposed to assist the process of meditation by allowing currents of psychic energy to flow more readily, for example causing the arousal of kundalini through the channel sushumna, which corresponds to the spinal cord. Other asanas include the 'lion', the 'serpent', and the 'bow'." (Drury, 2002, 18).

Astral "(Origin C17: from late L. *astralis*, from *astrum* 'star'). 1 of, relating to, or resembling the stars. 2 of or relating to a supposed non-physical realm of existence to which various psychic and paranormal phenomena are ascribed, and in which the physical human body is said to have a counterpart." (*The Concise Oxford Dictionary*, 1999).

Astral Body "Besides possessing an etheric body that complements the physical body, humans possess other higher spiritual bodies as well. One of these spiritual bodies, known as the astral body, participates in how we feel, how we express ourselves, and in how we are influenced by our emotions. Some clairvoyants actually refer to the astral body as the emotional body. Like the etheric body, the astral body is a kind of structured energy field that contributes certain types of energy information to the physical body..." (Gerber, 2000, 29).

"The 'double' of the human body, usually regarded by occultists as its animating force, providing the body with 'consciousness'. The astral body has a luminous, shining appearance, and is capable of passing through physical matter. The act of willed separation of the astral body from the physical is known as astral travel. Occultists believe that at death the astral body leaves its physical counterpart and finds a new existence on the astral plane. Some parapsychologists believe that ghostly apparitions are astral communications between persons who have just died and those who are dear to them. The astral body is often depicted as being joined to the physical body by a silver cord--an

23

etheric umbilical cord--and some subjects who experience out-of-body dissociation report seeing this cord." (Drury, 2002, 20).

Astral Field "A nexus between the physical and spiritual realms. Free of time and space." (Dale, 2009, 147).

Astral Travel "Sometimes known as the out-of-body experience. Astral travel is from the physical body resulting in an altered state of consciousness, and sometimes in different qualities of perception. Astral travel is achieved by a variety of active imagination techniques or trance-inducing methods. Many people who experience astral travel, like Robert Monroe, author of *Journey Out of The Body*, have reported conscious perception from a different vantage point (e.g. high up in the sky, enabling one to look down over a street or into rooms of another house at a distance). Professor Charles Tart, of the University of California at Davis, conducted a laboratory experiment in which a subject ('Miss Z') was asked to project her consciousness out of her body while it was monitored by electroencephalograph equipment. After four attempts Miss Z successfully read a five-digit random number located on a high shelf outside her normal range of vision and facing towards the ceiling. Tart believes it is his subject's ability to astral travel, rather than a facility for telepathy or clairvoyance, that enabled her to identify the number." (Drury, 2002, 20).

"Astral travel has been reported by some subjects who experience the near-death experience (i.e. those who, as a result of an accident or operation, are declared clinically dead, but subsequently revive). Typically, near-death subjects may witness details of their operation or resuscitation, as if from a location several feet above their body. They may report details of conversations among hospital staff and other activities that are subsequently verified." (Ibid).

"Sometimes astral travel also has a mythic dimension, where subjects report 'heaven and hell' imagery during an out-of-body experience. This may indicate that subjects are engaged in a dissociative encounter with positive and negative archetypal imagery from the unconscious mind." (Ibid).

Aura "The aura is an emanation that surrounds all living things, especially human beings, which many believers in the Western Esoteric community, claim to see and to be able to document. Many psychics, for example, claim to be able to see this emanation, completely invisible to the average person, and derive information from it, especially relative to the health of a person. Contemporary advocates of the existence of auras relate them historically to the lights said to shine around biblical and other holy figures, often pictured in Western art as halos. The aura is often said to be part of the invisible anatomy of the individual, which includes, among other invisible elements, the chakras." (Melton, 2008, 17).

"In occult terminology, the psychic energy field that surrounds both animate and inanimate bodies. The aura can be dull or brightly colored, and psychics–those who claim to perceive the auric colors directly–interpret the quality of the person or object according to the energy vibrations. Bright re, for example, indicates anger; yellow, strong intellectual powers; and purple, spirituality. Occultists generally believe that the halos depicted around the head of Jesus Christ and the saints are examples of mystically pure auras. Theosophists distinguish five auras: the health aura, the vital aura, the karmic aura, the character aura, and the aura of spiritual nature." (Drury, 2002, 23).

"Scientists have been investigating--and substantiating--the existence of the *aura*, the field that surrounds our entire body, for over a hundred years, adding to the knowledge our ancestor already possessed. This field consists of multiple bands of energy called *auric layers* or *auric fields*, that encompass the body, connecting us to the outer world." (Dale, 2009, 147).

"The aura has been known by many names in many cultures. The Kabbalists called it an astral light. Christian artists depicted Jesus and other figures as surrounded by coronas of light. The Vedic scriptures and teachings of the Rosicrucians, Tibetan and Indian Buddhists, and many Native American tribes describe the field in detail. Even Pythagoras discussed the field, which was perceived as a luminous body. In fact, John White and Stanley Krippner, authors of *Future Science*, list ninety-seven different cultures that reference the human aura, each culture calling it by a different name." (Ibid).

"Science has been actively involved in penetrating the mystery of the aura since the early 1800s. During that time period, Belgian mystic and physician Jan Baptist van Helmont visualized it as a universal fluid that permeates everything. The idea of the aura acting like a fluid--or flowing--as well as being permeable has remained consistent throughout history. Franz Mesmer, for whom the term 'mesmerism' was coined, suggested that both animate and inanimate objects were charged with a fluid, which he perceived as magnetic, through which material bodies could exert influence over each other, even at a distance. Baron Wilhelm von Reichenbach discovered several properties unique to this field, which he called the *odic force*. He determined that it shared similar properties to the electromagnetic field, which had previously been investigated by James Clerk Maxwell, one of the fathers of electricity. The odic field was composed of polarities or opposites, as is the electromagnetic field. In electromagnetism, however, opposites attract. Not so in the odic field, where like attracts like." (Ibid, 147-148).

"Reichenbach also found that the field related to different colors and that it could not only carry a charge, but also flow around objects. He described the field on the left side of the body as a negative pole and the right side as a positive pole, similar to the ideas of Chinese medicine." (Ibid, 148).

"These and other theories have revealed the aura to have a fluid or flowing state; to be comprised of different colors, therefore frequencies; to be permeable and penetrable; and to be magnetic in nature, although it also has electromagnetic properties. Other research has underscored these theories and expanded one additional element of the auric field: its connection to the inner sanctum of the human being." (Ibid).

"For example, in 1911 Dr. Walter Kilner examined the aura with colored filters and a special kind of coal tar. He discovered three zones: a dark layer next to the skin; a more ethereal layer flowing at a perpendicular angle to the body; and a delicate exterior with contours about six inches across. Most important, the conditions of this 'aura', as he called it, shifted in reaction to a subject's state of mind and health." (Ibid).

"In the early part of the 1900s, Dr. Wilhelm Reich furthered our knowledge of the human field and its qualities through experiments studying a universal energy that he name 'orgone'. During his studies, he observed energy pulsing in the sky and surrounding all animate and inanimate objects and beings. Many metaphysicians believe that orgone is equivalent to chi or prana. He also noticed that ears of congestion could be cleared to release negative mental and emotional patterns and thus affect change. This emphasized the connections between the subtle and the physical energies as well as emotional and mental energies." (Ibid).

"Then in the 1930s, Dr. Lawrence Bendit and Phoebe Bendit observed the human energy field and linked it to soul development, showing that the subtle forces are the foundation of health. Their observations are mirrored and expanded by those of Dr. Dora Kunz, a theosophist and intuitive, who saw that every organ has its own field--as does the overall body--which pulses with its own rhythm when healthy. When someone is ill, these rhythms alter, and problems can be intuitively seen in the field." (Ibid).

"When Dr. Zheng Rongliang of Lanzhou University in China measured the flow of chi form a human body with a unique biological detector, he showed that not only does the aura pulse, but that not everyone's field pulses at the same rate or intensity. This study was repeated by researchers at the Shanghai Atomic Nuclear Institute of Academia Sinica." (Ibid).

"Soviet scientists from the Bioinformation Institute, headed by A. S. Popow, actually measured the human field, or more specifically, the biocurrents manifested in the surrounding energy body. They discovered that living organisms emanate vibrations at a frequency between 300 and 2,000 nanometers. They called this field the 'biofield' and discovered that people with a strong and widespread biofield can transfer energy more successfully. This research was later confirmed by the Medical Science Academy in Moscow." (Ibid, 149).

"A special form of photography is actually able to take pictures of the auric field. In the 1930s, Russian scientist Semyon Kirlian and his wife, Valentina, invented a new photographic process that involves directing a high-frequency electrical field at an object. The object's pattern of luminescence--the auric field--can then be captured on film. Contemporary practitioners are using Kirlian photography to show how the aura responds to different emotional and mental states, and even to diagnose illness and other problems. Medical science is now using a heat aura, as well as other imaging processes, to show the different aspects of the body's electromagnetics." (Ibid).

"One of the more compelling sets of studies in this area was conducted by Dr. Valerie Hunt...In *A Study of Structural Neuromuscular, Energy Field, and Emotional Approaches*, she recorded the frequency of low-millivoltage signals emanating from the body during Rolfing sessions. She made the recordings using electrodes of silver and silver chloride on the skin. Scientists then analyzed the wave patterns recorded with a Fourier analysis and a sonogram frequency analysis. The field did, indeed, consist of a number of different color bands, which correlated to the chakras. The following results, taken from the February 1988 study, showed color--frequency correlations in hertz or cycles per second:

Blue - 250-275 plus 1,200 Hz

Green - 250-475 Hz

Yellow - 500-700 Hz
Orange - 950-1050 Hz
Red - 1,000-1,200 Hz
Violent - 1,000-2,000, plus 300-400; 600-800 Hz
White - 1,100-2,000 Hz." (Ibid).

"While mechanically measuring the subjects, healer and aura reader Reverend Rosalyn Bruyere provided her own input, separately recording the various colors she intuitively perceived. In all cases, her renderings were the same as those demonstrated mechanically. Hunt repeated this experiment with other psychics with the same results." (Ibid, 149, 151).

"We know it exits--but what is the auric field? Scientists including James Oschman, author of *Energy Medicine* (2002), consider it a biomagnetic field that surrounds the body. As Dr. Oschman says, 'It is a fact of physics that energy fields are unbounded.' This means that our biomagnetic fields extend indefinitely. Modern equipment can now measure the heart's fields--the strongest of those originating from an organ--up to fifteen feet away. As for the aura's job, science has determined that this magnetic field conveys information about events taking place inside the body, rather than on the skin. Its purpose is therefore vitally linked to our internal health." (Ibid, 151).

"The biomagnetic field is composed of information from each organ and every bodily tissue. The heart's currents determine its shape, as the heart is the body's strongest electrical producer. The primary electrical flow is therefore established by the circulatory system. As well, the nervous system interacts with the circulatory system and creates distinct flows, seen as whirling patterns, within the field." (Ibid).

"We cannot fully understand the function of the aura without knowing what it is made of--and we're still working on that. Barbara Ann Brennan summarizes scientific research to suggest that it is made of 'plasma,' tiny--perhaps subatomic--particles that move in clouds. Scientists propose that plasmas exist in a state between energy and matter. Brennan says that this 'bioplasma' is a fifth state of matter. Rudolf Steiner, a brilliant author and philosopher, suggested that the human energy field is made of ether, an element comparable to a negative mass, or a hollowed-out space. We can only surmise, but perhaps the field is actually made of both electromagnetic radiation (specifically magnetism) and an anti-matter that allows a shift of energy between this world and others. Thus the propensity of healers to deliver healing energy based on intention is a matter of creating enough intensity in the 'here and now' energies to access an equivalency in the anti-worlds. What we accomplish within our own field can be delivered like an instant message on the Internet to another individual's energy field." (Ibid, 151, 153).

"Barbara Ann Brennan proposes seven basic layers of the auric field. These graduate from the body, linked with each of the seven basic chakras. The chakras also attune to different subtle bodies, which combine to compose three basic planes. These planes are accessible through the auric fields." (Ibid, 151).

"Brennan is also able to intuitively perceive two levels beyond the ketheric, which she calls the cosmic plane. She associates these with the eighth and ninth chakras. The eighth appears fluid in her, while the ninth is composed of a crystalline template." (Ibid).

"The first modern description of chakra energies or of what we call the aura or auric field was made by Sir Isaac Newton in 1729 in his second paper on light and colors. In this paper Newton spoke of an 'electromagnetic' light, a 'subtle, vibrating, electric and elastic medium' that was excitable *and* exhibited phenomena such as repulsion, attraction, sensation, and motion, anticipating in many ways the electromagnetic field theories of Michael Faraday and James Clerk Maxwell a hundred years later." (Bruyere,1994, 59).

"It was not until this century, however, that the body's electrical nature became a fact of science. Beginning in the early 1930s Dr. Harold Saxton Burr spent over forty years scientifically researching what he called electrodynamic or 'L-fields' (the 'L' stands for 'Life'). These L-fields were detected and measured in men and women, in animals, trees, plants, seeds, eggs, and even in one of the lowest forms of life, slime molds. Burr theorized that the L-field is responsible for the body's capacity to regenerate new cells that act and function precisely as did the cells they replaced...the electro-dynamic field of the body serves as a matrix or mold, which preserves the 'shape' or arrangement of any material poured into it, however often the mater may be changed.' Furthermore, this 'invisible' and 'intangible' field 'can reveal the future 'shape' or arrangement of the materials it will mold.' In other words, an abnormality in the electrodynamic field can 'give warning of something 'out-of-shape' in the body, sometimes in advance of actual symptoms." (Ibid, 59-60).

"Over the past twenty years, the research of New York orthopedic surgeon Robert O. Becker and his colleagues has established with certainty the relationship between regeneration and electrical currents in living things. The flow of electrons (electric current) moving through the perineural cells (cells containing bundles of never fibers surrounded by an extensive layer of connective tissue) of the nervous system and the resultant magnetic field are the factors that affect an organism's ability to sense and evaluate damage occurring anywhere in the body; this electromagnetic flow also provides cells with the appropriate electrical environment to either sustain health within an uninjured cell or stimulate healing in a damaged cell. This same perineural structure is the passageway utilized by healers when they channel energy into a client to bring about healing. Both the L-field of Burr and the regeneration research of Becker have shed scientific light on the electromagnetic nature of the human body and consequently on the underlying electromagnetic nature of the chakra energies of the auric field." (Ibid, 61).

"The auric field is a metaphor for life. In other words, a person's energy field or the individual aura around the body, which is created and controlled by the chakras, reflects how one's life actually is lived; it mirrors the flow of that life. In this way, the auric field becomes more than a symbol for life. The aura is life." (Ibid).

Auric Egg "In theosophical terminology, the egg-shaped 'source of the human aura'--the seat of spiritual, mental, intellectual, and emotional faculties." (Drury, 2002, 23).

Auric layers or **auric fields** Barbara Ann Brennan suggests there are layers of the auric field, in accordance to the twelve--chakra system. The Physical Plane consists of a Mental Body aura layer, emanating closest to the physical body, an Emotional Body aura, and then an Etheric Body aura. The Astral Plane consists of an Astral Body aura layer. And the Spiritual Plane consists of a Ketheric Body aura layer, a Celestial Body aura layer, and an Etheric Template aura layer. (Dale, 2009, 150).

The "First Auric Layer" deals with the "protection of life energies"; the "Second Auric Layer screens feelings and emotions"; the "Third Auric Layer filters ideas and beliefs"; the "Fourth Auric Layer attracts and repels relationships"; the "Fifth Auric Layer attracts, repels, and sends guidance"; the "Sixth Auric Layer opens to choices, and enacts decisions"; the "Seventh Auric Layer connects with spirits and Spirit, and broadcasts spiritual decisions"; the "Eighth Auric Layer broadcasts karma and absorbs powers"; the "Ninth Auric Layer connects with other based on soul issues"; the "Tenth Auric Layer mirrors beliefs, and serves as a second self"; the "Eleventh Auric Layer commandeers force"; and the "Twelfth Auric Layer links with energy egg, and connects human and divine selves". (Ibid, 150).

"Auric fields are graduating layers of light that manage the energy outside of the body. Auric fields connect to the chakras, creating a symbiosis between what happens inside and outside of a person." (Ibid, 153).

"Our *auric* or *electromagnetic field* is generated by the spinning of the chakras...As it spins, each chakra produces its own electromagnetic field. This field then combines with fields generated by other chakras to produce the auric field. An individual's auric field is manifested via a combination of energies from three chakras. Generally these are the first, third, and fifth chakras, empowering the physical, intellectual, and etheric bodies. It is a combination of these three chakras that produces the *primary auric field* (the inner shell of the aura), which can be physically felt by the hand as it is passed over another's body. If one is sensitive enough, the *secondary auric field* (the outer shell) can also be felt. This secondary aura is produced from the interaction of all seven chakras." (Bruyere, 1989, 61).

"...The amount or intensity of energy produced by a particular chakra or group of chakras determines the color that dominates the auric field." (Ibid, 63).

"The auric field exists in different layers of color, sometimes referred to as *harmonics*. In other words, for people who can see the aura, it appears as a pattern of colors near the body and then another pattern of colors farther away from the body, and so on..." (Ibid, 64).

Axiatonal lines "Vibratory lines which connect levels of human electrochemical activity with astrobiological circuits that span the solar system and are connected with resonating star systems. The axiatonal lines connect the acupuncture mapping of the human biological system with superior astrobiological analogs." (Hurtak, 1977, 567-568).

Axon "A nerve fiber that conducts impulses through a single long process away from the cell body of a neuron to other cells or organs." (Hurtak, 1977, 568).

Ayahuasca "1 a tropical vine of the Amazon region, noted for its hallucinogenic properties. [Genus *Banisteriopsis*] 2 a hallucinogenic drink prepared from the bark of this." (*The Concise Oxford Dictionary*, 1999).

"There is a magic intoxicant in northwestern-most South

31

America which the Indians believe can free the soul from corporeal confinement, allowing it to wander free and return to the body at will. The soul, thus untrammeled, liberates its owner from the realities of everyday life and introduces him to wondrous realms of what he considers reality and permits him to communicate with his ancestors. The Quechuan term for this inebriating drink-- Ayahuasca ('**vine of the soul**')--refers to this freeing of the spirit. The plants involved are truly plants of the gods, for their power is laid to supernatural forces residing in their tissues, and they were divine gifts to the earliest Indians on earth." (Schultes and Hofmann, 1992, 120).

B

Banisteriopsis "Common ingredient in a number of psychedelic sacraments used by shamans in South America to contact the supernatural world. Yage, Caapi, and Ayahuasca all contain banisteriopsis and produce remarkable effects, including the separation of the 'soul' from the body, visions of predatory animals and distant locations, the experience of heaven and hell, and explanatory visions of thefts and homicides. The active ingredients of banisteriopsis are the alkaloids harmine, harmaline, and d--tetrahydroharmine." (Drury, 2002, 27).

Beta Brain-Wave State "A state of consciousness characterized by being alert, sharp, and focused; brain-wave activity of 14-27 Hz." (Backman, 2009, 230).

Bhakti yoga "The yoga of devotion and service to another, usually a guru." (Judith, 1999, 414).

Bhukti "Enjoyment. That which takes place when higher consciousness descends to the lower chakras." (Judith, 1999, 414).

Big Bang "The singularity at the beginning of the universe, about fifteen billion years ago." (Hawking, 2001, 203).

"The original explosion that created the universe, sending the galaxies hurtling in all directions. When the universe was created, the temperature was extremely hot, and the density of material was enormous. The big bang took place 13.7 billion years ago, according to the WMAP satellite. The afterglow of the big bang is seen today as the background microwave radiation. There are three experimental 'proofs' of the big bang: the redshift of the galaxies, the cosmic background microwave radiation, and nucleosynethsis of the elements." (Kaku, 2005, 382).

Biogenetic structuralism and religion "Biogenetic structuralism is an account of the way in which the gene-protein process in the formation of the human body, and especially of the brain, prepares human beings for characteristic behaviors and for a range of different competence. It thus prepares us for linguistic, sexual, musical, etc., competence, without dictating what we do with each competence. The claim is that we are prepared also for religious competence, and that religious beliefs and behaviors are consequently an inevitable part of human life. Biogenetic structuralism proposes two operators arising from different parts of the brain: the inferior parietal lobule on the dominant side, the anterior convexity of the frontal lobes (primarily on the dominant side), and their reciprocal neural interconnections account for causal sequencing of elements of reality abstracted from sense perceptions--especially in the operation of cross-modal transfer. This is the causal operator, which operates in the same way as a mathematical operator: it organizes a given 'strip of reality' into what is subjectively perceived as causal sequences taken back to the initial source of that strip. If the initiating source is not given by sense data, the causal operator generates a source automatically. When these are personalized, they produce the religious consequence of gods, powers, spirits, devils, demons, etc. when the strip of reality is the entire universe, the initial source produced by the causal operator is Brahman, the unproduced Producer of all that is Aristotle's unmoved Mover, and the like. While this accounts for those religious phenomena which allow interaction with personalized sources of power (e.g. myth, ritual, sacrifice, symbol), it does not eliminate the issue of ontology, i.e., whether there is in reality (in addition to the strip of reality which has evoked the causal operator) that which is claimed to be the source, allowing that it is necessarily described in approximate and corrigible language (see J. Bowker, *Licensed Insanities*, 1987): that is, the second level of phenomenology, to which the theory points. The second operator is distinct from that concerned with control. It produces those states commonly described as mystical. In the human autonomic system are two subsystems, the sympathetic (concerned with short-term energy expending, e.g. 'fight or flee', hence called ergotropic) and parasympathetic (concerned with energy-conserving in body-function maintenance, hence call trophotropic). Rhythmicity in the environment, whether visual, auditory, tactile, or proprioceptive, drives the sympathetic-ergotropic system, thus creating unusual subjective states. The non-dominant parieto-occipital region of the brain is progressively activated, and this constitutes the second operator, the holistic operator, creating an increasing sense of wholeness which

33

dominates progressively over the sense of multiplicity in ordinarily sensed reality. The suspension, or suppression, of rhythmicity produces the same consequence via the parasympathetic--trophotropic system. Other effects (e.g. the use of incense), by stimulating the pleasure system, reinforce the attainment of ecstatic unitary being (often summarized as AUB) is described in virtually all religions: the difference between one's self and nay other is obliterated, there is no sense of the passing of time, and all that remains is a perfect, timeless, undifferentiated consciousness. The state may in fact (and in time) be extremely brief, but qualitatively it leads to self-transcendence of such a kind that the contingencies of life (including death) seem comparatively unimportant. This is reported even by those (e.g. Bertrand Russell) who remain atheist. Since these fundamental constituents of religion have a gene-protein base in the brain, religions (for all that they do much more than this) will persist in human life in some form. Whereas the sign held up by prophets of doom used to read, 'Prepare to meet they God', biogenetic structuralism rewrites the sign to read, 'Prepare to meet thy God'." (*The Oxford Dictionary of World Religions*, 1997).

Black Body Radiation "The radiation emitted by a hot object in thermal equilibrium with its environment. If we take an object that is hollow (a black body), heat it up, wait for it to reach thermal equilibrium, and drill a small hole in it, the radiation emitted through the hole will be black body radiation. The Sun, a hot poker, and molten magma all emit approximately a black body radiation. The radiation has a specific frequency dependence that is easily measured by a spectrometer. The microwave background radiation filling up the universe obeys this black body radiation formula, giving concrete evidence for the big bang." (Kaku, 2005, 382).

Black Hole "A region of spacetime from which nothing, not even light, can escape because gravity is so strong." (Hawking, 2001, 203).

"An object whose escape velocity equals the speed of light. Because the speed of light is the ultimate velocity in the universe, this means that nothing can escape a black hole, once an object has crossed the event horizon. Black holes can be of various sizes. Galactic black holes, lurking in the center of galaxies and quasars, can weigh millions to billions of solar masses. Stellar black holes are the remnant of a dying star, perhaps originally up to forty times the mass of our Sun. Both of these black holes have been identified with our instruments. Mini-black holes may also exist, as predicted by theory, but they have not yet been seen in the laboratory." (Kaku, 2005, 382).

Body "The material or physical organism of man. The living electrochemical mechanism of animal nature and origin." (*The Urantia Book*, 1955, 8:7).

Boson "A particle or pattern of string vibration whose spin is a whole number." (Hawking, 2001, 203).

"A subatomic particle with integral spin, such as the photon or the conjectured graviton. Baryons are unified with fermions via supersymmetry." (Kaku, 2005, 383).

Boundary condition "The initial state of a physical system or, more generally, the state of the system at a boundary in time or space." (Hawking, 2001, 203).

Brane "An object, which appears to be a fundamental ingredient of M-theory, that can have a variety of spatial dimensions. In general, a p-brane has length in p directions, a 1-brane is a string, a 2-brane is a surface or a membrane, etc." (Hawking, 2001, 203).

"Abbreviation for membrane. Branes can be in any dimension up to eleven. They are the basis of M-theory, the leading candidate for a theory of everything. If we take a cross-section of an eleven-dimensional membrane, we obtain a ten-dimensional string. A string is therefore a one-brane." (Kaku, 2005, 383).

Breath "A vital constituent of life, associated with the element Air and also with the soul many cultures believe that the last breath of the dying person releases the soul from the body. In Hinduism, the breath or life-current is known as prana." (Drury, 2002, 37).

"As a necessary and manifest condition of life, breath and breathing have a literal and metaphorical importance in religions. Basic words which come to identify a real and continuing self originate as 'breath' (see e.g. *ruah* in Hebrew, Ruh [Nafs], Atman); and 'breath' becomes the vehicle of divine communication and presence hence Ruah ha-Qodesh, i.e., the Holy Spirit, and the invocation, 'Breathe on me, Breath of God, Fill me with life anew...'. in *Rg Veda* 10. 90. 13, the breath (prana) of the primordial Man, Purusa, becomes the origin of vayu, the wind, whose manifest form is Vayu. Prana as the source and persistent sustainer of life thus became the link between atman as (in the Vedic period) a reflexive pronoun and atman as the indestructible soul or self. The understanding and control of breath is therefore an important part of yoga, especially within Hatha-yoga, and as pranayama, the fourth in the eight stages (mentioned by Patanjali, I. 34, 2. 29 and 49, but later much elaborated). The control of breath, recognized as highly dangerous, has led to claims of extraordinary feats of retention, with practitioners being buried alive or submerged in water. But the purpose is not wonder-working, but the suffusion of the whole body with the divine, especially through the repetition, synchronized with the breathing in and out, of the Hamsa mantra, thereby sending the breath through the myriad channels of the body (nadi). In Tantrism, the even more specific object is to arouse the energies of kundalini. The importance of breathing in meditation was accepted by Buddhists, but also adapted. *Anapanasati* (*anapana*) is a relatively straightforward set of techniques; but in Tibet, breathing is a key means to visualization. In all these cases, breathing exercises are preparatory, but in China they are an end in themselves. They appear early (at least 6th cent. B.C.E.), and evidently underlie the Taoist practices which were aimed at the control of the energies (especially sexual energies) of the body, with the aim of achieving *ch'ang sheng* ('long life', the material immortality of the bodily elements): that would require, through practice, retention of breath for a period as long as a thousand normal breaths. Short of achieving that, the practice produces calmness through a deep breathing which imitates the hibernation of animals, or, more often, the breathing of an embryo in the womb: see further Ch'i. In W. religions, breathing is used for the control of the mind and for bringing a person without reserve or distraction into the presence of God. In Christianity, see Jesus Prayer; Hesychasm; in Islam, see Dhikr, in which a common technique is that of saying *la ilaha* ('there is no God') while breathing in, and *illa Allah* ('except God') while breathing out." (*The Oxford Dictionary of World Religions*, 1997).

C

Calabi-Yau manifold "A six-dimensional space that is found when we take ten-dimensional string theory and roll up or compactify six dimensions into a small ball, leaving a four-dimensional supersymmetric space. Calabi-Yau spaces are multiply connected--that is, they have holes in them, which can determine the number of quark generations that exist in our four-dimensional space. They are important in string theory because many of the features of these manifolds, such as the number of holes they have, can determine the number of quarks there are in our four-dimensional universe." (Kaku, 2005, 383).

Cannabis Commonly known as marijuana and by numerous

other names, it may be termed a psychoactive drug which has medicinal uses. "Pharmacologically, the principal psychoactive constituent of cannabis is tetrahydrocannabinol (THC); it is one of 483 known compounds in the plant, including at least 84 other cannabinoids, such as cannabidiol (CBD), cannabinol (CBN), tetrahydrocannabinvarin (THCV), and cannabigerol (CBG)." ("Marijuana," *Wikipedia*).

"Cannabis is often consumed for its psychoactive and physiological effects, which can include heightened mood or euphoria, relaxation, and an increase in appetite. Unwanted side-effects can sometimes include a decrease in short-term memory, dry mouth, impaired motor skills, reddening of the eyes, and feelings of paranoia or anxiety." (Ibid).

"Contemporary uses of cannabis are as a recreational or medicinal drug, and as part of religious or spiritual rites; the earliest recorded uses date from the 3rd millennium BC. Since the early 20th century cannabis has been subject to legal restrictions with the possession, use, and sale of cannabis preparations containing psychoactive cannabinoids currently illegal in most countries of the world; the United Nations has said that cannabis is the most-used illicit drug in the world. In 2004, the United Nations estimated that global consumption of cannabis indicated that approximately 4 percent of the adult world population (162 million people) used cannabis annually, and that approximately 0.6 percent (22.5 million) of people used cannabis daily." (Ibid).

Botanically, there are many different strains and hybrids of the Cannabis plant: *Cannabis sativa, Cannabis indica, Cannabis ruderalis*. Globally, major producing countries have included but are not limited to the following: Afghanistan, Burma, Canada, China, Colombia, India, Jamaica, Laos, Lebanon, Mexico, Netherlands, Pakistan, Paraguay, Thailand, Turkey, and the USA. (Ibid).

"Cannabis has psychoactive and physiological effects when consumed. The immediate desired effects from consuming cannabis include relaxation and mild euphoria (the 'high' or 'stoned' feeling), while some immediate undesired side-effects include a decrease in short-term memory, dry mouth, impaired motor skills and reddening of the eyes. Aside from a subjective change in perception and mood, the most common short-term physical and neurological effects include increased heart rate, increased appetite and consumption of food, lowered blood pressure, impairment of short-term and working memory, psychomotor coordination, and concentration." (Ibid).

"Cannabis has been used to reduce nausea and vomiting in chemotherapy and people with AIDS, and to treat pain and muscle spasticity. According to a 2013 review, 'Safety concerns regarding cannabis include the increased risk of developing schizophrenia with adolescent use, impairments in memory and cognition, accidental pediatric ingestions, and lack of safety packaging for medical cannabis formulations.'" (Ibid).

"A 2013 review comparing different structural and functional imaging studies showed morphological brain alterations in long-term cannabis users which were found to possibly correlate to cannabis exposure. A 2010 review found resting blood flow to be lower globally and in prefrontal areas of the brain in cannabis users, when compared to non-users. It was also shown that giving THC or cannabis correlated with increased blood flow in these areas, and facilitated activation of the anterior cingulate cortex and frontal cortex when participants were presented with assignments demanding use of cognitive capacity. Both reviews noted that some of the studies that they examined had methodological limitations, for example small sample sizes or not distinguishing adequately between cannabis and alcohol consumption." (Ibid).

"*Cannabis indica* may have a CBD:THC ratio four to five times that of *Cannabis sativa*. Cannabis strains with relatively high CBD:THC ratios are less likely to induce anxiety than those with a lower ratio. This may be due to CBD's antagonistic effects at the cannabinoid receptors, compared to THC's partial agonist effect. CBD is also a 5-HT1A receptor agonist, which may also contribute to an anxiolytic effect. This likely means the high concentrations of CBD found in Cannabis indica mitigate the anxiogenic effect of THC significantly. The effects of sativa are well known for their cerebral high, hence its daytime use as medical cannabis, while indica is well known for its sedative effects and preferred night time use as medical cannabis." (Ibid).

"According to the United Nations Office on Drugs and Crime (UNODC), 'the amount of THC present in a cannabis sample is generally used as a measure of cannabis potency.' The three main forms of cannabis products are the flower, resin (hashish), and oil (hash oil). The UNODC states that cannabis often contains 5 percent THC content, resin 'can contain up to 20 percent THC content', and that 'Cannabis oil may contain more than 60 percent THC content.'" (Ibid).

"A scientific study published in 2000 in the Journal of Forensic Sciences (JFS) found that the potency (THC content) of confiscated cannabis in the United States (US) rose from 'approximately 3.3 percent in 1983 and 1984', to '4.47 percent in 1997'. The study also concluded that 'other major cannabinoids (i.e., CBD, CBN, and CBC)' (other chemicals in cannabis) 'showed no significant change in their concentration over the years'. More recent research undertaken at the University of Mississippi's Potency Monitoring Project found that average THC levels in cannabis samples between 1975 and 2007 steadily increased, for example THC levels in 1985 averaged 3.48 percent by 2006 this had increased to an average of 8.77 percent." (Ibid).

"Australia's National Cannabis Prevention and Information Centre (NCPIC) states that the buds (flowers) of the female cannabis plant contain the highest concentration of THC, followed by the leaves…" (Ibid).

"Marijuana consists of the dried flowers and subtending leaves and stems of the female *Cannabis* plant. This is the most widely consumed form, containing 3 percent to 22 percent THC. In contrast, cannabis varieties used to produce industrial hemp contain less than 1 percent THC and are thus not valued for recreational use." (Ibid).

"Kief is a powder, rich in trichomes, which can be sifted from the leaves and flowers of cannabis plants and either is consumed in powder form or compressed to produce cakes of hashish…" (Ibid).

"Hashish (also spelled hasheesh, hashisha, or simply hash) is a concentrated resin cake or ball produced from pressed kief, the detached trichomes and fine material that falls off of cannabis flowers and leaves. It varies in color from black to golden brown depending upon purity and variety of cultivar it was obtained from. It can be consumed orally or smoked." (Ibid).

"There are many varieties of cannabis infusions owing to the variety of non-volatile solvents used. The plant material is mixed with the solvent and then pressed and filtered to express the oils of the plant into the solvent. Examples of solvents used in this process are cocoa butter, dairy butter, cooking oil, glycerine, and skin moisturizers. Depending on the solvent, these may be used in cannabis foods or applied topically." (Ibid).

"Cannabis is consumed in many different ways:

"Smoking, which typically involves inhaling vaporized cannabinoids ('smoke') from small pipes, bongs (portable versions of hookahs with water chamber), paper-wrapped joints or tobacco-leaf-wrapped blunts, roach clips, and other items." (Ibid).

39

"Vaporizer, which heats herbal cannabis to 165–190 degrees C (329–374 degrees F), causing the active ingredients to evaporate into a vapor without burning the plant material (the boiling point of THC is 157 degrees C (315 degrees F) at 760 mmHg pressure)." (Ibid).

"Cannabis tea, which contains relatively small concentrations of THC because THC is an oil (lipophilic) and is only slightly water-soluble (with a solubility of 2.8 mg per liter). Cannabis tea is made by first adding a saturated fat to hot water (e.g. cream or any milk except skim) with a small amount of cannabis." (Ibid).

"Edibles, where cannabis is added as an ingredient to one of a variety of foods." (Ibid).

"Marijuana vending machines for selling or dispensing cannabis are in use in the United States and are planned to be used in Canada." (Ibid).

"It is often claimed by growers and breeders of herbal cannabis that advances in breeding and cultivation techniques have increased the potency of cannabis since the late 1960s and early '70s, when THC was first discovered and understood. However, potent seedless cannabis such as 'Thai sticks' were already available at that time. *Sinsemilla* (Spanish for 'without seed') is the dried, seedless inflorescences of female cannabis plants. Because THC production drops off once pollination occurs, the male plants (which produce little THC themselves) are eliminated before they shed pollen to prevent pollination. Advanced cultivation techniques such as hydroponics, cloning, high-intensity artificial lighting, and the sea of green method are frequently employed as a response (in part) to prohibition enforcement efforts that make outdoor cultivation more risky. It is often cited that the average levels of THC in cannabis sold in United States rose dramatically between the 1970s and 2000, but such statements are likely skewed because of undue weight given to much more expensive and potent, but less prevalent samples." (Ibid).

"'Skunk' refers to several named strains of potent cannabis, grown through selective breeding and sometimes hydroponics. It is a cross-breed of Cannabis sativa and C. indica (although other strains of this mix exist in abundance). Skunk cannabis potency ranges usually from 6 percent to 15 percent and rarely as high as 20 percent. The average THC level in coffee shops in the Netherlands is about 18–19 percent." (Ibid).

History

"Cannabis is indigenous to Central and South Asia. Evidence

of the inhalation of cannabis smoke can be found in the 3rd millennium BCE, as indicated by charred cannabis seeds found in a ritual brazier at an ancient burial site in present day Romania. In 2003, a leather basket filled with cannabis leaf fragments and seeds were found next to a 2,500- to 2,800-year-old mummified shaman in the northwestern Xinjiang Uygur Autonomous Region of China. Evidence for the consumption of cannabis has also been found in Egyptian mummies dated about 950 BC." (Ibid).

"Cannabis is also known to have been used by the ancient Hindus of India and Nepal thousands of years ago. The herb was called ganjika in Sanskrit (ganja in modern Indo-Aryan languages). Some scholars suggest that the ancient drug soma, mentioned in the Vedas, was cannabis, although this theory is disputed." (Ibid).

"Cannabis was also known to the ancient Assyrians, who discovered its psychoactive properties through the Aryans. Using it in some religious ceremonies, they called it *qunubu* (meaning 'way to produce smoke'), a probable origin of the modern word 'cannabis'. Cannabis was also introduced by the Aryans to the Scythians, Thracians and Dacians, whose shamans (the *kapnobatai*--'those who walk on smoke/clouds') burned cannabis flowers to induce a state of trance." (Ibid).

"Cannabis has an ancient history of ritual use and is found in pharmacological cults around the world. Hemp seeds discovered by archaeologists at Pazyryk suggest early ceremonial practices like eating by the Scythians occurred during the 5th to 2nd century BCE, confirming previous historical reports by Herodotus. One writer has claimed that cannabis was used as a religious sacrament by ancient Jews and early Christians due to the similarity between the Hebrew word '*qannabbos*' ('*cannabis*') and the Hebrew phrase '*qene bosem*' ('aromatic cane'). It was used by Muslims in various Sufi orders as early as the Mamluk period, for example by the Qalandars." (Ibid).

"A study published in the *South African Journal of Science* showed that 'pipes dug up from the garden of Shakespeare's home in Stratford-upon-Avon contain traces of cannabis.' The chemical analysis was carried out after researchers hypothesized that the 'noted weed' mentioned in Sonnet 76 and the 'journey in my head' from Sonnet 27 could be references to cannabis and the use thereof. Examples of classic literature featuring cannabis include *Les paradis artificiels* by Charles Baudelaire and *The Hasheesh Eater* by Fitz Hugh Ludlow." (Ibid).

"John Gregory Bourke described use of 'mariguan', which he

identifies as *Cannabis indica* or Indian hemp, by Mexican residents of the Rio Grande region of Texas in 1894. He described its uses for treatment of asthma, to expedite delivery, to keep away witches, and as a love-philtre. He also wrote that many Mexicans added the herb to their *cigarritos* or mescal, often taking a bite of sugar afterward to intensify the effect. Bourke wrote that because it was often used in a mixture with toloachi (which he inaccurately describes as *Datura stramonium*), mariguan was one of several plants known as 'loco weed'. Bourke compared mariguan to hasheesh, which he called 'one of the greatest curses of the East', citing reports that users 'become maniacs and are apt to commit all sorts of acts of violence and murder', causing degeneration of the body and an idiotic appearance, and mentioned laws against sale of hasheesh 'in most Eastern countries'." (Ibid).

"Cannabis was criminalized in various countries beginning in the early 20th century. In the United States, the first restrictions for sale of cannabis came in 1906 (in District of Columbia). It was outlawed in South Africa in 1911, in Jamaica (then a British colony) in 1913, and in the United Kingdom and New Zealand in the 1920s. Canada criminalized cannabis in the Opium and Drug Act of 1923, before any reports of use of the drug in Canada. In 1925 a compromise was made at an international conference in The Hague about the International Opium Convention that banned exportation of 'Indian hemp' to countries that had prohibited its use, and requiring importing countries to issue certificates approving the importation and stating that the shipment was required 'exclusively for medical or scientific purposes'. It also required parties to 'exercise an effective control of such a nature as to prevent the illicit international traffic in Indian hemp and especially in the resin'." (Ibid).

"In the United States in 1937, the Marihuana Tax Act was passed, and prohibited the production of hemp in addition to cannabis. The reasons that hemp was also included in this law are disputed--several scholars have claimed that the act was passed in order to destroy the US hemp industry, with the primary involvement of businessmen Andrew Mellon, Randolph Hearst, and the Du Pont family. But the improvements of the decorticators, machines that separate the fibers from the hemp stem, could not make hemp fiber a very cheap substitute for fibers from other sources because it could not change that basic fact that strong fibers are only found in the bast, the outer part of the stem. Only about 1/3 of the stem are long and strong fibers." (Ibid).

"The United Nations' 2012 Global Drug Report stated that cannabis 'was the world's most widely produced, trafficked, and consumed drug in the world in 2010', identifying that between 119 million and 224 million users existed in the world's adult (18 or older) population." (Ibid).

Legal Status

"Since the beginning of the 20th century, most countries have enacted laws against the cultivation, possession or transfer of cannabis. These laws have impacted adversely on the cannabis plant's cultivation for non-recreational purposes, but there are many regions where, under certain circumstances, handling of cannabis is legal or licensed. Many jurisdictions have lessened the penalties for possession of small quantities of cannabis, so that it is punished by confiscation and sometimes a fine, rather than imprisonment, focusing more on those who traffic the drug on the black market." (Ibid).

"In some areas where cannabis use has been historically tolerated, some new restrictions have been put in place, such as the closing of cannabis coffee shops near the borders of the Netherlands, closing of coffee shops near secondary schools in the Netherlands and crackdowns on 'Pusher Street' in Christiania, Copenhagen in 2004."

"In some jurisdictions use free voluntary treatment programs and/or mandatory treatment programs for frequent known users. Simple possession can carry long prison terms in some countries, particularly in East Asia, where the sale of cannabis may lead to a sentence of life in prison or even execution. More recently however, many political parties, non-profit organizations and causes based on the legalization of medical cannabis and/or legalizing the plant entirely (with some restrictions) have emerged." (Ibid).

"In December 2012, the U.S. state of Washington became the first state to officially legalize cannabis in a state law (Washington Initiative 502) (but still illegal by federal law), with the state of Colorado following close behind (Colorado Amendment 64). On January 1, 2013, the first marijuana 'club' for private marijuana smoking (no buying or selling, however) was allowed for the first time in Colorado. The California Supreme Court decided in May 2013 that local governments can ban medical marijuana dispensaries despite a state law in California that permits the use of cannabis for medical purposes. At least 180 cities across California have enacted bans in recent years." (Ibid).

"In December 2013, Uruguay became the first country to legalize growing, sale and use of cannabis." (Ibid).

Cepheid Variable "A star that varies in brightness at a precise, calculable rate and hence serves as a 'standard candle' for distance measurements in astronomy. Cepheid variables were decisive in helping Hubble calculate the distance to the galaxies." (Kaku, 2005, 383).

Chakra "(Skt., 'wheel') a center of psychic energy in the body conceived as a lotus, especially in Tantrism. Six main chakras connected by the *susumna nadi* (in Buddhism called *avadhuti*) came to be recognized in Hinduism, the *muladhara* ('root support') at the base of the spine, the *svadhisthana* ('own place') in the genital region, the *manipura* ('jewel city') at the navel, the *anahata* ('unstruck') at the heart, the *visuddha* ('pure') at the throat, and the *ajna* ('command') between the eyebrows. Just above here are two minor chakras: the *manas* and *soma*. Above the top of the head is the thousand-petalled lotus (*sahasrara padma*; or *usnisa kamala* for Buddhists), the abode of bliss which is not classified as an ordinary chakra. Each chakra has a certain number of petals, and is associated with a particular color, shape, *tattva*, and *bija mantra*. For example, the *manipura* at the navel has ten petals, is red, and contains a triangle, Rudra is the presiding deity, *rupa tattva* dissolves in it, and its bija is *ram*. Thus the cosmos and all beings therein are contained in the totality of the chakras: 'all beings that exist in the seven worlds are to be found in the body', says the *Siva Samhita* (2.4). Tantric Buddhism (*Vajrayana*) only accepts four chakras, the *manipura, anahata, visuddha,* and *usnisa kamala*." (*The Oxford Dictionary of World Religions*, 1997).

"The texts are ambiguous as to whether the chakras are situated along the spinal column or at the nervous plexuses of the physical body. Indeed, there are discrepancies in the texts concerning the number and descriptions of the chakras, and it is unclear whether they are meant to be actually existent or whether they are heuristic devices of Tantric yoga used in visualization." (Ibid).

"1 a center for the reception, assimilation, and expression of life-force energies; 2 any of the seven energy centers of the body; 3 a disc-like vortex of energies made from the intersection of different planes; 4 wheel, as on a chariot; 5 discus, favorite weapon of Visnu; 6 the revolving wheel of the gods; 7 the wheel of time; 8 the wheel of law and celestial order; 9 a tantric ritual circle of people, alternating male and female."

"Each chakra we encounter is a step on the continuum

between matter and consciousness...ranging from the somatic level of physical and instinctual awareness through the interpersonal level of social interaction, and finally to the more abstract realms of transpersonal consciousness. When all of the chakras are understood, opened, and connected together, we have then bridge the gulf between matter and spirit, understanding that we, ourselves, are the Rainbow Bridge that connects Earth and Heaven once again." (Judith, 1999, 7).

"The chakras are inextricably linked with the science and practice of yoga. The word yoga means 'yoke,' and it is a system of philosophy and practice designed to yoke the mortal self to its divine nature of pure consciousness. The origin of yoga and earliest mention of the chakras goes back to the *Vedas*, meaning 'knowledge,' a series of hymns that are the oldest written tradition in India. These writings were created from an even older oral tradition of the Aryan culture, believed to be an invading Indo-European tribe that swept into India during the second century B.C.E." (Ibid, 9).

"Following the *Vedas* were the *Upanishads*, or wisdom teachings passed from teacher to disciple. There is some mention of the chakras as psychic centers of consciousness in the *Yoga Upanishads* (circa 600 B.C.E.) and later in the *Yoga Sutras of Patanjali* (circa C.E. 200). It is from Patanjali's sutras that we get the classic eightfold path of yoga tradition..." (Ibid, 10).

"The main text about chakras that has come to us in the West is a translation of Tantric texts by the Englishman Arthur Avalon in his book *The Serpent Power* published in 1916. These texts--the *Sat-Cakra-Nirupana*, written by an Indian pundit in 1577, and the *Padaka-Pancaka*, written in the tenth century--contain descriptions of the chakra centers and related practices..." (Ibid, 10-11).

"In these traditions, there are seven basic chakras, which exist within the subtle body, interpenetrating the physical body. The subtle body is the non-physical psychic body that is superimposed on our physical bodies. It can be measured as electromagnetic force fields within and around all living creatures...In the aura, which is the external manifestation of the subtle body, the energy field appears as a soft glow around the physical body, often made of spindle-like fibers...At the core of the body, the subtle field appears as spinning disks--chakras. The chakras are the psychic generators of the auric field. The aura itself is the meeting point between the core patterns generated by the chakras and the influence of the external world." (Ibid, 11).

45

"The chakras are gateways between various dimensions--centers where activity of one dimension, such as emotion and thought, connects and plays on another dimension, such as our physical bodies..." (Ibid, 17).

"The sum total of the chakras forms a vertical column in our bodies called *sushumna*. This column is a central integrating channel for connecting the chakras and their various dimensions..." (Ibid).

"Traveling beside, around, and through the sushumna, there are also many...acupuncture meridians, and the thousands of other *nadis*, subtle energy conduits, which Hindus have found within the subtle body." (Ibid).

"On a physical level, chakras correspond to nerve ganglia, where there is a high degree of nervous activity, and also to glands in the endocrine system...While chakras are interdependent with the nervous and endocrine systems, they are not synonymous with any portion of the physical body, but exist within the subtle body." (Ibid, 20).

"In metaphysical terminology, a chakra is a vortex...Chakras spin in a wheel-like manner, attracting or repelling activity on their particular plane by patterns analogous to a whirlpool. Anything the chakra encounters on its particular vibrational level gets drawn into the chakra, processed, and passed out again." (Ibid, 23).

"...chakras are made of symbolic patterns of our own mental and physical programming. This programming governs the way we behave. Like programming in a compute, it channels the way energy flows through the system and gives us different kinds of information..." (Ibid).

"Chakras send energy out form the core of the body, and they assimilate energy from outside that enters the core. In this way, once again, I define a chakra as an organizational center for the reception, assimilation, and transmission of life energy." (Ibid, 24).

"Chakras can be open or closed, excessive or deficient, or any of the various stages in between. These states may be basic aspects of someone's personality throughout most of their life, or something that changes from moment to moment in response to a situation..." (Ibid, 25).

In summary, "there are seven major and several minor chakras in the subtle body which act as gateways to dimensions spanning from matter to consciousness. In the human being, these seven planes correspond to archetypal levels of consciousness as well as various physical attributes. The chakras are created by the interpenetration of two major vertical currents. The lower chakras are of equal value and importance to the upper chakras for human beings at our present level of development...The system has immense value for personal growth and use in diagnosis and healing...These seven levels are proportional to the possible number of planes in a similar ration to the seven colors of the rainbow and the spectrum of electromagnetic waves. The seven basic chakras are merely the vibrations that we can perceive with our present 'equipment,'...The chakras are in constant interplay and can only be separated intellectually. The chakras can be opened through various physical exercises, tasks, meditation, healing methods, life experiences, and general understanding, leading to more profound states of consciousness." (Ibid, 46-47).

"...In addition to the major chakras, there are 122 smaller secondary chakras throughout the body..." (Bruyere, 1994, 41).

"...the chakras are connected by a non-physical channel running straight up the center of the body called the sushumna. Two alternate channels control the yin and yang energies, Ida and Pingala, twisting in figure-eight patterns around each chakra and running alongside the sushumna. These channels are among thousands of subtle energy channels called nadis, Sanskrit for 'flowing waters.' Ida and Pingala represent the luna and solar aspects, respectively." (Ibid, 113-114).

Chakra One, Root Chakra "Located at the base of the spine, [and] is associated with survival." (Judith, 1999, 24).

"Skt., '*Muladhara*'; Location: Perineum, base of spine, coccygeal plexus; Element: Earth; Psychological Function: Survival, grounding; Resulting in: Grounding; Identity: Physical identity; Developmental Stage: Womb-12 mos.; Glands: Adrenal; Other Body Parts: Legs, feet, bones, large intestine; Malfunction: Obesity, anorexia, Sciatica, constipation; Color: Red; Sephiroth: Malkuth; Gemstones: Ruby, garnet, hematite; Yoga Path: Hatha; Gunas: Tamas; Archangel: Auriel." (Ibid, 42, 58-59).

"The Sanskrit name for this chakra is *Muladhara*, which means 'root support.' The sciatic nerve, traveling from the sacral plexus down through the legs, is the largest peripheral nerve in the body (about as thick as your thumb) and functions much like a root for the nervous system...Our legs touch the ground below us and connect our nervous system with the earth, our first chakra element. We respond then, kinesthetically, to gravity--the basic underlying force of the earth--constantly pulling us downward. This force keeps us connected to our planet, rooted in material existence." (Ibid, 60).

"In the body, the first chakra is located at the base of the spine, or more accurately, the perineum, midway between the anus and the genitals. It corresponds to the section of the spine called the coccyx, as well as the coccygeal spinal ganglion and the lower lumbar vertebrae from which this ganglion sprouts..." (Ibid, 61).

"We have described chakras as vortices of energy. At the level of the first chakra, our vortex is the most dense of any chakra level..." (Ibid, 64).

"Consciousness in the Muladhara chakra is primarily concerned with physical survival. It is our instinctual fight or flight response..." (Ibid).

"Grounding is a process of dynamic contact with the Earth, with its edges, boundaries, and limitations. It allows us to become solidly real--present in the here and now--and dynamically alive with the vitality that comes from the Earth...Grounding involves opening the lower chakras, merging with gravity, and descending deeply into the vehicle of the body." (Ibid, 66).

"Without grounding, we are unstable; we lose our center, fly off the handle, get swept off our feet, or daydream in a fantasy world. We lose our ability to contain, to have, or to hold. Natural excitement, or charge, becomes dissipated, diluted, and ineffectual. When we lose our ground, our attention wanders from the present moment, and we appear to be 'not all here.' In this state, we feel powerless and, like a vicious circle, may no longer want to be here." (Ibid, 67).

"Measurements have shown that when the human body is standing on the ground, it is electrically grounded as well. There is an electrostatic field surrounding the Earth with a resonant frequency of about 7.5 cycles per second. The late Itzhak Bentov discussed a micro-motion of the body that consists of the constant vibration of the heart, cells, and bodily fluids. He determined that this micro-motion vibrates at a frequency of 6.8 to 7.5 cycles per second. Therefore, the body's natural frequency resonates with the Earth's ionosphere. Connecting physically to this great body...our own bodies enter into this resonance more deeply." (Ibid, 70).

"Grounding is a way of coping with stress..." (Ibid).

"Grounding brings clarity through stillness..." (Ibid, 71).

"Grounding forms a foundation..." (Ibid).

Chakra Two, Sacrum Chakra "Located in the lower abdomen,.[and] is associated with emotions and sexuality." (Judith, 1999, 24).

"Skt., '*Svadhisthana*'; Location: Sacrum; Element: Water;

Psychological Function: Desire; Resulting in: Sexuality; Identity: Emotional identity; Developmental Stage: 6-24 mos.; Glands: Gonads, ovaries, testicles; Other Body Parts: Womb, genitals, kidney, bladder, lower back, circulatory system; Malfunction: Impotence, frigidity, urinary, bladder or kidney trouble, stiff lower back; Color: Orange; Sephiroth: Yesod; Gemstones: Coral, carnelian, yellow zircon; Yoga Path: Tantra; Gunas: Tamas; Archangel: Gabriel." (Ibid, 42, 106-107).

"The second chakra is located in the lower abdomen centered between the navel and the genitals, although it encompasses the whole section of the body between these two points. It corresponds to the nerve ganglion called the sacral plexus. This plexus hooks into the sciatic nerve..." (Ibid, 110).

"This chakra is the center of sexuality as well as emotions, sensation, pleasure, movement, and nurturance..." (Ibid, 112).

"In Sanskrit, the chakra is called *Svadhisthana*, usually translated as 'one's own abode,' from the root *sva* meaning 'one's own.' We also find in it the root *svad* which means 'to taste sweet' or 'to taste with pleasure, to enjoy or take delight'." (Ibid).

"Clairsentience is the psychic sense of the second chakra, the first stirrings of 'higher' consciousness and the development of greater sensitivity toward others." (Ibid, 133).

"Clairsentience is the ability to sense other people's emotions, also called empathy." (Ibid).

Chakra Three, Solar Plexus Chakra "Located in the solar plexus, [and] is associated with personal power, will, and self-esteem." (Judith, 1999, 24).

"Skt., '*Manipura*'; Location: Solar Plexus; Element: Fire; Psychological Function: Will, power, assertiveness; Resulting in: Laughter, joy, anger; Identity: Ego identity; Developmental Stage: 18-24 mos.; Glands: Pancreas, adrenals; Other Body Parts: Digestive system, liver, gall bladder, muscles; Malfunction: Digestive system, ulcers, diabetes, hypoglycemia, chronic fatigue, hypertension; Color: Yellow; Sephiroth: Hod, Netzach; Gemstones: Amber, topaz, appetite; Yoga Path: Karma; Gunas: Rajas; Archangel: Michael." (Ibid, 43, 150-151).

"...Its purpose is transformation...the third chakra transforms the passive elements of earth and water into dynamic energy and power..." (Ibid, 152).

"In the body, the third chakra is located in the solar plexus, over the adrenal glands..." (Ibid, 154).

"As the name solar plexus implies, this is a fiery, solar chakra,

49

bring us light, warmth, energy, and power. It represents our 'get up and go,' our action, our will, our vitality...One of its associations with power comes from the belief that all the major nadis (psychic currents) originate from the navel..." (Ibid, 155).

"...the third chakra rules over metabolism, and is responsible for the regulation and distribution of metabolic energy throughout the body." (Ibid).

"In Sanskrit, this chakra is called *Manipura*, which means 'lustrous gem,' because it shines bright like the sun--a radiant, glowing center." (Ibid, 157).

"The third chakra attributes of power, will, vitality, and self-discipline are ultimately based on self-esteem. When our self-esteem is high, we are confident, assertive, proactive, disciplined, and basically excited about life..." (Ibid, 170).

Chakra Four, Heart Chakra "Located over the sternum, [and] is associated with love." (Judith, 1999, 24).

"Skt., '*Anahata*'; Location: Heart; Element: Air; Psychological Function: Love; Resulting in: Peace; Identity: Social identity, compassion, love; Developmental Stage: 3.5-7 years; Glands: Thymus; Other Body Parts: Lungs, heart, circulatory system, arms, hands; Malfunction: Asthma, high blood pressure, coronary and heart disease, lung disease; Color: Green; Sephiroth: Tiphareth; Gemstones: Emerald, tourmaline, jade; Yoga Path: Bhakti; Gunas: Rajas/Sattva; Archangel: Raphael." (Ibid, 43, 190-191).

"The symbol for the heart chakra is a circle of twelve lotus petals surrounding two intersecting triangles, forming a six pointed star...This symbol (also known as the Star of David) represents the Sacred Marriage: the balanced interpenetration of masculine and feminine. This is the star of radiance that emanates from an open heart chakra. The six points can also be seen as relating to the six other chakras, as they are each integrated at this center." (Ibid, 193).

"In the body, this chakra relates to the cardiac plexus, and rules over the heart, lungs, and thymus gland." (Ibid).

"The Sanskrit name for this chakra is *Anahata*, meaning 'sound that is made without any two things striking,' as well as 'unstruck,' 'unhurt,' 'fresh,' and 'clean.' When the chakra is free of grief from old hurts, its opening is innocent, fresh, and radiant..." (Ibid, 196).

"The element of the fourth chakra is air, the least dense of our physical elements so far...air represents breath, the vital process through which our cells are kept alive. The Hindus call it *prana*

50

(from *pra*, 'first,' and *na*, 'unit'). In yoga philosophy, prana is referred to as a vital energy in and of itself, a basic unit from which all like is made. This energy represents an interface between the physical world and the mental world. The mind, if it wishes to influence the body, can do so through control of the breath. Likewise, control of the breath can quiet the mind. Prana is considered a vital link between the two--just as the heart chakra is the integrator between upper and lower chakras." (Ibid, 196, 198).

"Opening the heart chakra requires a combination of technique and understanding. First, we learn to see the world in terms of relationships--what causes things to enter into and remain in combination with other things. This, of course, includes our personal relationships with others and with the world around us." (Ibid, 198).

"The heart requires an understanding and practice of balance--between mind and body, inner and outer realms, self and other, giving and receiving. Opening the heart requires a transcendence of ego, allowing us to surrender to forces larger than the self. Lastly, opening the heart chakra requires an understanding and control of the breath, for it is the tool of physical and mental transformation." (Ibid).

"Love is a unifying force--it draws things together, and keeps them in relationship. From this unity, we can touch an underlying continuity that allows our separate parts to be held in relationship to something larger. A binding force allows something to hold together long enough to evolve its patterns to deeper and more cohesive states. Love allows change and freedom, but keeps coherence at the center." (Ibid).

"In entering the fourth chakra, we transcend ego in order to loosen our self-defined boundaries and merge into the ecstasy of love. There is no greater way to invite love than to offer it first..." (Ibid).

"...If we see love as infinite, and approach it from abundance instead of scarcity, we see that in truth love is self-perpetuating." (Ibid).

"...The greater our understanding, the greater our capacity for love. The heart chakra perceives the world in its unity, not its separation." (Ibid).

Chakra Five, Throat Chakra "Located in the throat, [and] is associated with *communication and creativity*." (Judith, 1999, 24).

"Skt., '*Vishudda*'; Location: Throat; Element: Sound; Psychological Function: Communication; Resulting in: Creativity, synthesis of ideas into symbols; Identity: Creative identity; Developmental Stage: 7-12 yrs.; Glands: Thyroid, parathyroid; Other Body Parts: Throat, ears, mouth, shoulders, neck; Malfunction: Sore throat, neck and shoulder pain, thyroid troubles; Color: Bright blue; Sephiroth: Geburah, Chesed; Gemstones: Turquoise, aquamarine, celestite; Yoga Path: Mantra yoga; Gunas: Rajas/Sattva." (Ibid, 43, 234).

"Communication is the connecting principle that makes life possible. From DNA encoded messages of living cells to the spoken or written word, from the nerve impulses connecting mind and body to the broadcast waves connecting continent to continent, communication is the coordinating principle of all life. It is the means whereby consciousness extends itself from one place to another." (Ibid, 234-235).

"Within the body, communication is crucial. Without electrical communication between brain waves and muscle tissue, we couldn't move. Without chemical communication of hormones to cells there would be no growth, no cues for cyclic changes, no defenses against disease. If it were not for the ability of DNA to communicate genetic information, life could not exist." (Ibid, 236).

"Chakra five is the center related to communication through sound, vibration, self-expression, and creativity. It is the realm of consciousness that controls, creates, transmits, and receives communication, both within ourselves and between each other. It is the center of dynamic creativity, of synthesizing old ideas into something new. Its attributes include listening, speaking, writing, chanting, telepathy, and any of the arts--especially those related to sound and language." (Ibid).

"Communication is the process of transmitting and receiving information through symbols. As written or spoken words, as musical patterns, omens, or electrical impulses to the brain, the fifth chakra is the center that translates these symbols into information. Communication, due to its symbolic nature, is an essential key to ascending the inner planes." (Ibid).

"...Communication is our first level of physical transcendence in that it enables us to transcend the ordinary limitations of the body." (Ibid, 237).

"The associated element of the fifth chakra is ether, otherwise known as Akasha or spirit. It is in the fifth chakra that we refine our awareness enough to perceive the subtle field or vibration known as the etheric plane. This plane is the vibrating field of subtle matter that functions as both a cause and a result of our thoughts, emotions, and physical states." (Ibid, 239, 242).

"Richard Gerber, M.D., in his groundbreaking book, *Vibrational Medicine*, describes how 'in reality, it is the organizing principle of the etheric body which maintains and sustains the growth of the physical body.' Diseases tend to show up first in the etheric body, before they manifest in the tissues." (Ibid, 242).

Chakra Six, Third Eye Chakra "Located in the center of the forehead, [and] is associated with clairvoyance, intuition and imagination." (Judith, 1999, 24).

"Skt., '*Ajna*'; Location: Brow, center of the head slightly above eye level; Element: Light; Psychological Function: Seeing, intuition; Resulting in: Imagination; Identity: Archetypal identity; Developmental Stage: Puberty; Glands: Pineal; Other Body Parts: Eyes, base of skull, brow; Malfunction: Vision problems; headaches, nightmares; Color: Indigo; Sephiroth: Binah, Chokmah; Gemstones: Lapis, quartz; Yoga Path: Yantra; Gunas: Sattva." (Ibid, 44, 279-280).

"...With intuition, we see our way through situations, gleaning wisdom to guide us in difficult moments." (Ibid, 281).

"It is this gift of seeing--both inner and outer--that is the essence and function of chakra six. Through seeing, we have both a means of internalizing the outer world, and a symbolic language for externalization the inner world. Through our perception of spatial relationships, we have building blocks for both memory of the past and imagination of the future. Thus, this chakra transcends time." (Ibid).

"The 'brow chakra,' as it is often called, is located in the center of the head behind the forehead--either at eye level or slightly above, varying from person to person. It is associated with the third eye, an etheric organ of psychic perception floating between our two physical eyes. The third eye can be seen as the psychic organ of the sixth chakra, just as the physical eyes are tools of perception of the brain. The chakra itself includes the inner screen and vast storehouse of images that comprise our visual thinking process. The third eye sees beyond the physical world, bringing us added insight, just as reading between the lines of written material brings us deeper understanding." (Ibid).

"The Sanskrit name of this chakra is *ajna*, which originally meant 'to perceive' and later 'to command.' This speaks to the twofold nature of this chakra--to take in images through perception, but also to form inner images from which we command our reality, commonly known as creative visualization..."

53

(Ibid, 281-282).

"The corresponding element to this chakra is light. Through the sensory interpretation of light we obtain information about the world around us. How much we are able to see depends upon how open or developed this chakra is, including, to some degree, the acuity of our normal eyesight. The gamut of visual and psychic ability can run from those who are extremely observant of the physical world to those who are gifted in psychic perception, who can see auras, chakras, details of the astral plane, precognition (the 'seeing' of future events) and remote viewing (seeing things in other places)." (Ibid, 282).

"...the brow chakra ...is more mental than any of the previous chakras. Our visual perceptions must become translated into other forms, such as language, actions, or emotions, before they can be tangibly shared. As we become more mental, we leave behind the limitations of time and space and enter a transpersonal dimension." (Ibid, 284).

"As each chakra corresponds to a gland, chakra six is related to the pineal gland, a tiny (10 x 6 mm) cone-shaped gland located in the geometric center of the head at approximately eye level..." (Ibid).

"The pineal gland, sometimes called the 'seat of the soul,' acts as a light meter for the body, translating variations in light to hormonal messages relayed to the body through the autonomic nervous system. Over 100 body functions have daily rhythms which are influenced by exposure to light. The pineal reaches the height of its development at age seven, and has been thought to influence the maturation of the sex glands. Embryologically, the pineal gland is derived from a third eye that begins to develop early in the embryo and later degenerates." (Ibid).

Chakra Seven, Crown Chakra "Located at the top of the head, [and] is associated with knowledge, understanding and transcendent consciousness." (Judith, 1999, 24).

"Skt., 'Sahasrara'; Location: Top of Head; Element: Thought; Manifestation: Information; Psychological Function: Understanding; Resulting in: Bliss; Identity: Universal identity; Developmental Stage: Throughout life; Glands: Pituitary; Other Body Parts: Central nervous system, cerebral cortex; Malfunction: Depression, alienation, confusion, boredom, apathy, inability to learn; Color: Violet, white; Sephiroth: Kether; Gemstones: Diamond, amethyst; Yoga Path: Jnana; Gunas: Sattva." (Ibid, 44, 317-318).

"...seat of cosmic consciousness known as the seventh or crown chakra. This chakra connects us to divine intelligence and the source of all manifestation. It is the means through which we reach understanding and find meaning. As the final goal of our liberating current, it is the place of ultimate liberation." (Ibid, 319).

"...the crown chakra represents the ruling principle of life–the place where the underlying order and meaning of all things is ultimately perceived. It is the pervading consciousness that thinks, reasons, and gives form and focus to our activities. It is the true essence of being as the awareness that dwells within. In the unconscious, it is the wisdom of the body. In the conscious mind, it is the intellect and our belief system. In the superconscious, it is awareness of the divine." (Ibid).

"...this chakra reveals a pattern of such magnitude, complexity, and beauty, that it is almost overwhelming...a monad of intelligence...an overarching divine intelligence--sensitive, aware, responsive, and infinite..." (Ibid, 319-320).

"It is this chakra that yoga philosophy has deemed to be the seat of enlightenment. Its ultimate state of consciousness is beyond reason, beyond the senses, and beyond the limits of the world around us. Yoga practices advise withdrawing the senses (*pratyahara*) in order to achieve the mental stillness necessary to perceive this ultimate state. Tantric philosophy, on the other hand, regards the senses as a gateway to awakening consciousness. Chakra theory tells us that it is both--a stimulation of intelligence to give us information, and a withdrawal to the interior where information is sifted into ultimate knowledge." (Ibid, 320).

"The element of this chakra is thought, a fundamentally distinct and unmeasurable entity that is the first and barest manifestation of the greater field of consciousness around us. Accordingly, the function of the greater field of consciousness around us. Accordingly, the function of Sahasrara is knowing--just as other chakras are related to seeing, speaking, loving, doing, feeling, or having." (Ibid).

"The seventh chakra relates to what we experience as the mind especially the awareness that makes use of the mind. The mind is a stage for the play of consciousness..." (Ibid, 321).

"Through...thoughts, our mind assimilates experience into meaning and constructs our belief systems. These belief are the master programs from which we construct our reality. (In this way, the crown chakra is the master chakra, and relates to the master gland of the endocrine system, the pituitary.)" (Ibid).

"Physiologically, the crown chakra relates to the brain, especially the higher brain, or cerebral cortex. Our amazing human brain contains some thirteen billion interconnected nerve cells, capable of making more connections among themselves than the number of stars in the entire universe. This is a remarkable statement. Our brains, as instruments of awareness, are virtually limitless. Yet there are 100 million sensory receptors within the body, and ten trillion synapses in the nervous system, making the mind 100,000 times more sensitive to its internal environment than to its external one. So it is truly from a place within that we receive and assimilate most of our knowledge." (Ibid).

"From within, we access a dimension that has no locality in time and space...ultimate states of consciousness are described as omnipresent–by reducing the world to a pattern system occupying no physical dimension, we have infinite storage capacity for its symbols..." (Ibid).

"Pattern relates to the word for father, *pater*. The father gives the seed (DNA), the information or pattern which stimulates the creation of form...Mother comes from *mater*, as does the English word: matter..." (Ibid, 322).

"...Consciousness is the field of patterns from which manifestation emerges." (Ibid).

"...Higher consciousness is the awareness of a higher or deeper order–one that is more inclusive. Higher consciousness is sometimes called cosmic consciousness, and refers to awareness of a cosmic or celestial order. Where the lower chakras are full of millions of bits of information about the physical world and its cycles of cause and effect, cosmic consciousness reaches far into the galaxies and beyond, opening to the awareness of unifying truths. It is the perception of meta-patterns, overarching organizational principles of our cosmic ordering system. From this place we can descend again to lesser orders with an innate understanding of their structure and function as subsets of these meta-patterns." (Ibid).

"Some say Sahasrara is the seat of the soul, an eternal and dimensionless witness that stays with us throughout lifetimes. Others say it is the point through which the divine spark of Shiva enters the body and brings intelligence. It is the master processor of all awareness–the gateway to worlds beyond and worlds within, the dimensionless circumference that encompasses all that is. However we choose to describe it, we must remember that its scope is far greater than our words can convey. It can only be experienced." (Ibid, 323).

"The crown chakra is a meeting point between finite and infinite, mortal and divine, temporal and timeless. It is the gateway through which we expand beyond our personal self, beyond the limits of space time and experience primordial unity and transcendent bliss. It is also the point at which divine consciousness enters the body and descends, bringing awareness to all the chakras, giving us the means to operate in the world around us." (Ibid, 331-332).

Chakra System can be thought of "...as a profound system for spiritual growth, as well as a diagram of the sacred architecture in which we are embedded–the larger structure that holds us..." (Judith, 1999, xvi).

"...there are many other metaphysical systems featuring seven levels of man, nature, or physical planes. The Theosophists, for example, talk about seven cosmic rays of creation, with seven evolutionary races. The Christians talk about seven days of creation, as well as seven sacraments, seven seals, seven angels, seven deadly sins..." (Judith, 1999, 13).

Chandra X-Ray Telescope "The X-ray telescope in outer space that can scan the heavens for X-ray emissions, such as those emitted by a black hole or neutron star." (Kaku, 2005, 384).

Channeling "In contemporary Western culture, the term *channeling* refers to the ability of persons who claim to speak or write messages coming from personalities other than their own. With the mind or body in a light trance the person appears to be taken over by another personality, who communicates through the individual, often with messages of spiritual or psychological import. The idea is that the person is a 'channel' for some other, higher source that communicates through him or her. This source may be understood as having higher spiritual advancement, psychic skills, or special knowledge. It may identify itself as a teacher, spiritual guide, or even a deity, as well as a spirit of someone who has died." (Hastings, 1997, 198).

"The channeled entity often speaks as a spiritual and psychological guide, giving advice, teachings, information, and ideas to the channel personality or more publicly to others. Besides being spoken aloud, the messages may come mentally, or through automatic writing..." (Ibid).

"This phenomenon is not a new one. It is known from ancient religions, when the individuals who spoke in trances and ecstasy were considered prophets or oracles for the gods. Even now, in various mainstream and minority religions, within many cultures, possession by the holy spirit, speaking in ecstasy, or possession by spirits is considered a sign of spiritual development, and is often encourages and facilitated by ceremony and ritual. Channeling may be the current equivalent of ancient prophecy, bringing spiritual guidance and teachings for this time." (Ibid, 198-199).

Chaos "The primordial condition from which (or onto which) order is imposed, according to many religions, so that the cosmos can appear. This is often a matter of creation, but it can equally be a matter of evolution. Chaos may remain behind, or below, the appearance of order, so that it, or its agents, constantly threatens to reappear." (*The Oxford Dictionary of World Religions*, 1997).

Chaos Theory "is a field of study in mathematics, with applications in several disciplines including physics, engineering, economics, biology, and philosophy. Chaos theory studies the behavior of dynamical systems that are highly sensitive to initial conditions, an effect which is popularly referred to as the butterfly effect. Small differences in initial conditions (such as those due to rounding errors in numerical computation) yield widely diverging outcomes for such dynamical systems, rendering long-term prediction impossible in general. This happens even though these systems are deterministic, meaning that their future behavior is fully determined by their initial conditions, with no random elements involved. In other words, the deterministic nature of these systems does not make them predictable. This behavior is known as deterministic chaos, or simply chaos." ("Chaos Theory," *Wikipedia*).

Chaotic inflation "A version of inflation, proposed by Andrei Linde, whereby inflation occurs at random. This means that universes can bud off other universes in a continual, chaotic fashion, creating a multiverse. Chaotic inflation is one way to solve the problem of ending inflation, since we now have the random generation of inflated universes of all types." (Kaku, 2005, 384).

Chi "(Chin., 'air, breath, strength'). The vital energy (in Chinese religion, medicine and philosophy) which pervades and enables all things. Beginning from the elementary observation that the secret of a long life is to keep on breathing, it underlies the central Chinese, especially Taoist, concern with breathing exercises in relation to prolonging life and attaining immortality. 'Nourishing the life spirit' (*yang ch'i*) by a variety of exercises, including diet, breath control, and sexual control, became pervasive. It is thus closely associated with *yuan-ch'i* and *ne-ch'i*. It is gathered in the human body in the 'ocean of breath' (*ch'i-hai*) just below the navel, where it must be carefully fostered, especially through breathing practices, above all *hsing-ch'i*, which allows the breath/energy to permeate the whole body, by imagining the breath as a visible line or lines moving through the body; or *t'ai-hsi* which reverts one's breathing to that of an embryo or fetus in the womb, and which, by transferring ordinary breathing (outer ch'i or *wai-ch'i*) to dependent but directed breathing, is powerful in leading to cures and immortality. The harnessing of ch'i through breathing practices is thus indispensable to Taoist life, and to its understanding of what constitutes all manifest appearance: the cosmos is an expression of Tao, in which ch'i is brought into the balance of yin-yang. Their separation brought heaven and earth into being, their reunion in different degrees or patterns of association brings 'the ten thousand things' (*wan-wu*)--i.e. the totality of all entities and creatures--into being: 'In the beginning there was only the One, before heaven and earth were separated. When this One was divided, yin and yang came into being. That which received *yang-ch'i* rose light and clear, and became heaven; that which received *yin-ch'i* sand dark and heavy, and became earth; that which received both in right balance became human' (Miyuki, *Die Erfahrung der goldenen Blute* (1984), 185). Medically, ch'i was developed into the exercises of *ch'i-kung*, also known as outer exercises (*wai-kung*)." (*The Oxford Dictionary of World Religions*, 1997).

Ch'i "In Taoist mysticism and traditional Chinese medicine, the flow of energy in the body; also, 'the breath of life'. Practitioners of acupuncture believe that ch'i flows through channels of the body known as meridians and that an imbalance of ch'i leads to disease. Stimulation of acupuncture points along these meridians helps to rectify this imbalance. In Japan, ch'i is designated 'ki'." (Drury, 2002, 49).

Although the term *ch'i*, or vital breath, only appears three times in the *Tao Te Ching*, its' role is central to the development of Taoist meditation techniques. "Ch'i refers to the metaphysical concept of material energy coursing through our body and universe. The same concept exists in the Indian tradition as *prana*, in the Greek tradition of *pneuma*, in the Latin tradition as *spiritus*, and in the Hebrew tradition as *ruah*." (Mair, 1998, 137).

"In Chinese philosophy, the field idea is not only implicit in the notion of the *Tao* as being empty and formless, and yet producing all forms, but is also expressed explicitly in the concept of *ch'i*. This term played an important role in almost every Chinese school of natural philosophy and was particularly important in Neo-Confucianism; the school which attempted a synthesis of Confucianism, Buddhism and Taoism. The word *ch'i* literally means 'gas' or 'ether', and was used in ancient China to denote the vital breath or energy animating the cosmos. In the human body, the 'pathways of *ch'i*' are the basis of traditional Chinese medicine. The aim of acupuncture is to stimulate the flow of *ch'i* through these channels. The flow of *ch'i* is also the basis of the flowing movements of *T'ai Chi Ch'uan*, the Taoist dance of the warrior." (Capra, 2000, 213).

"The Neo-Confucians developed a notion of *ch'i* which bears the most striking resemblance to the concept of the quantum field in modern physics. Like the quantum field, *ch'i* is conceived as a tenuous and non-perceptible form of matter which is present throughout space and can condense into solid material objects. In the words of Chang Tsai: 'When the *ch'i* condenses, its visibility becomes apparent so that there are then the shapes (of individual things). When it disperses, its visibility is no longer apparent and there are no shapes. At the time of its condensation, can one say otherwise than that this is but temporary? But at the time of its dispensing, can one hastily say that it is then non-existent?'" (Ibid, 213-214).

"Thus *ch'i* condenses and disperses rhythmically, bringing forth all forms which eventually dissolve into the Void. As Chang Tsai says again, 'The Great Void cannot but consist of *ch'i*; this *ch'i* cannot but condense to form all things; and these things cannot but become dispersed so as to form (once more) the Great Void.' As in quantum field theory, the field--or the *ch'i*--is not only the underlying essence of all material objects, but also carries their mutual interactions in the form of waves." (Ibid, 214).

Children

Clairsentience "is the psychic sense of the second chakra, the first stirrings of 'higher' consciousness and the development of greater sensitivity toward others." (Judith, 1999, 133).

"Clairsentience is the ability to sense other people's emotions, also called empathy." (Ibid).

"Most people are clairsentient to some degree. The phenomenon usually occurs more strongly in people who have a proclivity for clairvoyance or telepathy, characteristics of the upper chakras..." (Ibid).

60

Clairvoyance "Paranormal acquisition of information about an object or contemporary physical event; in contrast to telepathy, the information is assumed to derive directly from an external physical source and not from the mind of another person." (Tart, 1997, 221).

COBE "The Cosmic Observer Background Explorer satellite, which gave perhaps the most conclusive proof of the big bang theory by measuring the black body radiation given off by the original fireball. Its results have since been improved greatly by the WMAP satellite." (Kaku, 2005, 384).

Collective Unconscious "Concept of psychologist Carl Jung, who believed that certain primordial images in the unconscious mind were not individual in origin, but 'collective'--being symbolic expressions of the 'constantly repeated experiences of humanity'. In Jung's view, these collective images were mostly religious motifs, acknowledged almost universally as significant. An example would be the mythic image of the sun, represented in numerous legends as the sun--hero and worshiped in Greece as Apollo, in Egypt as Osiris, and in ancient Persia as Ohrmazd." (Drury, 2002, 53).

"The collective unconscious began to crystallize as a fully formed idea in 1915, after Jung's split with Freud. Lying beneath the personal unconscious, like the sub-basement in Jung's dream, was the collective unconscious, which for Jung became the foundation of the psyche common to all humans. It was composed of 'latent memory traces inherited from man's ancestral past...The psychic residue of man's evolutionary development, a residue that accumulates as a consequence of repeated experiences over many generations.' A 'transpersonal' aspect of the human psyche, the collective unconscious is the very basis of the human mind, the primal mind that the child is born with. And upon this psychic template, or in Jung's words, 'virtual image' of the world, the child's sense of self, personality, and experiences are erected." (Seifer, 2011, 172-173).

Conscience "...is not a divine voice speaking to the human soul. It is merely the sum total of the moral and ethical content of the mores of any current stage of existence; it simply represents the humanly conceived ideal of reaction in any given set of circumstances." (*The Urantia Book*, 1955, 1005:2).

Conscious "(Origin C16: from L. *conscius* 'knowing with others or in oneself' (from *conscire* 'be a privy to' + **-ous**). 1 aware of and responding to one's surroundings. 2 (usu. **conscious of**) having knowledge of something..." (*The Concise Oxford Dictionary*,

1999).

"The spirit nature of the Universal Father is shared fully with his coexistent self, the Eternal Son of Paradise. Both the Father and the Son in like manner share the universal and eternal spirit fully and unreservedly with their *conjoint* personality coordinate, the Infinite Spirit. God's spirit is, in and of himself, absolute; in the Son it is unqualified, in the Spirit, universal, and in and by all of them, infinite." (*The Urantia Book*, 1955, 25:4).

"The worship experience consists in the sublime attempt of the betrothed Adjuster to communicate to the divine Father the inexpressible longings and the unutterable aspirations of the human soul--the *conjoint* creation of the God-seeking mortal mind and the God--revealing immortal Adjuster. Worship is, therefore, the act of the material mind's assenting to the attempt of its spiritualizing self, under the guidance of the associated spirit, to communicate with God as a faith son of the Universal Father. The mortal mind consents to worship; the immortal soul craves and initiates worship; the divine Adjuster presence conducts such worship in behalf of the mortal mind and the evolving immortal soul. True worship, in the last analysis, becomes an experience realized on four cosmic levels: the intellectual, the morontial, the spiritual, and the personal--the consciousness of mind, soul, and spirit, and their unification in personality." (66:4).

Consciousness "1 the state of being conscious; the fact of awareness by the mind of itself and the world. 2 one's awareness or perception of something." (*The Concise Oxford Dictionary*, 1999).

"From the Lat. *conscire*, 'to know', the faculty of being aware, of feeling and perceiving. Often equated with Mind. The conscious mind, which functions in the everyday world and determines what, for each of us, is our operative reality, is often distinguished from the unconscious mind of dreams, repressed memories, unfulfilled fantasies, delusions, and hallucinations, which are only experienced in an altered state of consciousness. Many mystical traditions teach that true enlightenment is not experienced unless the mind is transcended." (Drury, 2002, 54).

"In our work [The Institute of Noetic Sciences] *personal consciousness* is awareness--how an individual perceives and interprets his or her environment, including beliefs, intentions, attitudes, emotions, and all aspects of his or her subjective experience. *Collective consciousness* is how a group (an institution, a society, a species) perceives and translates the world around them." ("Consciousness," Institute of Noetic Sciences).

"...Man's *consciousness* of moral duty and his spiritual idealism represent a value level--an experiential reality--which is difficult of symbolization." (*The Urantia Book*, 1955, 3:14).

"*God-consciousness*, as it is experienced by an evolving mortal of the realms, must consist of three varying factors, three differential levels of reality realization. There is first the mind *consciousness*--the comprehension of the *idea* of God. Then follows the *soul consciousness*--the realization of the *ideal* of God. Last, dawns the spirit *consciousness*--the realization of the *spirit reality* of God. By the unification of these factors of the divine realization, no matter how incomplete, the mortal personality at all times overspreads all conscious levels with a realization of the *personality* of God. In those mortals who have attained the Corps of the Finality all this will in time lead to the realization of the *supremacy* of God and may subsequently eventuate in the realization of the *ultimacy* of God, some phase of the absonite superconsciousness of the Paradise Father." (69:6).

Consciousness transformation "A fundamental shift in perspective or worldview that results in an expanded understanding of self and the nature of reality." ("Consciousness," The Institute of Noetic Sciences).

Worldview can be defined as "the beliefs, attitudes through which we filter our understanding of the world and our place in it." (Ibid).

Conservation of Energy "The law of science that states that energy (or its equivalent in mass) can neither be created or destroyed." (Hawking, 2001, 204).

Conservation Laws "The laws that state that certain quantities never change with time. For example, the conservation of matter and energy posits that the total amount of matter and energy in the universe is a constant." (Kaku, 2005, 384).

Continuity of Consciousness "The recognition that soul energy remains constant from lifetime to lifetime and between lives." (Backman, 2009, 230).

Copenhagen School "The school founded by Niels Bohr, which states that an observation is necessary in order to 'collapse the wave function' to determine the state of an object. Before an observation is made, an object exists in all possible states, even absurd ones. Since we do not observe dead cats and live cats existing simultaneously, Bohr had to assume that there is (a) 'wall' separating the subatomic world from the everyday world we observe with our senses. This interpretation has been challenged because it separates the quantum world from the everyday, macroscopic world, while many physicists now believe that the macroscopic world must also obey the quantum theory. Today, because of nanotechnology, scientists can manipulate individual atoms, so we realize that there (is) no 'wall' separating the two worlds. Hence, the cat problem resurfaces today." (Kaku, 2005, 384-385).

Cosmic force "In discussing physical-energy manifestations, we generally use the terms *cosmic force*, emergent energy, and universe power. These are often employed as follows:" (*The Urantia Book*, 1955, 9:6).

"1. *Cosmic force* embraces all energies deriving from the Unqualified Absolute but which are as yet unresponsive to Paradise gravity." (9:7).

Cosmic horizon "Location in space beyond which light has not had time to reach us, since the beginning of the universe." (Greene, 2004, 538).

Cosmic insight "Cosmic insight, the grasp of universe meanings." (*The Urantia Book*, 1955, 194:12).

Cosmic microwave background radiation "The residual radiation left over from the big bang which is still circulating around the universe, first predicted in 1948 by George Gamow and his group. Its temperature is 2.7 degrees above absolute zero. Its discovery by Penzias and Wilson gave the most convincing 'proof' of the big bang. Today, scientists measure tiny deviations with this background radiation to provide evidence for inflation or other theories." (Kaku, 2005, 385).

"Remnant electromagnetic radiation (photons) from the early universe, which permeates space." (Greene, 2004, 538).

Cosmic String "A long, heavy object with a tiny cross section that may have been produced during the early stages of the universe. By now a single string could stretch across the entire universe." (Hawking, 2001, 204).

"A remnant of the big bang. Some gauge theories predict that some relics of the original big bang might still survive in the form of gigantic cosmic strings that are the size of galaxies or larger. The collision of two cosmic strings may allow for a certain form of time travel." (Kaku, 2005, 385).

Cosmo-"(Origin from Gk. *kosmos* 'order, world'). (comb. form) of or relating to the world or the universe: *cosmography*." (*The Concise Oxford Dictionary*, 1999).

Cosmological constant "A hypothetical energy and pressure, uniformly filling space; origin and composition unknown." (Greene, 2004, 538).

Cosmology "the science of the origin and development of the universe; an account or theory of the origin of the universe." (*The Concise Oxford Dictionary*, 1999).

"Study of origin and evolution of the universe." (Greene, 2004, 538).

"From the Greek *kosmos*, 'the universe', the study of the universe and its perceived attributes, including space, time, change, and eternity. In mystical and esoteric literature, it is often used to denote the study of gods and goddesses, the process of Creation, and the nature of Reality." (Drury, 2002, 57).

"(Gk., *kosmos* + *logos*). Reflection on, and account of the world/universe as a meaningful whole, as embodying or expressing an order or underlying structure that makes sense: cosmogony is concerned with the coming into being of the cosmos, and cosmography with the description of its extent. A cosmology either manifests the character of the world as an independent organism or expresses the intentions of a transcendent being or beings. In some conceptions the present order remains stable until ended by a transcendent power, but in other conceptions it is liable, or even certain, to be replaced by other orders in an unending cycle. In the latter conception, the notions of cosmogony and cosmology may resemble each other closely. In most pre-modern religions, the cosmological order of thought to affect all the different levels and types of existence so that human action and society should, or must, reflect the more general order. The particular ideas in a cosmology are often both so basic to a culture's thought and so different from each other that the ideas of one scheme--e.g. a neo-Confucian one may not be adequately expressible in the ideas of another scheme--e.g. a traditional Christian one. In so far as cosmologies are concerned with the origin of the cosmos or with the description of its nature and distribution, they are linked to (or include) cosmogony and cosmography." (*The Oxford Dictionary of World Religions*, 1997).

"It is rare for religions to give a single cosmology or cosmogony purporting to be a description of the origin of the universe, in the way in which a scientific cosmology might aim to give a critically realistic account of the origin and nature of the universe. Religious cosmologies give accounts of origin and nature, but principally in order to display the cosmos as an arena of opportunity; and for that reason, a religion may offer, or make use of, many cosmogonies without making much attempt to reconcile the contradictions between them. It is this aesthetic and spiritual relaxation which allows religions to address cosmological issues from the point of view of accountability and responsibility (as at the present time over issues of ecology), not as competitors with a scientific account: thus the Vancouver Assembly of World Council of Churches decided 'to engage member churches in a conciliar process of mutual commitment (covenant) to justice, peace, and the integrity of creation (subsequently known as JCIC)'; while this (especially the word 'covenant') depends on a particular understanding of creation, and thus of cosmogony, it has moved far beyond concerns about identifying the 'correct' account of the cosmos and its origins." (Ibid).

"(Judaism) *Tanach* (Jewish scripture) contains at least six different types of creation narrative, each of which 'gives voice to the viewpoints and values prevalent in diverse settings, priestly, agrarian, sapiential, prophetic, cultic, apocalyptic' (D. A. Knight, in R. W. Lowin and F. B. Reynolds, eds., *Cosmogony and Ethical Order*, 1985), but all of which are integrated to the overriding cult of Yahweh. Even within scripture, there is an exegesis going on, which changes the emphasis of cosmology. Thus it was early observed that the Bible begins with a grammatically anomaly: the word *bereshith*, 'in the beginning', is actually in the form, 'in the beginning of'; but the text does not state, 'in the beginning of what'. Attention to Proverbs 8:22 disclosed that Wisdom is called *reshith*, 'the beginning', so that Genesis 1:1 could be translated 'by means of Wisdom God created', thereby locating a Wisdom cosmogony in Genesis, in a way which was to be fruitful in the interpretation of Jesus in early Christianity. Nevertheless, the controlling accounts are those in Genesis: God created everything that exists in six days and rested on the seventh (1-2:4). A second, more anthropocentric account (Genesis 2:4-24), although differing in details, also emphasizes that God is the origin of everything. These stories have been compared with Mesopotamian accounts, such as the Babylonian *Emuna Elish* and the *Gilgamish* epic, but they differ in that the Hebrew God is portrayed as the single omnipotent creator. There are no primeval battles between deities (though traces of those cosmogonies are in Psalms and Job). The world is created solely in obedience to the divine will. The rabbis of the Talmudic period were anxious to refute any gnostic suggestions that the world was created by angelic intermediaries. Although

66

influenced by the cosmogonies of their time (R. Abbahu, for example, believed that there was a succession of experimental worlds), the rabbis insisted that the world was created out of nothing, solely by the word of God--'With ten words was the world created' (*Avot* 5.1). In common with their Christian counterparts, Jewish philosophers tried to harmonize the biblical account with philosophical theories. Philo, for example, based his ideas on Plato's *Timaeus*; Sa'adiah Gaon was influenced by Aristotle; and Solomon ibn Gabirol tried to reconcile the biblical view with Neoplatonism. Speculations about the nature of the visible cosmos (*ma'aseh bereshit*) and the transcendent world (*ma'aseh merkabah*) are found in Jewish mysticism; and the kabbalists taught that the gulf between God and the material world is bridged by the 'sefirot' (emanations) which have their origin in God (se e.g. Cordovero). The Jewish prayer book liturgy maintains that God is 'He who renews the work of creation every day', and 20th century theologians have emphasized the continuing nature of creation: 'Creation happens to us, burns itself in us, recasts us in burning...We take part in creation, meet the Creator, reach out to him, helpers and companions' (M. Buber, *I and Thou*, 1958)." (Ibid).

"(Christianity) Christians inherited the Jewish cosmology, but virtually from the outset (as early as Paul's letters) they associated Christ with the activity of the Father in creation. He is 'the one Lord through whom all things exist and by whom we are' (1 Corinthians 8:6). He is the Wisdom of God (ibid 1:24), the 'image of the invisible God and the first-born of all creatures', in whom all things were created and now subsist (Colossians 1:15 f.). Furthermore, creation now has its end and purpose in him. Not surprisingly, therefore, Christian interest in cosmology and creation has seen them as a matter, not of technique, but of relationship--i.e. the relation of dependence which the created order has on its creator, not just for its origin, but for its sustenance. The General Thanksgiving in the *Book of Common Prayer* encourages Christians to give thanks 'for our creation, preservation and all the blessings of this life'; but creation and preservation are the same thing. The creativity of God is continuous: if God as creator withdrew his creative presence from an entity, it would cease to be. Thus God is the cause, not simple of things coming to be, but also of their being. For that reason, it because obvious, at least as early as the time of Aquinas, that the Greek argument, to the effect that the created world need not necessarily have had a beginning, was correct, but that this did not militate against a theistic understanding of creation: it would still be in a relation (albeit an unending relation) of createdness to its creator--a point lucidly argued by Leibniz in *On the Ultimate Origination of Things* (1697). However, it was also accepted that if revelation discloses a finite beginning, then on those grounds it should be accepted. It has become an issue subsequently whether revelation makes disclosures of that quasi-scientific kind at all. The claim that God creates the world *ex nihilo* (out of nothing) has sometimes confused the point: *ex nihilo* does not mean that 'nothing' is the sort of no-thing that God creates out of (which happens to be nothing rather than something), but rather that everything owes its existence to God, and that the creator and the created are ontologically distinct. The prevailing cosmography for millennia was one of a 'three-decker' universe (heaven above, earth in the middle, and hell below), but its 'correction' by modern cosmologies has not affected the more fundamental point of the earlier (or of any) religious cosmology which mapped the universe as an arena of opportunity. For that reason, a three-decker universe may well persist indefinitely in liturgy. Nevertheless, alternative cosmologies have been developed to reflect changing scientific understandings of the cosmos. However, the necessity for these is not altogether apparent: from at least the time of Aquinas, a distinction has been made between God as first cause (as above) who produces and sustains a creation in which both natural and free causes (secondary causes) operate, and those effective and efficient causes which are real and not nominal." (Ibid).

"(Islam) The Quran strongly affirms God as creator and disposer of all that is. By a simple word, *kun* ('Be'), he commands and it is (2.117, 6.73). God is *al-Khaliq* (the Creator, from *khalaqa*, 'he created'), and has the power and authority to bring about all things as he disposes (*qadar*, Allah). Everything that he has crated is a sign (*aya*), not only *of* God for those who have eyes to see, but also *that* God has power to continue his creative act in relation to humans by bringing them from the grave for judgment (e.g. 50.6-11). Because all things are derived from God, this becomes the fundamental argument that all people must constitute a single *'umma* (community) in *islam* (allegiance which constitutes true safety) to God. So strong and immediate a doctrine of creation gave rise to many disputes (e.g. about the place of human freedom and responsibility, or about the direct involvement of God in his creation). Attempts to make God the first of a series of delegated emanations and causes (e.g. in ibn Rushd or ibn Sina) were resisted--so much so that it came to be held that God was the creator of each specific occasion or event, hence the name 'occasionalism'. The creation of a first man and first woman, and of the earth and seven heavens in two days, and of the cosmos in six, is described in such a way that, given the nature of the Quran, any apparent conflict with other accounts (e.g. in the natural sciences) would have to be resolved in favor of the Quran." (Ibid).

"(Hinduism) Vedic religion displays a clear sense of an ordered universe in which rta prevails. There are many different accounts of how the universe came into being, some implying agency, others emanation from a pre-existing state in which there is neither beginning nor end. Important examples are: Brahmanda (the cosmic egg from which all creatures come forth: *Rg Veda* 10.121.1; *Katha Upanisad* 3.10); Hiranyagarbha (the golden embryo, the everlasting plan), or *aksara purusa*, the indestructible person, who becomes the vibrating energy from which all life is generated); Visvakarma as creator (the first to come forth from Brahmanda, the architect of the gods, *Rg Veda* 10.82); and Brahma ('the source of the universe, presiding over all creation, preserving like Visnu, destroying like Siva', *Markandeya Purana* 46.14). Equally well-known was the understanding of the universe coming forth from the primordial sacrifice, described in *Rg Veda* 10.90: see Purusa. Yet the universe may also have had no point of origin, but may rather be an emanation (*anadisrsti*) from a ground or source of being, later to be identified as Brahman. Thus Sankara understood the emanation as a progress from the subtle to the gross constituents of the world. But earlier than that, there had developed a sense of an unending process like a wave, with elements rising up into organized appearance, but then lapsing into a corresponding trough during 'the sleep of Brahma', a period of dissolution (*pralaya*). It was thus possible that the cosmos arose from infinite space and consciousness, a belief expressed through Aditi. In truth, Indian religion accepted that the origin of the cosmos could not be known, but that the conditions of ordered life could be extremely well-known. Cosmology lays out the terms for achieving that understanding--cosmology, again, as the arena of opportunity-- while remaining agnostic about detail, as in the so-called 'Hymn of Creation' (*Nasadiya Sukta*, *Rg Veda* 10.129): 'Neither being (*sat*) nor non-being was as yet. There was no air, no sky that lies beyond it. What was concealed? And where? And in whose protection?...Who really knows? Who can declare it? Whence was it born, and whence came this creation? The gods were born later than this world's creation, so who knows from where it came into existence? None can know from where creation has arisen, and whether he has or has not produced it. He who surveys it in the highest heaven, he alone knows--or perhaps does not know.' In philosophy, the self-generating nature of the universe was worked out particularly in Samkhya. In theistic terms, the universe is produced through maya, the power to bring all things into appearance." (Ibid).

"There was a greater confidence in cosmography. Vertically, the world was understood to be made up of seven continents (*dvipas*), ranged in circles with intervening oceans around the central point of Mount Meru. Vertically, if one takes a cross-section of the Brahmanda, one finds a series of layers. At the top are the lokas of the gods and high attainers; next are the planets, sky, and earth; then the underworlds, and finally the twenty-eight narakas or hells." (Ibid).

"(Jainism and Buddhism) The Indian scepticism about the work of the gods or God in creating this cosmos was taken to a further extreme in both Jainism and Buddhism. Such gods as there are (and there are many, especially in Buddhism) are subject to rebirth and are certainly incapable of creating anything. The Jains inherited the *triloka* (see Loka), and envisaged it as something like an hour-glass, squeezed in at the middle. Above (*Urdhvaloka*) are a series of heavens of increasing brightness, at the top of which is 'the slightly curved place' (*Isatpragbhara*) where dwell the liberated and disembodied souls. In the middle is the *Madhyaloka*, which includes the continent inhabited by humans. Below is the *Adholoka*, a series of increasingly terrible hells--from which release is eventually certain, though the intervening time may be unimaginably long." (Ibid).

"In Buddhism, there is an equal rejection of any kind of creator--though there are stories of how it came about that Brahma (a kindly and well-disposed god in Buddhism, but just as much in quest of enlightenment as anyone else) deceived himself into thinking that he must have been the creator (*Digha Nikaya* 1.18). Buddhism inherited the same basic cosmography, but adapted it greatly. It envisages a series of levels, all of which are open to the process of reappearance: at the summit are the four realms of purely mental rebirth, (*arupa-avacara*); below them are the realms of pure form (*rupa-avacara*) where the gods dwell in sixteen heavens, five of which are known as 'pure abodes' (*suddhavasa*), the remaining eleven of which arise out of the *jhanas* (meditational states). Lower still are the sense-desire heavens, including those of

70

the Tavatimsa gods (the thirty-three Vedic gods, the chief of whom, Indra, known as Sakka, has become a protector of Buddhism) and of the Tusita gods (where bodhisattva spend their penultimate birth, and in which Maitreya now dwells). In the sense-desire realms are the levels on which live asuras, humans and animals. Below these are pretaloka and the hells of torment (*niraya/naraka*). All worlds are made up of transient and impermanent moments, and are therefore the product, neither of a creator, nor even of some eternal process, as in the interaction between Purusa and Prakrti in Samkhya. The world is imply a process, passing through cycles (*kappa*) of immense length. In Mahayana, beyond the three domains of *kama*, *rupa*, and *arupa*, there are added a further dimension of the *Buddha-ksetras* (Buddha-fields)." (Ibid).

Curandero, Curandera "In Mexico and Peru, a folk-healer or shaman skilled in summoning spirits to heal the sick. One of the most famous contemporary healers in Peru is Eduardo Calderon, a shaman who uses San Pedro cactus in an all-night curing ceremony that combines Indian and Christian rituals and features a selection of power-objects. The anthropologist R. Gordon Wasson documented in several books the healing vigil, or *velada*, of the Mexican Mazatec shaman Maria Sabina, who made use of sacred mushrooms as a healing sacrament." (Drury, 2002, 62).

D

Dance "Rhythmic bodily movements, often accompanied by music, chanting and clapping, which--from an occult point of view--may result in an altered state of consciousness or trance state, especially when performed in a ritual setting. Dance has this function in many forms of primitive worship..." (Drury, 2002, 64).

Dark Energy "The energy of empty space. First introduced by Einstein in 1917 and then discarded, this energy of nothing is now known to be the dominant form of matter/energy in the universe. Its origin is unknown, but it may eventually drive the universe into a big freeze. The amount of dark energy is proportional to the volume of the universe. The latest data shows that 73 percent of the matter/energy of the universe is in the form of dark energy." (Kaku, 2005, 385).

"A hypothetical energy and pressure, uniformly filling space; more general notion than a cosmological constant as its energy/pressure can vary with time." (Greene, 2004, 538).

Dark Matter "Matter in galaxies and clusters, and possibly between clusters, that cannot be observed directly but that can be

71

detected by its gravitational field. As much as ninety percent of the matter in the universe is dark matter." (Hawking, 2001, 204).

"Invisible matter, which has weight but does not interact with light. Dark matter is usually found in a huge halo around galaxies. It outweighs ordinary matter by a factor of 10. Dark matter can be indirectly measured because it bends starlight due to its gravity, somewhat similar to the way glass bends light. Dark matter, according to the latest data, makes up 23 percent of the total matter/energy content of the universe. According to string theory, dark matter may be made of subatomic particles, such as the neutralino, which represent higher vibrations of the superstring." (Kaku, 2005, 385).

"Matter suffused through space, exerting gravity but not emitting light." (Greene, 2004, 538).

Delta Brain-Wave State "An altered state of consciousness characterized by detachment, physical healing, and sleep; brain-wave activity of 0.5-4 Hz." (Backman, 2009, 230).

Destiny "the events that will necessarily happen to a particular person in the future; the hidden power believed to control this; fate." (*The Concise Oxford Dictionary*, 1999).

Destiny, spiritual "...Spiritual destiny is dependent on faith, love, and devotion to truth--hunger and thirst for righteousness--the wholehearted desire to find God and to be like him." (*The Urantia Book*, 1955, 1739:2).

Determinism "(Philosophy) the doctrine that all events and actions are ultimately determined by causes regarded as external to the will." (*The Concise Oxford Dictionary*, 1999).

"The view that events and behaviors are determined before they occur, by the laws of the universe or by God. In religions, determinism takes different forms: in Christianity, see Augustine and Calvin; in Islam, *qadar* and *kasb*, Allah; in Hinduism *et al.*, karma. The religious problem is how to reconcile the omnipotence of God or the inevitable effect of karma with the freedom and responsibility of the human agent." (*The Oxford Dictionary of World Religions*, 1997).

"Man, in his spiritual domain, does have a free will. Mortal man is neither a helpless slave of the inflexible sovereignty of an all-powerful God nor the victim of the hopeless fatality of a mechanistic cosmic *determinism*. Man is most truly the architect of his own eternal destiny." (*The Urantia Book*, 1955, 1134:8).

"The philosophy that everything is predetermined, including the future. According to Newtonian mechanics, if we know the velocity and position of all the particles in the universe, then we can in principle calculate the evolution of the entire universe. The uncertainty principle, however, has proven that determination is incorrect." (Kaku, 2005, 386).

"Determinism, or 'causal' determination, is the belief that everything that happens to us is predictable--has a cause, so to speak, according to previous events. Thus, what happens to us in terms of actions, behaviors, and experiences is based upon what happened just before that, and just before that, and so on, and so on. Causal law rules the universe according to the philosophy of determinism, in a chain of events that lead from A to Z in a recognizable and rational manner." (Jones, 2011, 20).

"There are different types of determinism, because philosophers, if nothing else, like to break ideas down into the smallest possible denominations, so here are a few:" (Ibid).

Determinism, Biological: Our behaviors, desires, and actions are all genetic in nature. (Jones, 2011, 20).

Determinism, Behavioral: All actions and events are reactions to our environment condition. (Jones, 2011, 20).

Determinism, Cultural: Same behavioral determinism, but substitute cultural for environmental. (Jones, 2011, 20).

Determinism, Environment: Our geographical location and physical environment determine our actions and responses. (Jones, 2011, 20).

Determinism, Historical: Various forces determine the historical and political course of events, related to the Marxist concept of dialectical materialism. (Jones, 2011, 20).

Determinism, Logical: All propositions about past, present, and future are either true or false. Future events, because already fixed, take away free will/choice. (Jones, 2011, 20).

Determinism, Psychological: Human beings act according to reason and their own best interest. (Jones, 2011, 20).

Determinism, Technological: Reductionist theory stating that technology drives the social structure and cultural makeup of society. (Jones, 2011, 20).

Determinism, Theological: God determines in advance everything that humans will do, think, act upon, become. Again, little or no free will leg-room here. (Jones, 2011, 20).

Dialectic "(usually treated as sing.) 1 the art of investigating or discussing the truth of opinions. 2 inquiry into metaphysical contradictions and their solutions. 3 the existence or action of opposing social forces, concepts, etc." (*The Concise Oxford Dictionary*,

1999).

Dimension "(Origin ME: via OFr. from L. *dimensio(n)*, from *dimetiri* 'measure out'). 1 a measurable extent, such as length, breadth, or height. (Physics) an expression for a derived physical quantity in terms of fundamental quantities such as mass, length, or time, raised to the appropriate power (acceleration, for example, having the dimension of *length* x *time*^{2}). 2 an aspect or feature: *water can add a new dimension to your garden.* (v.) cut or shape to particular dimensions." (*The Concise Oxford Dictionary*, 1999).

"A coordinate or parameter by which we measure space and time. Our familiar universe has three dimensions of space (length, width, and depth) and one dimension of time. In string and M-theory, we need ten (eleven) dimensions in which to describe the universe, only four of which can be observed in the laboratory. Perhaps the reason why we don't see these other dimensions is either that they are curled up or that our vibrations are confined to the surface of a membrane." (Kaku, 2005, 386).

Directions, Four "In Western magic, the four directions are symbolized in ritual by the four archangels: Raphael (east), Michael (south), Gabriel (west), and Uriel (north); representing the elements Air, Fire, Water, and Earth respectively. According to the *Grimoire of Honorius*, the four directions also have four demons associated with them: Magoa (east), Egym (south), Baymon (west), and Amaymon (north)." (Drury, 2002, 74).

Doppler Effect "The shift of frequency and wavelength of sound waves or light waves that an observer perceives if the source is moving relative to that observer." (Hawking, 2001, 204).

"The change in frequency of a wave, as an object approaches or moves away from you. If a star moves toward you, the frequency of light increases, so a yellow star appears slightly bluish. If a star moves away from you, the frequency of its light decreases, so a yellow star appears slightly reddish. This change in light frequency can also be created by expanding space itself between two points, as in the expanding universe. By measuring the amount of shift in the frequency, you can calculate the velocity with which a star is moving away from you." (Kaku, 2005, 386-387).

Dream "Occurrence during the period of sleep associated with rapid eye movements (REM). Sigmund Freud regarded dreams as an expression of the wish-fulfillment of repressed desires and an amalgamation of memories and associations based on recent events. However, dreams sometimes also have mysterious and inexplicable contents that have led them to be linked with extrasensory perception. Mark Twain had a vivid dream in which he 'saw' his brother's corpse resting in a metal coffin with a bouquet of crimson flowers on his chest. A few weeks later, Twain's brother was fatally injured when the boiler of a boat exploded. A metal coffin was donated by friends, and when Twain arrived at the funeral service the scene was as he had dreamed it-- except the flowers were a different color." (Drury, 2002, 79).

"Prophetic dreams seem to be comparatively rare, however, and most dreams appear to derive from a familiar external stimulus that triggers patterns of association. The nineteenth-century researcher Alfred Maury described how, when eau de Cologne was place near his nostrils, he dreamed he was in an exotic Egyptian bazaar; and how, when a section of his bed fell across his neck, he dreamed that he was being guillotined in the French Revolution. While most Freudian psychologists believe that the contents of dreams usually reflect wish-fulfillment or image-association, Carl Jung proposed that sometimes dreams also reveal sacred archetypes--profound mythic symbols that are central to religious and mystical experience. According to Jung, these archetypes are symbols not from one's personal unconscious, but from the collective unconscious--universal psychic motifs representing the 'constantly repeated experiences of humanity'. Dreams that include visionary archetypes and symbolic revelations of this type are sometimes known as high dreams." (Ibid, 79-80).

Dream, High "A dream in which sacred or transcendental images appear and which invariably has a profound effect on the dreamer." (Drury, 2002, 80).

Dream, Lucid "Term used by Celia Greene of the Institute of Psychophysical Research in Oxford to describe the situation where the dreamer is aware that he or she is dreaming and therefore is conscious within the dream state. There are close parallels between the lucid dream, the out-of-body experience, and the paranormal phenomenon popularly known as astral travel. The definitive study is Celia Green's *Lucid Dreams* (1968)." (Drury, 2002, 80).

E

Eagle "Bird with many occult associations. The eagle is linked in astrology to Scorpio, which with Taurus, Leo and Aquarius is one of the 'fixed' signs of the zodiac. Occultists also identify these signs with the four letters of the sacred Tetragrammaton YHVH, the eagle being associated with the first H. In general terms, the eagle symbolizes height (and therefore transcendence), light, spirit, and the powers of the imagination." (Drury, 2002, 83).

earth "1 (also **Earth**) the planet on which we live, the third planet of the solar system in order of distance from the sun. 2 the substance of the land surface; soil; one of the four elements in ancient and medieval philosophy and in astrology..." (*The Concise Oxford Dictionary*, 1999).

"One of the four alchemical elements, the others being Fire, Water, and Air. The spirits of the Earth are gnomes and goblins. The three astrological signs linked to Earth are Taurus, Virgo, and Capricorn." (Drury, 2002, 83).

Earthbound "Term used in spiritualism to describe discarnate beings, or spirits, who remain close to the domain where they lived in real life. They are often accused of hauntings, but can be dispelled by exorcism." (Drury, 2002, 83).

Earth Plane "The physical domain of everyday reality, as distinct from the astral plane, the ether, the spirit dimension, or the higher worlds. In the Kabbalah this place of existence is called Malkuth, the Kingdom." (Drury, 2002, 83).

East "The direction of the rising sun, and therefore associated with new life, light, spiritual illumination, and initiation. All white magic rituals commence with salutations to the eastern quarter, and in kabbalistic magic this direction is ruled by the archangel Raphael, symbolizing the element Air." (Drury, 2002, 83).

Ecstasy "A state of you, rapture, or spiritual enlightenment in which a person feels lifted up into a state of visionary transcendence. Ecstasy is a profound altered state of consciousness and is often associated with trance." (Drury, 2002, 84).

Ego "One's personal identity. Mystics and occultists tend to regard the ego as essentially illusory and believe that the self may assume many personalities in different lifetimes, as part of the spiritual quest towards self-realization." (Drury, 2002, 86).

Eighth Chakra "The template through which the higher energy systems surrounding the body are united with the human bio-computer system controlled by the seven chakra stations of energy flow. The Eighth Chakra allows for the unification between the Overself Body and the human biological system as the energy center for the 'divine Light,' the 'flame of salvation' and eternal Light appearing over the head." (Hurtak, 1977, 573).

Electromagnetic field "The field which exerts the electromagnetic force." (Greene, 2004, 538).

Electromagnetic force "The force of electricity and magnetism. When they vibrate in unison, they create a wave that can describe ultraviolet radiation, radio, gamma rays, and so on, which obeys Maxwell's equations. The electromagnetic force is one of the four forces governing the universe." (Kaku, 2005, 387).

"The force that arises between particles with electric charge of a similar (or opposite) sign." (Hawking, 2001, 204).

Electromagnetic wave "A wavelike disturbance in an electric field. All waves of the electromagnetic spectrum travel at the speed of light, e.g., visible light, x-rays, microwaves, infrared, etc." (Hawking, 2001, 204).

Electron "A particle with negative charge that orbits the nucleus of an atom." (Hawking, 2001, 204).

"A negatively charged subatomic particle that surrounds the nucleus of an atom. The number of electrons surrounding the nucleus determines the chemical properties of the atom." (Kaku, 2005, 387).

Emotional Body "Alternative term for the astral or desire body." (Drury, 2002, 91).

Empathize "understand and share the feelings of another." (*The Concise Oxford Dictionary*, 1999).

Empathy "the ability to empathize." (*The Concise Oxford Dictionary*, 1999).

Empiric "(adj.) another term for empirical. (n.) (archaic) 1 a scientist who relies solely on observation and experiment. 2 a quack doctor." (*The Concise Oxford Dictionary*, 1999).

Empirical "based on, concerned with, or verifiable by observation or experience rather than theory or pure logic." (*The Concise Oxford Dictionary*. 1999).

Endemic "1 (of a disease or condition) regularly found among particular people or in a certain area. 2 (of a plant or animal) native or restricted to a certain area." (*The Concise Oxford Dictionary*, 1999).

Energy "1 the strength and vitality required for sustained activity. (**energies**) a person's physical and mental powers as applied to a particular activity. 2 power derived from physical or chemical resources to provide light and heat or to work machines. 3 (Physics) the property of matter and radiation which is manifest as a capacity to perform work." (*The Concise Oxford Dictionary*, 1999).

"Energy we use as an all-inclusive term applied to spiritual, mindal, and material realms..." (*The Urantia Book*, 1955, 9:4).

"*Physical energy* is a term denoting all phases and forms of phenomenal motion, act, and potential." (9:5).

"In discussing physical-energy manifestations, we generally

use the terms cosmic force, emergent energy, and universe power. These are often employed as follows:" (9:6).

"1. *Cosmic force* embraces all energies deriving from the Unqualified Absolute but which are as yet unresponsive to Paradise gravity." (9:7).

"2. *Emergent energy* embraces those energies which are responsive to Paradise gravity but are as yet unresponsive to local or linear gravity. This is the pre-electronic level of energy-matter." (9:8).

"3. *Universe power* includes all forms of energy which, while still responding to Paradise gravity, are directly responsive to linear gravity. This is the electronic level of energy-matter and all subsequent evolutions thereof." (9:9).

"Pattern may configure energy, but it does not control it. Gravity is the sole control of energy-matter..." (10:3).

"...Viewed as an unspiritual phenomenon, God is energy..." (47:1).

"...The light and energy of the eternal God thus swing on forever around his majestic circuit, the endless but orderly procession of the starry hosts composing the universe of universes..." (47:2).

"All physical force, energy, and matter are one..." (123:2).

"All forms of force-energy--material, mindal, or spiritual--are alike subject to those grasps, those universal presences, which we call gravity..." (131:4).

Energy Body "...at the atomic level, the human body is really composed of different kinds of vibrating energy..." (Gerber, 2000, 6).

"The concept of the body as a complex energetic system is part of a new scientific worldview gradually gaining acceptance in the eyes of modern medicine..." (Ibid, 7).

"...the newly emerging vibrational model of human functioning provides physicians with the bridge they need in order to go beyond Newtonian medicine to grasp the contributions of the human mind and spirit in various states of health and illness. What is already known about the body in terms of mechanistic function can be put into the framework of the larger dynamic energy system that more fully describes the 'multidimensional' human being..." (Ibid, 9).

"The new vibrational model of human beings sees consciousness as playing an integral role in health and illness. Consciousness is not merely a by-product of electrical and chemical signal-processing in the human brain. Consciousness is a kind of energy itself...From the perspective of vibrational medicine, our consciousness is not limited to the brain and central nervous system but is also seen as an integral aspect of the human heart...In the vibrational-medicine view of human functioning, our emotions are not just the result of neurochemical reactions in the limbic system or the emotional centers of our brain. Our emotions are also influenced by a greater, spiritual energy field that encompasses and influences the entire physical body and nervous system..." (Ibid, 10).

"...we now know that the cells of the body actually emit weak pulses of light. Those weak cellular light pulses seem to be part of a light-based communication system that helps to coordinate the actions of the cells within each organ. The pulses of light emitted by cells are just one of the many different informational codes the human body and its individual cells use to regulate the function of organs on a day-to-day and moment-to-moment basis. Our cells communicate through the coded messages carried by hormones and biochemicals, as well as through electrical signals (such as those carried by the nerves of the body), and also through weak light signals. The cells of the body appear to have their own inherent intelligence that allows them to understand and use this coded information in its many forms in order to maintain the body in a state of health." (Ibid, 11).

Energy Healing "encompasses all forms of allopathic medicine--which only works with the relatively lower, or measurable, energy structures--as well as modalities that work with the subtle structures." (Dale, 2009, 13-14).

"Vibrational medicine is the intentional use of frequency to positively affect another frequency or to bring an organism into balance. It is one component of *energy healing*, which also uses information, and information and vibration together, to effect change..." (Ibid, 13).

Enlightenment "(n.) 1 the action of enlightening or the state of being enlightened; the attainment of spiritual insight, in particular (in Buddhism) that awareness which frees a person from the cycle of rebirth. 2 (**the Enlightenment**) a European intellectual movement of the late 17th and 18th centuries emphasizing reason and individualism rather than tradition." (*The Concise Oxford Dictionary*, 1999).

"Attainment of insight, illumination, wisdom, truth, etc." (*The Oxford Dictionary of World Religions*, 1997).

Entanglement, quantum "Quantum phenomenon in which spatially distant particles have correlated properties." (Greene, 2004, 538).

Entrainment "The alignment of forces, or fields of energy, to allow maximum transfer of information or communication." (Braden, 1993, 191-192).

Entropy "A measure of the disorder of a physical system; the number of different microscopic configurations of a system that leave its macroscopic appearance unchanged." (Hawking, 2001, 205).

"The measure of disorder or chaos. According to the second law of thermodynamics, the total entropy in the universe always increases, which means that everything must eventually run down. Applied to the universe, it means that the universe will tend toward a state of maximum entropy, such as a uniform gas near absolute zero. To reverse the entropy in a small region (such as a refrigerator), the addition of mechanical energy is required. But even for a refrigerator, the total entropy increases (which is why the back of a refrigerator is warm). Some believe that the second law ultimately predicts the death of the universe." (Kaku, 2005, 388).

"A measure of the disorder of a physical system; the number of rearrangements of a system's fundamental constituents that leave its gross, overall appearance unchanged." (Greene, 2004, 538).

Ephemeral "lasting or living for a very short time (chiefly of plants) having a very short life cycle." (*The Concise Oxford Dictionary*, 1999).

Eros "(Origin Lat., from Gk. *eros*, lit. 'sexual love' (also the name of the god of love in Gk. mythology)). 1 sexual love or desire. 2 (in Freudian theory) the life instinct. Often contrasted with Thanatos. 3(in Jungian psychology) the principle of personal relatedness in human activities, associated with the anima. Often contrasted with Logos." (*The Concise Oxford Dictionary*, 1999).

Esalen Institute "Famous 'growth' institute founded by Michael Murphy and Dick Price, located on a cliff edge at Big Sur, California. Esalen Institute offers workshops that specialize in different consciousness-expanding modalities, including t'ai chi, meditation, gestalt therapy, and shamanism. Esalen Institute is closely associated with the international transpersonal psychology movement, a philosophical school that emerged from humanistic psychology and which is dedicated to studying visionary and peak experiences, mysticism, and altered states of consciousness."

(Drury, 2002, 93-94).

Ether "(Origin ME: from OFr. or via L. from Gk. *aither* 'upper air', from the base of *aithein* 'burn, shine'). (Physics, historical) a substance formerly postulated to permeate all space and to transmit light." (*The Concise Oxford Dictionary*, 1999).

"A hypothetical non-material medium once supposed to fill all space. The idea that such a medium is required for the propagation of electromagnetic radiation is no longer tenable." (Hawking, 2001, 205).

"According to occult belief, the fluidic substance that fills all space, pervades all matter, and is active in all processes of life." (Drury, 2002, 95).

"The associated element of the fifth chakra is ether, otherwise known as Akasha or spirit." (Judith, 1999, 239).

"The element ether represents a world of vibrations--the emanations of living things that we experience as the aura, as sound, and as the subtle plane of whispered impressions on the mind into which more solid realities are enfolded." (Ibid, 242).

"While most metaphysical systems postulate four elements (earth, water, fire, and air), ether, or spirit, is the generally universal element added when a system encompasses five elements...In these systems, the four elements describe the physical world and the spirit is left for the unexplainable non-physical realm." (Ibid).

"Ether can be equated with the all-encompassing and unifying field of subtle vibrations found throughout the universe. Any vibration, be it a sound wave or a dancing particle, is in contact with other vibrations, and all vibrations can and do affect each other." (Ibid, 243).

"...The etheric field is a kind of blueprint for the vibrational patterns of our tissues, organs, emotions, activities, experiences, memories, and thoughts." (Ibid, 244).

"We are convinced that the Unqualified Absolute is not an undifferentiated and all-pervading influence comparable either to the pantheistic concepts of metaphysics or to the sometime *ether* hypothesis of science. The Unqualified Absolute is force unlimited and Deity conditioned, but we do not fully perceive the relation of this Absolute to the spirit realities of the universes." (*The Urantia Book*, 1955, 14:7).

"Many comets are unestablished wild offspring of the solar mother wheels, which are being gradually brought under control of the central governing sun. Comets also have numerous other origins. A comet's tail points away from the attracting body or sun

81

because of the electrical reaction of its highly expanded gases and because of the actual pressure of light and other energies emanating from the sun. This phenomenon constitutes one of the positive proofs of the reality of light and its associated energies; it demonstrates that light has weight. Light is a real substance, not simply waves of hypothetical *ether*." (173:3).

"The so-called *ether* is merely a collective name to designate a group of force and energy activities occurring in space. Ultimatons, electrons, and other mass aggregations of energy are uniform particles of matter, and in their transit through space they really proceed in direct lines. Light and all other forms of recognizable energy manifestations consist of a succession of definite particles which proceed in direct lines except as modified by gravity and other intervening forces. That these processions of energy particles appear as wave phenomena when subjected to certain observations is due to the resistance of the undifferentiated force blanket of all space, the hypothetical *ether*, and to the inter-gravity tension of the associated aggregation of matter. The spacing of the particle-intervals of matter, together with the initial velocity of the energy beams, establishes the undulatory appearance of many forms of energy-matter." (475:10).

"Primordial-force behavior does give rise to phenomena which are in many ways analogous to your postulated *ether*. Space is not empty; the spheres of all space whirl and plunge on through a vast ocean of outspread force-energy; neither is the space content of an atom empty. Nevertheless there is no *ether*, and the very absence of this hypothetical *ether* enables the inhabited planet to escape falling into the sun and the encircling electron to resist falling into the nucleus." (476:2).

"But not all the suppositions of natural philosophy are valid; for example, the hypothetical *ether*, which represents an ingenious attempt of man to unify his ignorance of space phenomena. The philosophy of the universe cannot be predicated on the observations of so-called science. If such a metamorphosis could not be seen, a scientist would be inclined to deny the possibility of developing a butterfly out of a caterpillar." (480:2).

Ethereal "(Origin C16: via L. from Gk. *aitherios* [from *aither* 'ether']). Extremely delicate and light in a way that seems not to be of this world." (*The Concise Oxford Dictionary*, 1999).

"Spirit beings do not dwell in nebulous space; they do not inhabit *ethereal* worlds; they are domiciled on actual spheres of a material nature, worlds just as real as those on which mortals live.

The Havona worlds are actual and literal, albeit their literal substance differs from the material organization of the planets of the seven superuniverses." (*The Urantia Book*, 1955, 154:3).

Etheric Body "In addition to the spiritual- and life-energy inputs to the body from the chakras and the acupuncture-meridian system, other energy and information systems influence our health and well-being. Surrounding and interpenetrating our physical body is an energy field or structure known as the 'etheric body.' The etheric body is a kind of invisible duplicate of the physical body that actually occupies the same space as the physical body (but at a higher vibratory rate or energy frequency than the physical). It is the first in a series of what are called the 'higher spiritual bodies.' In a very real sense, our soul, our 'true self,' expresses itself through a physical body that is subtly influenced and molded by these various higher spiritual bodies. Each of our spiritual bodies is formed from vibrating life-energy fields of progressively higher and finer levels of energy and matter." (Gerber, 2000, 23).

"Beyond the human etheric and astral bodies resides another spiritual body known as the mental body. The mental body, also composed of a subtle magnetic energy, vibrates faster than astral energy. As its name implies, the mental body is intimately involved in the energy of thought, creativity, invention, and inspiration. Just as with the astral body, strong ideas and mental energy patterns create mental thought forms that can sometimes be observed by clairvoyants who are able to perceive the higher aspects of the human energy field..." (Ibid, 31).

"In occultism, the matrix that holds the physical body together and which, at death, separates completely. The etheric body is affected by the nature of the astral body and the mental body, and ensures that the physical body is a reflection of the type of being inhabiting that form. In occult belief, therefore, the physical form is a reflection of more 'subtle' internal bodies, and the etheric body is midway between the physical and astral forms." (Drury, 2002, 95).

"The etheric body, ether-body, aether body, a name given by neo-Theosophy to a vital body or subtle body propounded in esoteric philosophies as the first or lowest layer in the 'human energy field' or aura. It is said to be in immediate contact with the physical body, to sustain it and connect it with 'higher' bodies." ("Etheric Body," *Wikipedia*).

"The English term 'etheric' in this context seems to derive from the Theosophical writings of Madame Blavatsky, but its use was formalized by C. W. Leadbeater and Annie Besant due to the elimination of Hindu terminology from the system of seven planes and bodies. (Adyar School of Theosophy)." (Ibid).

"The term gained some general popularity after the 1914-18 war, Dr. Walter John Kilner having adopted it for a layer of the 'human atmosphere' which, as he claimed in a popular book, could be rendered visible to the naked eye by means of certain exercises." (Ibid).

"The classical element aether of Platonic and Aristotelian physics continued in Victorian scientific proposals of a luminiferous ether as well as the cognate chemical substance ether. According to Theosophists and Alice Bailey the etheric body inhabits an etheric plane which corresponds to the four higher sub-planes of the physical plane. The intended reference is therefore to some extremely rarefied matter, analogous in usage to the word 'spirit' (originally 'breath'). In selecting it as the term for a clearly defined concept in an Indian-derived metaphysical system, the Theosophists aligned it with ideas such as the prana-maya-kosha (sheath made of prana, subtle breath or life-force) of Vedantic thought." (Ibid).

"In popular use it is often confounded with the related concept of the astral body as for example in the term astral projection--the early Theosophists had called it the 'astral double'. Others prefer to speak of the 'lower and higher astral'." (Ibid).

"Linga sarira is a Sanskrit term for the invisible double of the human body, the etheric body or etheric double (or astral body in some Theosophical concepts). It is one of the seven principles of the human being, according to Theosophical philosophy." (Ibid).

"Rudolf Steiner, the founder of Anthroposophy, often referred to the etheric body (Ätherleib or 'Life Body') in association with the etheric formative forces and the evolution of man and the cosmos. According to him, it can be perceived by a person gifted with clairvoyance as being of 'peach-blossom color'." (Ibid).

"Steiner considered the etheric reality or life principle as quite distinct from the physical material reality, being intermediate between the physical world and the astral or soul world. The etheric body can be characterized as the life force also present in the plant kingdom. It maintains the physical body's form until death. At that time, it separates from the physical body and the physical reverts to natural disintegration." (Ibid).

"According to Max Heindel's Rosicrucian writings, the etheric body, composed of four ethers, is called the 'Vital Body' since the ether is the way of ingress for vital force from the Sun and the field of agencies in nature which promote such vital activities as assimilation, growth, and propagation. It is an exact counterpart of our physical body, molecule for molecule, and organ for organ, but it is of the opposite polarity. It is slightly larger, extending about one and one-half inches beyond the periphery of the physical body." (Ibid).

"Samael Aun Weor teaches that the vital body is the tetra-dimensional part of the physical body and the foundation of organic life. He states that in the second Initiation of Fire, which is reached through working with sexual magic with a spouse, the Kundalini rises in the vital body. Then the initiate learns how to separate the two superior ethers from the others in order for them to serve as a vehicle to travel out of the physical body." (Ibid).

"On the Tree of Life of the Kabbalah, the vital body is often related to the sephirah Yesod." (Ibid).

"Some clairvoyants and occultists have produced drawings and paintings that record their perceptions of the etheric body; see Leadbeater's *Man Visible and Invisible* for one example. The images produced by Kirlian photography bear obvious resemblances to these graphics, showing a spiky-looking energy field extending a few inches around the human body (as well as other biological specimens, like leaves, and objects like coins). The fact that Kirlian photography can capture the acupuncture points of the body links the technology with concepts of prana, qi, bioplasma, and related ideas and theories. For some believers in the etheric body, Kirlian photography provides important supporting evidence--though skeptics are generally not swayed." (Ibid).

"In the teachings of Theosophy, Devas are regarded as living either in the atmospheres of the planets of the solar system (Planetary Angels) or inside the Sun (Solar Angels) (presumably other planetary systems and stars have their own angels) and they help to guide the operation of the processes of nature such as the process of evolution and the growth of plants; their appearance is reputedly like colored flames about the size of a human being. It is believed by Theosophists that devas can be observed when the third eye is activated. Some (but not most) devas originally incarnated as human beings." (Ibid).

"It is believed by Theosophists that nature spirits, elementals (gnomes, ondines, sylphs, and salamanders), and fairies can be also be observed when the third eye is activated. It is maintained by

Theosophists that these less evolutionarily developed beings have never been previously incarnated as human beings; they are regarded as on a separate line of spiritual evolution called the "deva evolution"; eventually, as their souls advance as they reincarnate, it is believed they will incarnate as devas." (Ibid).

"It is asserted by Theosophists that all of the above mentioned beings possess etheric bodies (but no physical bodies) that are composed of etheric matter, a type of matter finer and more pure that is composed of smaller particles than ordinary physical plane matter." (Ibid).

Ethic "(Origin ME: from OFr. *ethique*, from L. *ethice*, from Gk. [*he*] *ethike* [*tekhne*] '[the science of] morals', based on *ethos*). A set of moral principles." (*The Concise Oxford Dictionary*, 1999).

Eugenics "pl. (treated as sing.) The science of using controlled breeding to increase the occurrence of desirable heritable characteristics in a population." (*The Concise Oxford Dictionary*, 1999).

Event "A point in spacetime specified by its place and time." (Hawking, 2001, 205).

Event Horizon "The edge of a black hole; the boundary of the region from which it is not possible to escape to infinity." (Hawking, 2001, 204).

"The point of no return surrounding a black hole, often called the horizon. It was once believed to be a singularity of infinite gravity, but this was shown to be an artifact of the coordinates used to describe it." (Kaku, 2005, 388).

"Imaginary sphere surrounding a black hole delineating the points of no return; anything crossing the event horizon cannot escape the black hole's gravity." (Greene, 2004, 538)

Evolution "1 the process by which different kinds of living organisms are believed to have developed from earlier forms, especially by natural selection. 2 gradual development. 3 (Chemistry) the giving off of a gaseous product, or of heat. 4 a pattern of movements or maneuvers." (*The Concise Oxford Dictionary*, 1999).

"...a process of unrolling or opening out. In biology, originally applied to the development of individual plants and animals, which according to the doctrine of preformation depended on the unrolling or unfolding of pre-existing parts. Only in the 1830s was this word first applied to the historical transmutation of organisms; by the 1860s and 1870s it had come to refer to a general process of transmutation, which was generally assumed to be directional or progressive. Darwin's theory of evolution by natural selection enabled this process to be thought of as blind and purposeless, and this interpretation is central to Neo-Darwinism (q.v.), the dominant orthodoxy in modern biology. A variety of other evolutionary philosophies postulate an inherently creative principle in matter or in life; and some see in the evolutionary process the manifestation of a directional or purposive principle. According to modern cosmology, the entire universe is an evolutionary system." (Sheldrake, 1988, 367).

Evolve "1 develop gradually. 2 (of an organism or biological feature) develop over successive generations by evolution. 3 (Chemistry) give off (gas or heat)." (*The Concise Oxford Dictionary*, 1999).

Exotic Matter "A new form of matter with negative energy. It is different from antimatter, which has positive energy. Negative matter would have antigravity, so it would fall up instead of down. If it exists, it could be used to drive a time machine. However, none has ever been found." (Kaku, 2005, 388).

Expiate "(Origin C16 {earlier [ME] as *expiation*}: from L. *expiat-*, *expiare* 'appease by sacrifice' (based on *pius* 'pious'). Atone for (guilt or sin)." (*The Concise Oxford Dictionary*, 1999).

Extrasensory perception (ESP) "Paranormal cognition; the acquisition of information about an external event, object, or influence (mental or physical; past, present, or future) in some way other than through any of the known sensory channels." (Tart, 1997, 223).

"General term used to describe phenomena that cannot be perceived through the normal senses. These events and data are often referred to collectively as psi phenomena. ESP includes mental telepathy, clairvoyance, automatism, clairaudience, psychometry, precognition, and certain forms of divination. It may also involve using supernormal faculties inaccessible to most people, such as the ability to project the astral body; the ability to enter states of dissociation, mediumism, or trance..." (Drury, 2002, 97-98).

Extrasolar planet "A planet orbiting a star other than our own. Over a hundred such planets have now been detected, at a rate of about two a month. Most of them, unfortunately, are Jupiter-like and are not favorable to the creation of life. Within a few decades, satellites will be sent into outer space that will identify Earth-like extrasolar planets." (Kaku, 2005, 388).

Extraspiritual "...the Isle of Paradise is nonpersonal and

87

extraspiritual, being the essence of the universal body, the source and center of physical matter, and the absolute master pattern of universal material reality." (*The Urantia Book*, 1955, 8:5).

Extraterrestrial "of or from outside the earth or its atmosphere. (n.) a hypothetical or fictional being from outer space." (*The Concise Oxford Dictionary*, 1999).

"A being from another planet or dimension. The term is commonly used in accounts of unidentified flying objects where the inhabitants of flying saucers and 'mother ships' are said to have come to earth from elsewhere in space..." (Drury, 2002, 98).

F

Family "(n.) 1 (treated as sing. or plur.) a group consisting of two parents and their children living together as a unit; a group of people related by blood or marriage; the children of a person or couple. 2 all the descendants of a common ancestor; all the languages ultimately derived from a particular early language, regarded as a group. 3 a group united by a significant shared characteristic. (Biology) a principal taxonomic category ranking above genus and below order. (adj.) designed to be suitable for children as well as adults." (*The Concise Oxford Dictionary*, 1999).

"In human context, a family (from Latin: *familia*) is a group of people affiliated by consanguinity (by recognized birth), affinity (by marriage), or co-residence/shared consumption. Members of the immediate family may include a spouse, parent, brother and sister, and son and daughter. Members of the extended family may include grandparent, aunt, uncle, cousin, nephew and niece, or sibling-in-law. In most societies the family is the principal institution for the socialization of children. As the basic unit for raising children, anthropologists most generally classify family organization as matrifocal (a mother and her children); conjugal (a husband, his wife, and children; also called nuclear family); avuncular (for example a brother, his sister, and her children); or extended family in which parents and children co-reside with other members of one parent's family. As a unit of socialization, the family is the object of analysis for anthropologists and sociologists of the family. Sexual relations among the members are regulated by rules concerning incest such as the incest taboo." ("Family," *Wikipedia*).

"'Family' is used metaphorically to create more inclusive categories such as community, nationhood, global village and humanism." (Ibid)

"Genealogy is a field which aims to trace family lineages

through history." (Ibid).

"Family is also an important economic unit studied in family economics." (Ibid).

"One of the primary functions of the family is to produce and reproduce persons, biologically and/or socially. This can occur through the sharing of material substances (such as food); the giving and receiving of care and nurture (nurture kinship); jural rights and obligations; and moral and sentimental ties. Thus, one's experience of one's family shifts over time. From the perspective of children, the family is a 'family of orientation': the family serves to locate children socially and plays a major role in their enculturation and socialization. From the point of view of the parent(s), the family is a 'family of procreation,' the goal of which is to produce and enculturate and socialize children. However, producing children is not the only function of the family; in societies with a sexual division of labor, marriage, and the resulting relationship between two people, it is necessary for the formation of an economically productive household." (Ibid).

"The diverse data coming from ethnography, history, law and social statistics, establish that the human family is an institution and not a biological fact founded on the natural relationship of consanguinity. The different types of families occur in a wide variety of settings, and their specific functions and meanings depend largely on their relationship to other social institutions. Although the concept of consanguinity originally referred to relations by 'blood,' cultural anthropologists have argued that one must understand the idea of 'blood' metaphorically and that many societies understand family through other concepts rather than through genetic distance. Sociologists have a special interest in the function and status of these forms in stratified (especially capitalist) societies." (Ibid).

"According to the work of scholars Max Weber, Alan Macfarlane, Steven Ozment, Jack Goody and Peter Laslett, the huge transformation that led to modern marriage in Western democracies was 'fueled by the religio-cultural value system provided by elements of Judaism, early Christianity, Roman Catholic canon law and the Protestant Reformation'." (Ibid).

"Much sociological, historical and anthropological research dedicates itself to the understanding of this variation, and of changes in the family that form over time. Times have changed; it is more acceptable and encouraged for mothers to work and fathers to spend more time at home with the children. The way roles are balanced between the parents will help children grow and learn valuable life lessons. There is great importance of communication and equality in families, in order to avoid role strain." (Ibid).

"The term 'nuclear family' is commonly used, especially in the United States, to refer to conjugal families. A 'conjugal' family includes only the husband, the wife, and unmarried children who are not of age. Sociologists distinguish between conjugal families (relatively independent of the kindred of the parents and of other families in general) and nuclear families (which maintain relatively close ties with their kindred)." (Ibid).

"A 'matrifocal' family consists of a mother and her children. Generally, these children are her biological offspring, although adoption of children is a practice in nearly every society. This kind of family is common where women have the resources to rear their children by themselves, or where men are more mobile than women." (Ibid).

Members of the conjugal (or nuclear) families include the following:

Father - a male parent;

Mother - a female parent;

Son - a male child of the parent(s);

Daughter - a female child of the parent(s);

Brother - a male sibling;

Sister - a female sibling;

Grandfather - the father of a parent;

Grandmother - the mother of a parent; and

Cousins - two people who share at least one grandparent in common, but neither the same parents. (Ibid).

"Such systems generally assume that the mother's husband is also the biological father. In some families, a woman may have children with more than one man or a man may have children with more than one woman. The system refers to a child who shares only one parent with another child as a 'half-brother' or 'half-sister'. For children who do not share biological or adoptive parents in common, English-speakers use the term 'stepbrother' or 'stepsister' to refer to their new relationship with each other when one of their biological parents marries one of the other child's biological parents. Any person (other than the biological parent of a child) who marries the parent of that child becomes the 'stepparent' of the child, either the 'stepmother' or 'stepfather'. The same terms generally apply to children adopted into a family as to

90

children born into the family." (Ibid).

"Typically, societies with conjugal families also favor neo-local residence; thus upon marriage a person separates from the nuclear family of their childhood (family of orientation) and forms a new nuclear family (family of procreation). However, in western society the single parent family has been growing more accepted and has begun to make an impact on culture. Single parent families are more commonly single mother families than single father. These families sometimes face difficult issues besides the fact that they have to rear their children on their own, for example low income making it difficult to pay for rent, child care, and other necessities for a healthy and safe home. Members of the nuclear families of members of one's own (former) nuclear family may class as lineal or as collateral. Kin who regard them as lineal refer to them in terms that build on the terms used within the nuclear family:" (Ibid).

"Grandparent; Grandfather - a parent's father; Grandmother - a parent's mother." (Ibid).

"Grandchild; Grandson - a child's son; Granddaughter - a child's daughter." (Ibid).

"For collateral relatives, more classification terms come into play, terms that do not build on the terms used within the nuclear family:" (Ibid).

"Uncle - father's brother, mother's brother, father's sister's husband, mother's sister's husband." (Ibid).

"Aunt - father's sister, mother's sister, father's brother's wife, mother's brother's wife." (Ibid).

"Nephew - brother's son, sister's son, husband's brother's son, husband's sister's son, wife's brother's son, wife's sister's son." (Ibid).

"Niece - brother's daughter, sister's daughter, husband's brother's daughter, husband's sister's daughter, wife's brother's daughter, wife's sister's daughter.

"Cousin - the most classificatory term; the children of uncles and aunts..." (Ibid).

"Contemporary society generally views the family as a haven from the world, supplying absolute fulfillment. Zinn and Eitzen discuss the image of the 'family as haven [...] a place of intimacy, love and trust where individuals may escape the competition of dehumanizing forces in modern society'. During industrialization, 'the family as a repository of warmth and tenderness (embodied by the mother) stands in opposition to the competitive and aggressive world of commerce (embodied by the father). The family's task was to protect against the outside world.' However, Zinn and Eitzen note, 'The protective image of the family has waned in recent years as the ideals of family fulfillment have taken shape. Today, the family is more compensatory than protective. It supplies what is vitally needed but missing in other social arrangements.'" (Ibid).

"'The popular wisdom', according to Zinn and Eitzen, sees the family structures of the past as superior to those today, and families as more stable and happier at a time when they did not have to contend with problems such as illegitimate children and divorce. They respond to this, saying, 'there is no golden age of the family gleaming at us in the far back historical past.' 'Desertion by spouses, illegitimate children, and other conditions that are considered characteristics of modern times existed in the past as well.'" (Ibid).

The Postmodern Family

"Others argue that whether or not one views the family as 'declining' depends on one's definition of 'family'. Married couples have dropped below half of all American households. This drop is shocking from traditional forms of the family system. Only a fifth of households were following traditional ways of having married couples raising a family together. In the Western World, marriages are no longer arranged for economic, social or political gain, and children are no longer expected to contribute to family income. Instead, people choose mates based on love. This increased role of love indicates a societal shift toward favoring emotional fulfilment and relationships within a family, and this shift necessarily weakens the institution of the family." (Ibid).

"Margaret Mead considers the family as a main safeguard to continuing human progress. Observing, 'Human beings have learned, laboriously, to be human', she adds: 'we hold our present form of humanity on trust, [and] it is possible to lose it'...'It is not without significance that the most successful large-scale abrogations of the family have occurred not among simple savages, living close to the subsistence edge, but among great nations and strong empires, the resources of which were ample, the populations huge, and the power almost unlimited'". (Ibid).

"The model, common in the western societies, of the family triangle, husband-wife-children isolated from the outside, is also called the oedipal model of family, and it is a form of patriarchal family..." (Ibid).

"As it has been explained by Deleuze, Guattari and Foucault,

92

as well as other philosophers and psychiatrists such as Laing and Reich, the patriarchal-family conceived in the West tradition serves the purpose of perpetuating a propertarian and authoritarian society. The child grows according to the oedipal model, which is typical of the structure of capitalist societies, and he becomes in turn owner of submissive children and protector of the woman." (Ibid).

Family Rights and Laws

"Reproductive rights are legal rights and freedoms relating to reproduction and reproductive health. These include the right to decide on issues regarding the number of children born, family planning, contraception, and private life, free from coercion and discrimination; as well as the right to access health services and adequate information. According to UNFPA, reproductive rights 'include the right to decide the number, timing and spacing of children, the right to voluntarily marry and establish a family, and the right to the highest attainable standard of health, among others'." (Ibid).

"Mothers' rights movements focus on maternal health, workplace issues such as labor rights, breastfeeding, and rights in family law." (Ibid).

"The fathers' rights movement is a movement whose members are primarily interested in issues related to family law, including child custody and child support, that affect fathers and their children." (Ibid).

"Children's rights are the human rights of children, with particular attention to the rights of special protection and care afforded to minors, including their right to association with both parents, their right to human identity, their right to be provided in regard to their other basic needs, and their right to be free from violence and abuse." (Ibid).

"Marriage rights - Each jurisdiction has its own marriage laws. These laws differ significantly from country to country; and these laws are often controversial. Areas of controversy include women's rights as well as same sex marriage." (Ibid).

"Work-family balance is a concept involving proper prioritizing between work/career and family life. It includes issues relating to the way how work and families intersect and influence each other. At a political level, it is reflected through policies such as maternity leave and paternity leave." (Ibid).

Marriage Laws

"Marriage law refers to the legal requirements which

93

determine the validity of a marriage, which vary considerably between countries." ("Marriage laws," *Wikipedia*).

"A marriage, by definition, bestows rights and obligations on the married parties, and sometimes on relatives as well, being the sole mechanism for the creation a affinal ties (in-laws). These may include:" (Ibid).

"Giving a husband/wife or his/her family control over a spouse's labor, and property." (Ibid).

"Giving a husband/wife responsibility for a spouse's debts." (Ibid).

"Giving a husband/wife visitation rights when his/her spouse is incarcerated or hospitalized." (Ibid).

"Giving a husband/wife control over his/her spouse's affairs when the spouse is incapacitated." (Ibid).

"Establishing the second legal guardian of a parent's child." (Ibid).

"Establishing a joint fund of property for the benefit of children." (Ibid).

"Establishing a relationship between the families of the spouses." (Ibid).

"These rights and obligations vary considerably between societies, and between groups within society." (Ibid).

father "(n.) 1 a man in relation to his natural child or children; a male animal in relation to its offspring; an important figure in the origin and early history of something; a man who gives care and protection; the oldest member or doyen of a society or other body. (**the Father**) (in Christian belief) the first person of the Trinity; God; (**Father**) used in proper names to suggest an old and venerable character: *Father Thames*. 3 (**Fathers** or **Fathers of the Church**) early Christian theologians who are regarded as especially authoritative. (v.) 1 be the father of; (usually as noun **fathering**) treat with fatherly protective care; be the source or originator. 2 (**father someone/thing on**) assign paternity of a child or responsibility for something to." (*The Concise Oxford Dictionary*, 1999).

"A father (or dad) is a male parent who has raised a child, supplied the sperm through sexual intercourse or sperm donation which grew into a child, and/or donated a body cell which resulted in a clone. The adjective 'paternal' refers to a father and comparatively to 'maternal' for a mother. The verb 'to father' means to procreate or to sire a child from which also derives the

94

noun 'fathering'. Fathers determine the sex of their child through a sperm cell which either contains an X chromosome (female), or Y chromosome (male). Related terms of endearment are dad, daddy, pa, papa, poppa, pop, and pops. A male role-model that children can look up to is sometimes referred to as a father-figure." ("Father," *Wikipedia*).

"Traditionally, fathers act in a protective, supportive and responsible way towards their children. Involved fathers offer developmentally specific provisions to their sons and daughters throughout the life cycle and are impacted themselves by doing so. Active father figures may play a role in reducing behavior and psychological problems in young men and women. An increased amount of father–child involvement may help increase a child's social stability, educational achievement, and their potential to have a solid marriage as an adult. Their children may also be more curious about the world around them and develop greater problem solving skills. Children who were raised with fathers perceive themselves to be more cognitively and physically competent than their peers without a father. Mothers raising children together with a father reported less severe disputes with their child." (Ibid).

"The father figure does not always have to be a child's biological father and some children will have a biological father as well as a step- or nurturing father. When the biological father dies, or divorces, the mother may marry a second man who becomes the stepfather of the child. Where a child is conceived through sperm donation, the donor will be the 'biological father' of the child, and if the mother has a male partner, he will be the nurturing father." (Ibid).

"Fatherhood as legitimate identity shared by specific men and their children can be dependent on domestic factors and behaviors. For example, a study of the relationship between fathers, their sons, and home computers found that the construction of fatherhood and masculinity required fathers display computer expertise." (Ibid).

"According to the anthropologist Maurice Godelier, the parental role assumed by human males is a critical difference between human society and that of humans' closest biological relatives--chimpanzees and bonobos--who appear to be unaware of their 'father' connection. Studies show that fathers with smaller testicles are more likely to bathe, feed and nappy change their babies." (Ibid).

"*Soul.* The soul of man is an experiential acquirement. As

95

mortal creature chooses to 'do the will of the Father in heaven,' so the indwelling spirit becomes the *father* of a new reality in human experience. The mortal and material mind is the mother of this same emerging reality. The substance of this new reality is neither material nor spiritual--it is morontial..." (*The Urantia Book*, 1955, 8:10).

"No ascending mortal can escape the experience of rearing children--their own or others--either on the material worlds or subsequently on the finaliter world or on Jerusem. *Fathers* must pass through this essential experience just as certainly as mothers. It is an unfortunate and mistaken notion of modern peoples on Urantia that child culture is largely the task of mothers. Children need fathers as well as mothers, and fathers need this parental experience as much as do mothers." (531:4).

"No affectionate *father* is ever precipitate in visiting punishment upon an erring member of his family..." (617:4).

"While wrongdoing is always deleterious to a family, wisdom and love admonish the upright children to bear with an erring brother during the time granted by the affectionate *father* in which the sinner may see the error of his way and embrace salvation." (617:5).

"...*father* and mother are equal contributors of the living inheritance factors which initiate offspring..." (932:2).

Fatherly "(adj.) of, resembling, or characteristic of a father, especially in being protective and affectionate." (*The Concise Oxford Dictionary*, 1999).

Fermion "A particle or a pattern of string vibration whose spin is half of a whole number." (Hawking, 2001, 204).

"A subatomic particle with half-integral spin, such as the proton, electron, neutron, and quark. Fermions can be unifies with bosons via supersymmetry." (Kaku, 2005, 388).

Findhorn "Spiritual community located in northeast Scotland. The Findhorn foundation was founded in 1962 by Peter and Eileen Caddy on the site of a derelict caravan park. At the time the land was overgrown with gorse and nettles, and the soil was very poor. However, the Caddys developed the land and began to grow crops there. Eileen Caddy maintains that she was guided by a spirit-entity known as 'Elixir'--God's voice--who spoke to her and provided details of how the community should develop. Findhorn now has a large vegetable garden, which supports a community of around two hundred, and is based very much on the principle of cooperating with Nature. Some members of the Findhorn

Foundation believe that Nature spirits, or devas, have helped to make the crops grow under difficult environmental conditions." (Drury, 2002, 104-105).

Fifth dimension "The next 'garment of light' that our matter-energy body enters, in the process of spiritual evolution. A less gross-material body with the restored 'similitude' of God governing the physical processes. Enoch said three-dimensional humanity will be transposed into the fifth dimension upon completing its education in this realm of 'image and similitude'." (Hurtak, 1977, 576).

Fire "One of the four alchemical elements, the others being Earth, Water, and Air. The spirits of Fire are known as salamanders (a mythic variety not related to the small, newt-like amphibian that is an actual species). The three astrological signs linked to Fire are Aries, Leo, and Sagittarius." (Drury, 2002, 105).

Fusion "The process of combining protons or other light nuclei so they form higher nuclei, releasing energy in the process. The fusion of hydrogen to helium creates the energy of a main sequence star, like our Sun. The fusion of the light elements in the big bang gives us the relative abundance of light elements, like helium." (Kaku, 2005, 389).

G

Geller, Uri "(b. 1946) Israeli psychic who has become internationally famous for his alleged ability to use his mental powers to bend metal keys and cutlery without touching them. Geller has performed before large gatherings of people and submitted himself for experimental tests at the Stanford Research Institute. However, he declined to be investigated by a *New Scientist* panel of experts and the British Society of Psychical Research. Despite the controversy that surrounds him, and the claims by some stage magicians that the so-called 'Geller effect' of bending cutlery by mind-power can be achieved by conjuring. Geller has impressed many scientists with his alleged psi abilities." (Drury, 2002, 117).

Gene "(Biology) a unit of heredity which is transferred from a parent to offspring and is held to determine some characteristic of the offspring: in particular, a distinct sequence of DNA forming part of a chromosome." (*The Concise Oxford Dictionary*, 1999).

Gene pool "the stock of different genes in an inter-breeding population." (*The Concise Oxford Dictionary*, 1999).

Genera "plural form of Genus." (*The Concise Oxford Dictionary*, 1999).

Genetic "1 of or relating to genes or heredity; of or relating to genetics. 2 of or relating to origin, or arising from a common origin." (*The Concise Oxford Dictionary*, 1999).

Genetic code "the means by which DNA and RNA molecules carry genetic information in living cells." (*The Concise Oxford Dictionary*, 1999).

Genetics "(treated as sing.) The study of heredity and the variation of inherited characteristics. 2 (treated as sing. or pl.) the genetic properties or features of an organism." (*The Concise Oxford Dictionary*, 1999).

Genome "(Biology) 1 the haploid set of chromosomes of an organism. 2 the complete set of genetic material of an organism." (*The Concise Oxford Dictionary*, 1999).

Genotype "(Biology) the genetic constitution of an individual organism. Often contrasted with Phenotype." (*The Concise Oxford Dictionary*, 1999).

Genus "1 (Biology) a principal taxonomic category that ranks above species and below family, denoted by a capitalized Latin name, e.g. *Leo*. 2 a class of things which have common characteristics and which can be divided into subordinate kinds." (*The Concise Oxford Dictionary*, 1999).

Gluons "Messenger particles of the strong nuclear force." (Greene, 2004, 538).

Grand unification "Theory attempting to unify the strong, weak, and electromagnetic forces." (Greene, 2004, 538).

Gravitational field "The means by which gravity communicates its influence." (Hawking, 2001, 204).

Gravitational force "The weakest of the four fundamental forces of nature." (Hawking, 2001, 204).

Gravitational wave "A wavelike disturbance in a gravitational field." (Hawking, 2001, 204).

Graviton "A conjectured subatomic particle that is the quanta of gravity. The graviton has spin 2. It is too small to be seen in the laboratory." (Kaku, 2005, 390).

"Hypothetical messenger particles of the gravitational force." (Greene, 2004, 538).

Gravity Wave "A wave of gravity, predicted by Einstein's general relativity theory. This wave has been indirectly measured by looking at the aging of pulsars rotating around each other." (Kaku, 2005, 390).

Grid "Reference to a two dimensional framework, providing a preferred pathway for energy-information-light to travel from point

A to point B. The grid may be thought of as the substance that exists in the nothingness, the thread of fundamental intelligence that is the underlying fabric of creation." (Braden, 1993, 192).

"Conceptually, a grid may be considered as an etheric network of guidelines, a meshed framework along which pulses of energy are directed. These ordered patterns of energy are typically formed of a single uniformly shaped pattern, repeating itself over and over as equally spaced expressions of the identical geometry in any two dimensional direction..." (Ibid, 193).

Gunas "Qualities. The three threads that weave together the qualities found in all things: tamas, rajas, sattva." (Judith, 1999, 415).

H

Harner, Michael J "(b. 1929) American anthropologist who spent many years of field research in the Upper Amazon, Mexico, and western North America learning techniques of shamanism from native Indians. Harner has now adapted the traditional shamanic techniques for western practitioners, using a method that combines drumming and visualization to allow people to enter 'the magical reality'. This 'journey' entails visualizing the cosmic tree, entering its root system, and traveling through to the lower world, where one may make contact with a power animal or magical ally. A variant on this is to ascend to the upper world through a tunnel of smoke." (Drury, 2002, 134).

"Harner has been visiting professor at Columbia, Yale, and the University of California, Berkeley, and is at present Chairman of the Foundation for Shamanic Studies in Mill Valley, California. He is the author of a practical book on shamanism titled *The Way of the Shaman* (1980), and has also published two academic books on the subject: *The Jivaro* (1972), and *Hallucinogens and Shamanism* (1973)." (Ibid).

Hatha Yoga "Form of yoga that teaches techniques relating to the physical control of the body. It makes use of special postures known as asanas and rhythmic breathing methods known as pranayama. Yoga recognizes the interrelatedness of mind and body, and the word *hatha* itself consists of two polar opposites: *ha*, meaning 'sun' (masculine), and *tha*, meaning 'moon' (feminine). Hatha Yoga is the best known and most popular form of yoga." (Drury, 2002, 135).

"The yoga through the path of training the body." (Judith, 1999, 416).

Hawking Radiation "The radiation that slowly evaporates

from a black hole. This radiation is in the form of black body radiation, with a specific temperature, and is due to the fact that quantum particles can penetrate the gravitational field surrounding a black hole." (Kaku, 2005, 390).

Heartfulness "is a calm awareness of one's bodies feelings, the vibration of consciousness; the united sounding of the sacred word or conscious feeling itself, i.e. compassionate mindfulness." ("Heartfulness," *Wikipedia*).

"It can be related to the Hindu idea of transcendence, (not the process of transcendental meditation as TM by Brahmananda Saraswati) the process of moving beyond the bodies limitations created by the mind and to connect the body itself directly with the source." (Ibid).

"(Skt. *Śruti*, 'cosmic sound of truth') is one of the many teachings of shakyamuni where he claims that "hearing, listening, heartfulness. (Skt. *samyak-śrúti*) is one of the key aspects of understanding on the path to liberation and subsequent enlightenment. It has been shown that regulating the subtle rhythms of the heart can create a state of harmonic balance within the syncopation of the heartbeats i.e. Heartfulness--a state of peaceful heart meditation."

"The American journal of physiology recently published findings that state 'The effects of different breathing frequencies and patterns on cardiovascular regulation have been investigated extensively in recent years. In this context, various effects of poetry recitation on cardiovascular parameters, especially on heart rate oscillations, have been demonstrated. Bernardi et al. found a frequency adjustment of breathing oscillations with endogenous blood pressure fluctuations Mayer waves and even cerebral blood flow oscillations during the recitation of the rosary and the 'OM' mantra. This effect was attributed to the breathing frequency of 6 breaths/min induced by the metric of both religious verses. Furthermore, they noticed an increased arterial baroreflex sensitivity, which is a favorable long-term prognostic factor in cardiac patients. In another study, Bernardi et al. observed a significant increase in arterial oxygen saturation (SaO2) during controlled breathing at frequencies of 15/6/3 breaths/min in patients with chronic heart failure and healthy controls. The strongest increase was found at a breathing frequency of 6 breaths/min. Thus recitation of specific poetry as a means to control breathing patterns was proposed and the rosary prayer to be "viewed as a health practice as well as a religious practice."'

(Ibid).

Heredity "1 the passing on of physical or mental characteristics genetically from one generation to another; a person's ancestry. 2 inheritance of title, office, or right." (*The Concise Oxford Dictionary*, 1999).

"The transmission of characters from ancestors to their descendants. Originally understood in a broad sense which included the inheritance of acquired characteristics and habits of life; restricted in modern biology to mean the inheritance of genes According to the hypothesis of formative causation, heredity includes both genetic inheritance and the inheritance of morphic fields by morphic resonance." (Sheldrake, 1995, 368).

Heterogeneous "1 diverse in character or content. 2 (Chemistry) denoting a process involving substances in different phases (solid, liquid, or gaseous): *heterogeneous catalysis*." (*The Concise Oxford Dictionary*, 1999).

Heterotic String Theory "The most physically realistic string theory. Its symmetry group is E(8) x E(8), which large enough to incorporate the symmetry of the Standard Model. Via M-theory, the heterotic string can be shown to be equivalent to the other four string theories." (Kaku, 2005, 390).

Higgs boson "The Higgs boson or Higgs particle is an elementary particle initially theorized in 1964, and tentatively confirmed to exist on 14 March 2013. The discovery has been called 'monumental' because it appears to confirm the existence of the Higgs field, which is pivotal to the Standard Model and other theories within particle physics. It would explain why some fundamental particles have mass when the symmetries controlling their interactions should require them to be massless, and--linked to this--why the weak force has a much shorter range than the electromagnetic force. The discovery of a Higgs boson should allow physicists to finally validate the last untested area of the Standard Model's approach to fundamental particles and forces, guide other theories and discoveries in particle physics, and potentially lead to developments in 'new' physics." ("Higgs boson," *Wikipedia*).

"This unanswered question in fundamental physics is of such importance that it led to a search of more than 40 years for the Higgs boson and finally the construction of one of the world's most expensive and complex experimental facilities to date, the Large Hadron Collider, able to create Higgs bosons and other particles for observation and study. On 4 July 2012, it was announced that a previously unknown particle with a mass between 125 and 127 GeV/c2 (134.2 and 136.3 amu) had been detected; physicists suspected at the time that it was the Higgs boson. By March 2013, the particle had been proven to behave, interact and decay in many of the ways predicted by the Standard Model, and was also tentatively confirmed to have positive parity and zero spin, two fundamental attributes of a Higgs boson. This appears to be the first known scalar particle discovered in nature. More data is needed to know if the discovered particle exactly matches the predictions of the Standard Model, or whether, as predicted by some theories, multiple Higgs bosons exist." (Ibid).

"The Higgs boson is named after Peter Higgs, one of six physicists who, in 1964, proposed the mechanism that suggested the existence of such a particle. Although Higgs's name has come to be associated with this theory, several researchers between about 1960 and 1972 each independently developed different parts of it. In mainstream media the Higgs boson has often been called the 'God particle', from a 1993 book on the topic; the nickname is strongly disliked by many physicists, including Higgs, who regard it as inappropriate sensationalism. In 2013 two of the original researchers, Peter Higgs and François Englert, were awarded the Nobel Prize in Physics for their work and prediction (Englert's co-researcher Robert Brout had died in 2011)." (Ibid).

"In the Standard Model, the Higgs particle is a boson with no spin, electric charge, or color charge. It is also very unstable, decaying into other particles almost immediately. It is a quantum excitation of one of the four components of the Higgs field, constituting a scalar field, with two neutral and two electrically charged components, and forms a complex doublet of the weak isospin SU(2) symmetry. The field has a 'Mexican hat' shaped potential with nonzero strength everywhere (including otherwise empty space) which in its vacuum state breaks the weak isospin symmetry of the electroweak interaction. When this happens, three components of the Higgs field are 'absorbed' by the SU(2) and U(1) gauge bosons (the 'Higgs mechanism') to become the longitudinal components of the now-massive W and Z bosons of the weak force. The remaining electrically neutral component separately couples to other particles known as fermions (via Yukawa couplings), causing these to acquire mass as well. Some versions of the theory predict more than one kind of Higgs fields and bosons. Alternative 'Higgsless' models would have been considered if the Higgs boson were not discovered." (Ibid).

Higgs Field "The field that breaks the symmetry of GUT theories when it makes the transition from the false vacuum to the real vacuum. Higgs fields are the origin of mass in GUT theory and also can be used to drive inflation. Physicists hope that the LHC will finally discover the Higgs field." (Kaku, 2005, 390-391).

Higgs ocean "Shorthand...for a Higgs field vacuum expectation value." (Greene, 2004, 539).

Hologram and **Holographic Theory** "A hologram is a three-dimensional image formed by two intersecting laser beams." (Judith, 1999, 293).

"A recursive pattern of energy (geometric, emotional, feeling, thought, consciousness or mathematical) that stands whole and complete unto itself while serving as a portion of a greater whole...By definition, each element of a holographic pattern mirrors all other elements of the pattern. This is the beauty of the holographic model of consciousness. Change introduced anywhere in the system is mirrored throughout the entire system." (Braden, 1993, 193).

"In the creation of a hologram, a beam of light produced by a laser is reflected from an object, and recorded on a light-sensitive plate. The plate also receives another beam of the same frequency, called the reference beam, which goes directly from the source to the plate. Looking at the plate itself, we would see only a meaningless pattern of dark and light swirls. This is the coded information of the intersection of the two beams, much as the grooves on a record are the coded representation of a sound track." (Judith, 1999, 293).

"When the plate is later 'reenacted' by a reference beam that contains the same frequency as the original laser, the image of the holographed object eerily jumps out at you in three dimensions. You can move to the side of the hologram and see the side of the object as if it were really there, yet since it is only light you can pass your hand right through it." (Ibid).

"There are many remarkable things about holograms. The first is that the information is stored 'omnipresently' on the plate...The second remarkable thing about holograms is that they are non-spatial. Many holograms can be superimposed upon one another in one 'space,' or on one plate by using lasers of different frequencies. Karl Pribram's theory states that the brain itself functions like a hologram through constant interpretations of interference patterns between brain waves." (Ibid, 293-294).

"Pribram...working with Karl Lashley...found that memory

seemed to be stored omnipresently throughout the brain." (Ibid).

"When we view an object, light is transformed into neural frequency patterns in the brain. The brain is filled with some thirteen billion neurons. The number of possible connections between these neurons numbers in the trillions. Where scientists have previously looked at the neurons themselves as significant to brain activity, they are now looking at the junctions between the neurons. While the actual cells exhibit a kind of on-off reflex action, the junctions at the nerve endings exhibit wavelike qualities when viewed as a whole." (Ibid).

"As impulses travel through the brain, the wavelike qualities create what we experience as perception and memory. These perceptions are stored as encoded wave-front frequencies in the brain and can be activated by an appropriate stimulus, triggering the original wave forms..." (Ibid, 295).

"Our perception of the world around us seems to be a reconstruction of a neural hologram within the brain. This applies to language, thought, and all the senses as well as to the perception of visual information." (Ibid).

"Because this model hints at each of our brains containing access to all information, even that of other time dimensions, it can explain many things beyond the normal functions of memory and perception such as remote viewing, clairvoyance, mystic visions, and precognition." (Ibid).

"...theoretical physicist David Bohm has described a model which suggests that the universe itself may be a kind of hologram." (Ibid).

"According to Bohm, the universe is 'enfolded' or spread as a whole throughout a kind of cosmic medium...This enfoldment allows for an infinite number of interference capabilities, giving us the forms and energies that we experience with our holographic minds. In this context, the, the brain itself is part of a larger hologram, and would therefore contain information about the whole." (Ibid).

"...each of our minds also contains the encoded information of a greater intelligence, just waiting for the right reference beam to trigger the image." (Ibid, 296).

Holotropic consciousness "Consciousness aiming toward wholeness and totality of existence, characterizes certain non-ordinary psychological states, such as meditative, mystical, or psychedelic experiences..." (Grof, 1988, 38-39).

"In the holotropic mode of consciousness, it is possible to

reach, in addition, all the remaining aspects of existence. These include not only access to one's biological, psychological, social, racial, and spiritual history and the past, present, and future of the entire phenomenal world, but access to many other levels and domains of reality described by the great mystical traditions of the world. Comparative study of mystical literature shows that most of these systems seem to agree on a complex, layered, and hierarchical model of reality that includes phenomenal as well as transphenomenal aspects of existence (Wilber, 1980)." (Ibid).

Horizon "The farthest point you can see. Surrounding a black hole there is a magic sphere, at the Schwarzschild radius, which is the point of no return." (Kaku, 2005, 391).

Hubble's constant "The velocity of a red-shifted galaxy divided by its distance. Hubble's constant measures the rate of expansion of the universe, and its inverse correlates roughly to the age of the universe. The lower the Hubble constant, the older the universe. The WMAP satellite has placed the Hubble constant at 71 km/s per million parsecs, or 21.8 km/s per million light-years, ending decades of controversy." (Kaku, 2005, 391).

Hubble's Law "The farther a galaxy is from Earth, the faster it moves. Discovered by Edwin Hubble in 1929, this observation agrees with Einstein's theory of an expanding universe." (Kaku, 2005, 391).

Human Potential Movement "Term given to the movement that arose in the late 1960s and early 1970s as humanistic psychologists and other social thinkers began systematically to explore the potential of human consciousness. This included research into the mind/body relationship, the study of left- and right-brain hemisphere functions, peak experiences, and mystical states of consciousness. To some extent, the movement combines elements of the aftermath of the psychedelic era of the 1960s with the revival of interest in Eastern philosophies and holistic health. It has strong links with transpersonal psychology and with the activities of the Esalen Institute in California." (Drury, 2002, 148-149).

Hyperspace "Dimensions higher than four. String theory (M-theory) predicts that there should be ten (eleven) hyperspatial dimensions. At present, there is no experimental data indicating the existence of these higher dimensions, which may be too small to measure." (Kaku, 2005, 391).

Hypnosis "A form of trance in which the subject's powers of concentration are mobilized and subconscious memories and perceptions brought to the surface. The hypnotherapist provides the subject with cues which allow the individual the individual to overcome personal barriers and emotional blockages, and bring into consciousness abilities and memories formerly neglected. The term 'hypnotism' was coined by the Scottish surgeon Dr. James Braid, who rejected the theory of Anton Mesmer that magnetic force could be transmitted from one person to another. Braid believed that mesmerism produced a state of consciousness combining relaxation and enhanced awareness. He derived the name 'hypnotism' from the Greek god of sleep, Hypnos, although in coining this expression he clearly misnamed the process in question." (Drury, 2002, 150).

"An altered state of consciousness when a subject is in alpha or theta brain-wave state." (Backman, 2009, 231).

Hypnotherapy "The experience of being guided into an altered state of consciousness to benefit at a human and soul level." (Backman, 2009, 231).

I

Ida "One of the three central nadis which represent the lunar, feminine energy of a person. It is also linked with the Ganges. Its color is yellow." (Judith, 1999, 416).

"In Kundalini Yoga, the negatively charged lunar current that circles around the central axis of the nervous system, sushumna. It counterbalances the positively charged solar current known as pingala." (Drury, 2002, 152).

"...the chakras are connected by a non-physical channel running straight up the center of the body called the sushumna. Two alternate channels control the yin and yang energies, Ida and Pingala, twisting in figure-eight patterns around each chakra and running alongside the sushumna. These channels are among thousands of subtle energy channels called nadis, Sanskrit for 'flowing waters.' Ida and Pingala represent the luna and solar aspects, respectively." (Judith, 1999, 113-114).

Individuation "In the analytical psychology of Carl Jung, the concept of 'making the self-whole'. For Jung, this process included harmonizing the forces of one's external life with the events of both the human unconscious and the collective unconscious. Jung was interested in mystical systems that could lead people towards spiritual transformation." (Drury, 2002, 155).

Inductive Linkage "Man's world of information is dependent on perception. Information through Inductive Linkage is the ordering of perceptual reality for the purpose of interaction with higher intelligence. It is the formation of neural patterns for the subsequent reordering of consciousness in relation to new information. By way of focusing Light on the neural pathways or patterns, a system of ordering the perceptual reality of being is manifest. Thus, the configuration of all ordered neural impulses gives the resultant form of activity, which becomes the organism's perceptual reality, its perspective." (Hurtak, 1977, 580).

Infinity "A boundless or endless extent or number." (Hawking, 2001, 205).

Inflation "A brief period of accelerated expansion during which the very early universe increased its size by an enormous factor." (Hawking, 2001, 205).

"The theory which states that the universe underwent an incredible amount of superliminal expansion at the instant of its birth. Inflation can solve the flatness, monopole, and horizon problems." (Kaku, 2005, 391).

Inflationary cosmology "Cosmological theory incorporating a brief but enormous burst of spatial expansion in the early universe." (Greene, 2004, 539).

Inflation field "The field whose energy and negative pressure drives inflationary expansion." (Greene, 2004, 539).

Information "To inform literally means to put into form or shape. Information is now generally taken to be the source of form or order in the world; information is informative and plays the role of a formative cause, as for example in the concept of 'genetic information'." (Sheldrake, 1995, 369).

Information theory "A branch of cybernetics that attempts to define the amount of information required to control a process of given complexity. Information in this narrow technical sense is measured in bits. A bit is the amount of information required to specify one of two alternatives, for example to distinguish between 1 and 0 in the binary notation used in computers." (Sheldrake, 1995, 369).

Infrared Radiation "Heat radiation, or electromagnetic radiation, that is slightly below visible light in frequency." (Kaku, 2005, 391).

Institute of Noetic Sciences (IONS) "The term *noetic sciences* was first coined in 1973 when the Institute of Noetic Sciences (IONS) was founded by Apollo 14 astronaut Edgar Mitchell, who two years earlier became the sixth man to walk on the moon. Ironically, it was the trip back home that Mitchell recalls most, during which he felt a profound sense of universal

107

connectedness—what he later described as a *Samadhi* experience. In Mitchell's own words, 'The presence of divinity became almost palpable, and I knew that life in the universe was not just an accident based on random processes…The knowledge came to me directly." ("Noetic Sciences," The Institute of Noetic Sciences).

"It led him to conclude that reality is more complex, subtle, and mysterious than conventional science had led him to believe. Perhaps a deeper understanding of consciousness (inner space) could lead to a new and expanded understanding of reality in which objective and subjective, outer and inner, are understood as co-equal aspects of the miracle of being. It was this intersection of knowledge systems that led Dr. Mitchell to launch the interdisciplinary field of noetic sciences." (Ibid).

Intellect "(Origin ME: from L. *intellectus* 'understanding', from *intellegere*). (n.) 1 the faculty of reasoning and understanding objectively; one's mental powers. 2 a clever person." (*The Concise Oxford Dictionary*, 1999).

"The cognitive and rational powers of the mind. In Western magic, the human intellect is symbolized by the eighth sephirah on the Tree of Life, Hod, which is characterized as masculine." (Drury, 2002, 158).

"…The existence of God is utterly beyond all possibility of demonstration except for the contact between the God-consciousness of the human mind and the God-presence of the Thought Adjuster that indwells the mortal *intellect* and is bestowed upon man as the free gift of the Universal Father." (*The Urantia Book*, 1955, 24:6).

"In the inner experience of man, mind is joined to matter. Such material-linked minds cannot survive mortal death. The technique of survival is embraced in those adjustments of the human will and those transformations in the mortal mind whereby such a God-conscious *intellect* gradually becomes spirit taught and eventually spirit led. This evolution of the human mind from matter association to spirit union results in the transmutation of the potentially spirit phases of the mortal mind into the morontia realities of the immortal soul. Mortal mind subservient to matter is destined to become increasingly material and consequently to suffer eventual personality extinction; mind yielded to spirit is destined to become increasingly spiritual and ultimately to achieve oneness with the surviving and guiding divine spirit and in this way to attain survival and eternity of personality existence." (26:1).

"If the finite mind of man is unable to comprehend how so

great and so majestic a God as the Universal Father can descend from his eternal abode in infinite perfection to fraternize with the individual human creature, then must such a finite *intellect* rest assurance of divine fellowship upon the truth of the fact that an actual fragment of the living God resides within the intellect of every normal-minded and morally conscious Urantia mortal. The indwelling Thought Adjusters are a part of the eternal Deity of the Paradise Father. Man does not have to go farther than his own inner experience of the soul's contemplation of this spiritual-reality presence to find God and attempt communion with him." (62:1).

"...Limitations of *intellect*, curtailment of education, deprivation of culture, impoverishment of social status, even inferiority of the human standards of morality resulting from the unfortunate lack of educational, cultural, and social advantages, cannot invalidate the presence of the divine spirit in such unfortunate and humanly handicapped but believing individuals..." (69:8).

"Infinite mind ignores time, ultimate mind transcends time, cosmic mind is conditioned by time. And so with space: The Infinite Mind is independent of space, but as descent is made from the infinite to the adjutant levels of mind, *intellect* must increasingly reckon with the fact and limitations of space." (102:4).

"Mind transmutes the values of spirit into the meanings of *intellect*; volition has power to bring the meanings of mind to fruit in both the material and spiritual domains. The Paradise ascent involves a relative and differential growth in spirit, mind, and energy. The personality is the unifier of these components of experiential individuality." (102:6).

"Though it is hardly possible for the mortal mind to comprehend the seven levels of relative cosmic reality, the human *intellect* should be able to grasp much of the meaning of three functional levels of finite reality:" (140:5).

"1. *Matter.* Organized energy which is subject to linear gravity except as it is modified by motion and conditioned by mind." (140:6).

"2. *Mind.* Organized consciousness which is not wholly subject to material gravity, and which becomes truly liberated when modified by spirit." (140:7).

"3. *Spirit.* The highest personal reality. True spirit is not subject to physical gravity but eventually becomes the motivating influence of all evolving energy systems of personality dignity." (140:8).

"Morontia progression pertains to continuing advancement of *intellect*, spirit, and personality form…" (342:2).

"The characteristics of the mystical state are diffusion of consciousness with vivid islands of focal attention operating on a comparatively passive *intellect*. All of this gravitates consciousness toward the subconscious rather than in the direction of the zone of spiritual contact, the superconscious…" (1099:7).

"The certainties of science proceed entirely from the *intellect*…" (1119:3).

"…The *intellect* is the harmonizer and the ever-present conditioner and qualifier of the sum total of mortal experience. Both energy-things and spirit values are colored by their interpretations through the mind media of consciousness." (1136:1).

"When the mortal *intellect* attempts to grasp the concept of reality totality, such a finite mind is face to face with infinity-reality…" (1152:2).

"Mortal mind is a temporary *intellect system* loaned to human beings for use during a material lifetime…" (1216:6).

"…Set your mind at work to solve problems; teach your *intellect* to work for you…" (1437:3).

"…the truly reflective human *intellect* is not altogether bound by the limits of time…" (1480:3).

Intellectual "(adj.) of, relating to, or appealing to the intellect; having a highly developed intellect. (n.) a person with a highly developed intellect." (*The Concise Oxford Dictionary*, 1999).

"…in the *intellectual* world we may discern eternal truth…" (*The Urantia* Book, 1955, 40:5).

"*Intellectual* self-consciousness can discover the beauty of truth, its spiritual quality, not only by the philosophic consistency of its concepts, but more certainly and surely by the unerring response of the ever-present Spirit of Truth…" (42:7).

"…The plan for your *intellectual* evolution is, indeed, one of sublime perfection…" (103:4).

"…All true and genuine *intellectual* values, all divine thoughts and perfect ideas, are unerringly drawn into this absolute circuit of mind." (103:7).

"Self-consciousness consists in *intellectual* awareness of personality actuality; it includes the ability to recognize the reality of other personalities…" (194:6).

"There is a definite requirement of the pilgrims of time on each of the Havona circles; and while every pilgrim continues under the tutelage of supernaphim by nature adapted to helping that particular type of ascendant creature, the course that must be mastered is fairly uniform for all ascenders who reach the central universe. This course of achievement is quantitative, qualitative, and experiential--*intellectual,* spiritual, and supreme." (291:4).

"On mansion world number one (or another in case of advanced status) you will resume your *intellectual* training and spiritual development at the exact level whereon they were interrupted by death. Between the time of planetary death or translation and resurrection on the mansion world, mortal man gains absolutely nothing aside from experiencing the fact of survival. You begin over there right where you leave off down here." (533:6).

"Mansonia number two more specifically provides for the removal of all phases of *intellectual* conflict and for the cure of all varieties of mental disharmony..." (535:4).

"...your planet seems most confused and greatly retarded in all phases of *intellectual* progress and spiritual attainment." (578:2).

"...Beauty is the *intellectual* recognition of the harmonious time-space synthesis of the far-flung diversification of phenomenal reality, all of which stems from pre-existent and eternal oneness." (647:2).

"Even truth, beauty, and goodness--man's *intellectual* approach to the universe of mind, matter, and spirit--must be combined into one unified concept of a divine and supreme ideal..." (647:6).

"To finite man truth, beauty, and goodness embrace the full revelation of divinity reality. As this love-comprehension of Deity finds spiritual expression in the lives of God-knowing mortals, there are yielded the fruits of divinity: *intellectual* peace, social progress, moral satisfaction, spiritual joy, and cosmic wisdom..." (648:3).

"...Sin enormously retards *intellectual* development, moral growth, social progress, and mass spiritual attainment..." (761:5).

"If one is disposed to recognize a theoretical subconscious mind as a practical working hypothesis in the otherwise unified intellectual life, then, to be consistent, one should postulate a similar and corresponding realm of ascending *intellectual* activity as the superconscious level, the zone of immediate contact with the indwelling spirit entity..." (1099:4).

"The enlightened spiritual consciousness of civilized man is not concerned so much with some specific *intellectual* belief or with any one particular mode of living as with discovering the truth of

111

living, the good and right technique of reacting to the ever-recurring situations of mortal existence…" (1115:6).

"Theology deals with the *intellectual* content of religion, metaphysics (revelation) with the philosophical aspects…" (1140:7).

"Mortal man is passing through a great age of expanding horizons and enlarging concepts on Urantia, and his cosmic philosophy must accelerate in evolution to keep pace with the expansion of the *intellectual* arena of human thought…" (1146:4).

Intelligence "(n.) 1 the ability to acquire and apply knowledge and skills. 2 a person with this ability. 3 the gathering of information of military or political value; information gathered in this way. 4 (archaic) news." (*The Concise Oxford Dictionary*, 1999).

"All finite knowledge and creature understanding are relative. Information and *intelligence*, gleaned from even high sources, is only relatively complete, locally accurate, and personally true." (*The Urantia Book*, 1955, 42:2).

"*Intelligence* alone cannot explain the moral nature. Morality, virtue, is indigenous to human personality. Moral intuition, the realization of duty, is a component of human mind endowment and is associated with the other inalienables of human nature: scientific curiosity and spiritual insight. Man's mentality far transcends that of his animal cousins, but it is his moral and religious natures that especially distinguish him from the animal world." (192:8).

"…*Intelligence* alone can discriminate as to the best means of attaining indiscriminate ends, but a moral being possesses an insight which enables him to discriminate between ends as well as between means. And a moral being in choosing virtue is nonetheless intelligent. He knows what he is doing, why he is doing it, where he is going, and how he will get there." (193:3).

"…From the standpoint of *intelligence*, man ascends to the level of a moral being because he is endowed with personality." (193:7).

"…Those accredited beings who have, for any reason, been unable to attain that level of *intelligence* mastery and endowment of spirituality which would entitle them to personal guardians, cannot thus immediately and directly go to the mansion worlds. Such surviving souls must rest in unconscious sleep until the judgment day of a new epoch, a new dispensation, the coming of a Son of God to call the rolls of the age and adjudicate the realm, and this is the general practice throughout all Nebadon…" (341:1).

"…*Intelligence* may control the mechanism of civilization,

wisdom may direct it, but spiritual idealism is the energy which really uplifts and advances human culture from one level of attainment to another." (909:8).

"Throughout the mind functions of cosmic *intelligence*, the totality of mind is dominant over the parts of intellectual function. Mind, in its essence, is functional unity; therefore does mind never fail to manifest this constitutive unity, even when hampered and hindered by the unwise actions and choices of a misguided self. And this unity of mind invariably seeks for spirit coordination on all levels of its association with selves of will dignity and ascension prerogatives." (1217:5).

"It requires *intelligence* to secure one's share of the desirable things of life. It is wholly erroneous to suppose that faithfulness in doing one's daily work will insure the rewards of wealth. Barring the occasional and accidental acquirement of wealth, the material rewards of the temporal life are found to flow in certain well-organized channels, and only those who have access to these channels may expect to be well rewarded for their temporal efforts. Poverty must ever be the lot of all men who seek for wealth in isolated and individual channels. Wise planning, therefore, becomes the one thing essential to worldly prosperity. Success requires not only devotion to one's work but also that one should function as a part of some one of the channels of material wealth. If you are unwise, you can bestow life upon your generation without material reward; if you are an accidental beneficiary of the flow of wealth, you may roll in luxury even though you have done nothing worthwhile for your fellow men." (1779:2).

"...Modern men and women of *intelligence* evade the religion of Jesus because of their fears of what it will do to them--and with them. And all such fears are well founded. The religion of Jesus does, indeed, dominate and transform its believers, demanding that men dedicate their lives to seeking for a knowledge of the will of the Father in heaven and requiring that the energies of living be consecrated to the unselfish service of the brotherhood of man." (2083:2).

Interference "The mixing of two waves that are slightly different in phase or frequency, creating a characteristic interference pattern. By analyzing this pattern, one may be able to detect tiny differences between two waves which differ only by an extremely small amount." (Kaku, 2005, 391).

"Phenomenon in which overlapping waves create a distinctive pattern; in quantum mechanics, involves seemingly exclusive alternatives combining together." (Greene, 2004, 539).

Interference pattern "The wave pattern that appears from the merging of two or more waves that are emitted from different locations or at different times." (Hawking, 2001, 205).

Intuition "Subjective faculty of the mind that often produces insights and perceptions that cannot be attained by the rational intellect. In Western magic, human intuition is symbolized by the seventh sephirah on the Tree of Life, Netzach, and is characterized as feminine." (Drury, 2002, 158).

"The act or faculty of knowing or sensing without the use of rational processes." (Backman, 2009, 231).

J

Jiva "The individual soul or psyche, embodied as a life force, as opposed to atman, a more universal, spiritual sense of soul." (Judith, 1999, 416).

"Skt. term for a 'living being', the individual or egoic consciousness. According to yogic tradition, when jnana, or knowledge, overcomes maya, or illusion, the notion of jiva ceases to exist." (Drury, 2002, 162).

Jivanmukta "In yoga, a 'liberated soul', a yogi who has attained this state of self-knowledge in his present incarnation has no further need to reincarnate and, after death, his soul merges with the Absolute." (Drury, 2002, 162).

Jivatman "Skt. term, similar to jiva in meaning but emphasizing that the atman, or true self, is the most significant aspect of one's individual consciousness." (Drury, 2002, 162).

Journey of the Soul "In shamanism, the 'journey' undertaken by a medicine-man or healer in order to recover the soul of a person who is bewitched or inflicted with disease; or alternatively, to communicate with the gods. The journey occurs in a state of trance--dissociation and often employs the use of drum rhythms and the ingestion of psychedelic sacramental plants." (Drury, 2002, 162).

K

Kaluza-Klein Theory "The theory of Einstein formulated in five dimensions. When reduced down to four dimensions, we find Einstein's usual theory coupled to Maxwell's theory of light. Thus, this was the first nontrivial unification of light with gravitation. Today, Kaluza-Klein theory is incorporated within string theory." (Kaku, 2005, 392).

"Theory of universe involving more than three spatial dimensions." (Greene, 2004, 539).

Karma "(Skt., Pali: 'action', 'deed'; Chin., *yin-yuan*; Korean, *inyon*). Karma, the law of consequence with regard to action, which is the driving force behind the cycle of reincarnation or rebirth (*samsara*) in Asian religions. According to karma theory, every action has a consequence which will come to fruition in either this or a future life; thus morally good acts will have positive consequences, whereas bad acts will produce negative results. An individual's present situation is thereby explained by reference to actions in his past history, in his present or in previous lifetimes. Karma is not itself 'reward and punishment', but the strict law producing consequence. The origin of the idea of karma is uncertain, but its beginnings could well be in non-Vedic, heterodox groups such as the Ajivikas and Jains (who have an extensive karma literature)." (*The Oxford Dictionary of World Religions*, 1997).

"In Hinduism, the word karma first appears in the *Rg Veda*, where it means religious action, specifically sacrifice; there is no hint here of its later meaning as the force driving beings through samsara. There is some hint of this in the Brahmanas, but only with the Upanisads do we really find karma in the sense of causality of action--e.g. *Brhadaranyaka Upanisad* 4.4.5. 'As a man acts, as he behaves, so does he become. Who so does good actions becomes good; who so does evil actions becomes evil. Whatever action (karma) he does, that he attains.' Some schools of Indian thought, such as Pasupata Saivism, believed karma to be transferable or transactional, that the results of action could pass from one person to another, but Vedanta and Yoga had non-transactional karma theories. Purva-Mimamsa, which continued Vedic ways of thinking and emphasized dharma, at first excluded karma from its literature, but later incorporated it in the notion of apurva, a store of efficacy of ritual. The early Mimamasa rejection of karma points to its non-Vedic origin." (Ibid).

"Action creates impressions (*samskaras*) or tendencies (*vasanas*) in the mind which in time will come to fruition in further action. The subtle body (*linga* or *suksma sarira*), in which the individual soul (*jiva*) transmigrates, carries the seeds of karma; and the gross body (*sthula sarira*) is the field (*ksetra*) in which the fruit (*phala*) of action is experienced, and which also creates more karma." (Ibid).

"Vedanta and Yoga speak of three kinds of karma: (i) *prarabdha*, karma to be experienced during the present lifetime, (ii) *sancita*, latent karma, or the store of karma which has yet to reach fruition, and (iii) *agamin* or *sanciyama*, the karma sown in the present life which will be reaped in a future life. Liberation (*moksa*) is

115

freedom from karma. When moksa is attained, the great sore of *sancita karma* is burnt up, but the *prarabdha* remains to complete its course. The liberated person (*jivanmukta*) creates no more new karma and at death, having no more karma, is no longer reborn." (Ibid).

"In Buddhism, much of the same basic sense of a law of consequence is retained, but there is no 'self' to be reborn. Stress is laid, not so much on the action as such, as on the intention which lies behind it. When an action cannot be performed, the intention will nevertheless produce the karmic consequence. Equally, intentions (and actions) which produce good karmic consequence are also a hindrance toward progress to enlightenment, because they form a rewarding future in the stream of reappearance (*punabbhava*)--i.e. they do not lead away from reappearance. Only intentions and actions free of desire, hate, and delusion are free of karmic consequence. Karma/kamma is neither fatalistic nor deterministic, since true insight enables one to direct the stream of continuity, or even to bring it to cessation." (Ibid).

"Among Jain, karma is a kind of subtle matter which attaches itself to the jiva and weighs it down in bondage and rebirth. All actions, good as well as evil, cause karmic matter to attach to the soul. Therefore, the abandoning of action, in complete ascetic renunciation (even to the extent of voluntary starvation), is necessary." (Ibid).

"For Sikhs, karma (Panjabi, *karamu*) is accepted as consequential action, but against it is set karma (Arab., *karam*, 'favor') meaning the grace of God. Instead of adjudicating on the issue of whether a soul is propelled by (bad) karma to rebirth, or whether it lives in one body only, Sikhs concentrate on bringing karma (grace) to bear on karma, leading to union with God." (Ibid).

"Action; the continual cycle of cause and effect in which the individual is caught by the effects of past and present actions." (Judith, 1999, 416).

"A universal law of cause and effect which provides the soul with opportunities for physical, mental and spiritual growth. In incarnation: the soul's entry into a cycle of the lower 'life' from the 'firstborn' thresholds of the Living Light. Karma is subordinate to 'Eternal Life' as demonstrated by Elijah (1 Ki. 17:17-24); Elisha (2Ki. 4:32-37); Jesus (Matt. 9; John 11); Peter (Acts 9:40); and Paul (Acts 20:9, 10)." (Hurtak, 1977, 583).

Karma can be defined as "past-life propensities, learnings, and good and bad conditioning that are carried from one incarnation to the next." (Goswami, 2001, 260).

"Literally, *karma* means 'something that is done.' Often it can be translated as 'deed' or 'action'. The law of karma states simply that every event is both a cause and an effect. Every act has consequences of a similar kind, which in turn have further consequences and so on; and every act, every karma, is also the consequence of some previous karma." (Easwaran, 1985, xxvii).

"Karma also refers to our mental thoughts. In their analysis of the phenomenal world and the world within, the sages of the Upanishads found that there is not merely an accidental but an essential relationship between mental and physical activity. Given appropriate conditions to develop further, thoughts breed actions of the same kind, as a seed can grow only into one particular kind of tree." (Ibid, xxviii).

"...The law of karma states unequivocally that, though we cannot see the connections, we can be sure everything that happens to us, good and bad, originated once in something we did or thought. It follows that we can change what happens to us by changing ourselves; we can take our destiny into our own hands." (Ibid, xxix).

"Karma is sometimes considered punitive, a matter of getting one's just deserts. But it is much more illuminating to consider karma an educative force whose purpose is to teach the individual to act in harmony with dharma--not to pursue selfish interests at the expense of others but to contribute to life and consider the welfare of the whole. In this sense life is like school: one can learn, one can graduate, one can skip a grade or stay behind. As long as a debt of karma remains, however, a person has to keep coming back for further education. That is the basis of *samsara*, the cycle of birth and death." (Ibid, xxix-xxx).

"The *karma* principle of causality continuity is, again, very close to the truth of the repercussional synthesis of all time--space actions in the Deity presence of the Supreme; but this postulate never provided for the coordinate personal attainment of Deity by the individual religionist, only for the ultimate engulfment of all personality by the Universal Oversoul." (*The Urantia Book*, 1955, 1030:5).

Karma Yoga "The path of yoga that approaches liberation through right action." (Judith, 1999, 416).

"One of the four main types of yoga in Hinduism, leading to union with God. It consists of detachment, not from action as such, but from the fruits of all action, offering them instead as a

117

sacrifice to God. It follows that karma-yoga is the opposite to abstention from works: it is the cultivation of the proper attitude to works, especially religious duties." (*The Oxford Dictionary of World Religions*, 1997).

Kinesiology "also known as human kinetics, is the scientific study of human movement. Kinesiology addresses physiological, mechanical, and psychological mechanisms. Applications of kinesiology to human health include: biomechanics and orthopedics; strength and conditioning; sport psychology; methods of rehabilitation, such as physical and occupational therapy; and sport and exercise..." ("Kinesiology," *Wikipedia*).

"Kinesiology [muscle testing] is a diagnostic process that has been popular in chiropractic for some time, and is now making inroads in meridian therapy." (Dale, 2009, 368).

"The word kinesiology comes from the Greek word *kinesis*, which means 'motion.' It is the study of muscles and the movement of the body and is considered a form of biofeedback. Through it, a practitioner concentrates on a subject and then tests the muscular strength of a client, usually using his or her arm. Depending upon the system, muscular weakness signifies an imbalance concerning the subject, and muscular strength indicates a balance in regard to the subject..." (Ibid, 368).

Kundalini "1 Serpent goddess who lies coiled three and one-half times around the Muladhara chakra. As she awakens she climbs the Sushumna and pierces each chakra. 2 The activating energy force that connects and activates the chakras. 3 a kind of awakening typified by rising currents of psychic energy." (Judith, 1999, 416-417).

"It was in the non-dual Tantric tradition that the chakras and Kundalini came to be an integral part of yoga philosophy. The Tantric teachings are a syncretic weaving of many spiritual traditions of India, which came to popularity during the sixth and seventh century A.D., in reaction to the dualistic philosophy which preceded it..." (Judith, 1999, 10).

"Kundalini is generally a unique and powerful experience that results in a profound consciousness change. This change may be experienced as increased alertness, sudden insight, visions, voices, a feeling of weightlessness, a sense of purity within the body, or transcendental bliss. There is some evidence that Kundalini sets up a wave-like movement of the cerebrospinal fluid, which triggers the pleasure centers of the brain, giving us the 'blissful state' so often described by mystics." (Ibid, 36--37).

118

"Kundalini does produce a profound state of consciousness, and this resulting state of consciousness may make it very difficult to get along in a world so predominantly 'unenlightened.' It may not support our current paradigm or be harmonious to the circumstances in our lives or the physical state of purity within the body. These discrepancies may make for a great deal of discomfort, but are not always to be avoided. Kundalini is basically a healing force, and pain is felt only when it encounters tension and impurities we are not quite ready to release. Learning to open the chakras allows a clear path for Kundalini that is less apt to be painful." (Ibid, 38).

"Theoretically, Kundalini produces a force that helps open the crown chakra, located at the top of the head. Because blocks in the chakra may trap our spinal energy, this chakra is often the hardest to reach. Classically, the crown chakra is considered the seat of enlightenment; however, I believe that it is the combined presence and connection of all the chakras together, given conscious attention, that brings enlightenment." (Ibid).

Kundalini Yoga "In Kundalini Yoga, psychic energy is raised through the channel sushumna, which corresponds to the spinal cord; an ida and pingala, which are coiled within it, corresponding to the sympathetic nerve ganglion on either side of the spine. The kundalini energy is aroused from the base of the spine and passes through the seven chakras: 1) Muladhara, located near the coccyx; 2) Svadhisthana, below the navel in the sacral region; 3) Manipura, above the navel in the lumbar region; 4) Anahata, located near the heart; 5) Vishudda, associated with the cervical region and the throat; 6) Ajna, located between, and just slightly above the eyes; 7) Sahasrara, located on the crown of the head and associated with the attainment of cosmic consciousness." (Drury, 2002, 335).

L

Lambda "The cosmological constant, which measures the amount of dark energy in the universe. At present, the data supports Omega + Lambda = 1, which fits the prediction of inflation for a flat universe. Lambda, which was once thought to be zero, is now known to determine the ultimate destiny of the universe." (Kaku, 2005, 392).

Lepton "A weakly interacting particle, such as the electron and neutrino, and its higher generations, such as the muon. Physicists believe that all matter consists of hadrons and leptons (strongly and weakly interacting particles)." (Kaku, 2005, 392).

Leys "Alignments of ancient megaliths, dolmens, and stone circles, whose patterns are said to constitute grids of 'power', or ley lines..." (Drury, 2002, 182).

LHC "The Large Hadron Collider, a particle accelerator for creating energetic beams of protons, based in Geneva, Switzerland. When finally completed, it will collide particles with energies not seen since the big bang. It is hoped that the Higgs particle and sparticles will be found by the LHC after it opens in 2007." (Kaku, 2005, 392).

Light "--spirit luminosity--is a word symbol, a figure of speech, which connotes the personality manifestation characteristic of spirit beings of diverse orders. This luminous emanation is in no respect related either to intellectual insight or to physical-light manifestations." (*The Urantia Book*, 1955, 10:1).

Light second "Distance traveled by light in one second." (Hawking, 2001, 205).

Light, visible "Visible light consists of wave packets called photons, which exhibit either wave-like or particle-like properties, depending on the method of observation. Because light is wavelike...waveforms can be coherent. Variations in frequency give us the different colors...we can think of it as discreet packets or photons, each containing information that allows us to see." (Judith, 1999, 287).

"Light travels the fastest of any of the elements...at 186,000 miles per second--the fastest known speed of any material phenomenon." (Ibid).

"Light is electromagnetic energy. Though the photons are without mass, light can induce an electric current upon striking metal, a phenomenon known as the photoelectric effect. Photons, striking the metal, displace electrons in the metal, which induces a current. The interesting thing about this effect is that the lower frequencies of light--such as red light, for example--do not have enough energy to induce a current, regardless of their intensity. At higher frequencies, such as blue or violet, a current is produced, which then will vary with the intensity of the light." (Ibid, 287-288).

"Color is the form through which we perceive light...The 'hotter' colors--such as reds, oranges, and yellows--are of a lower frequency than the 'cooler' colors of Green, blue and violet, and therefore the photons have less energy. (Hot and cool are our own subjective assessments, and say little about the actual energy of light." (Ibid, 288).

"Light is produced by the excitation and de-excitation of electrons within the atom. Electrons loose or gain energy by 'leaping' from one energy level to another. Each leap is called a quantum jump, a discrete step and amount of energy much like the steps on a stairway. When an electron jumps to a higher level, it must absorb a certain amount of energy. When it falls back again toward the nucleus, that energy is released as a photon of light. An electron falling through two levels releases more energy than an electron falling through only one level. Therefore, the photon emits light at a higher frequency, giving us the blues and violets of the upper chakras." (Ibid).

Light year "Distance traveled by light in one year." (Hawking, 2001, 205).

"The distance light travels in one year, or approximately 5.88 trillion miles (9.46 trillion kilometers). The nearest star is about four light-years away, and the Milky Way galaxy is about 100,000 light-years across." (Kaku, 2005, 393).

LIGO "The Laser Interferometry Gravitational-Wave Observatory, based in Washington state and Louisiana, is the world's largest gravity wave detector. It went online in 2003." (Kaku, 2005, 393).

Lingam "Phallic symbol, usually associated with Shiva. A sign of generative power, even though Shiva was believed to never ejaculate in his sexual activities. Symbol of male potential." (Judith, 1999, 417).

Life Plan "The intention, or script, set in place for an individual prior to an incarnation." (Backman, 2009, 231).

Life Purpose "The overall mission, or intention, for each incarnation." (Backman, 2009, 231).

LISA "The Laser Interferometry Space Antenna is a series of three space satellites using laser beams to measure gravity waves. It may be sensitive enough to confirm or disprove the inflationary theory and possibly even string theory, when it is launched in a few decades." (Kaku, 2005, 393).

Lotus Posture "A classical asana in yoga. The yogi sits on a mat with the left foot over the right thigh and the right foot over the left thigh. The hands may be placed either in the lap or over the knees, palm upwards. This posture is used during meditation: the yogi concentrates his attention on the region of the third eye and seeks spiritual self-knowledge." (Drury, 2002, 187).

Lourdes "Sacred healing site at the foot of the Central Pyrenees in France, where many people have claimed miraculous cures and remissions from disease. It was here in 1858 that a young shepherdess, Bernadette Soubirous, had eighteen visions of the

Virgin Mary and was instructed to bathe in a spring near the River Gave. Bernadette herself suffered from asthma, and this continued to recur, even after her visions of the Virgin. She also had rheumatism and a tumor, and died at the premature age of thirty-five. These aspects notwithstanding, the Roman Catholic Church recognized the unique nature of Bernadette's visionary experience and established a bureau to authenticate miracles occurring at this site. Around two million visitors go to Lourdes each year, and thousands of pilgrims have been healed by their faith." (Drury, 2002, 187-188).

Love (n.) 1 an intense feeling of deep affection; a deep romantic or sexual attachment to someone; a great interest and pleasure in something; affectionate greetings. 2 (**Love**) love personified, often as the Roman and Cupid. 3 a person or thing that one loves. (Brit. informal) a friendly form of address. (v) feel a deep romantic or sexual attachment to; like very much. (as adj.) (**loving**) showing love or great care." (*The Concise Oxford Dictionary*, 1999).

"Divinity is creature comprehensible as truth, beauty, and goodness; correlated in personality as love, mercy, and ministry…" (*The Urantia Book*, 1955, 3:4).

"…God is spirit and God is love, and these two attributes are most completely revealed to the universe in the Eternal Son." (26:2).

"Mercy is the natural and inevitable offspring of goodness and love…" (38:4).

"…God's love is universal…" (39:1).

"…God's love is by nature a fatherly affection…" (39:2).

"The Father's love follows us now and throughout the endless circle of the eternal ages…" (40:1).

"…Selflessness is inherent in parental love…" (41:2).

"…The love of God saves the sinner…" (41:6).

"The religious challenge of this age is to those farseeing and forward-looking men and women of spiritual insight who will dare to construct a new and appealing philosophy of living out of the enlarged and exquisitely integrated modern concepts of cosmic truth, universe beauty, and divine goodness. Such a new and righteous vision of morality will attract all that is good in the mind of man and challenge that which is best in the human soul. Truth, beauty, and goodness are divine realities, and as man ascends the scale of spiritual live, these supreme qualities of the Eternal become increasingly coordinated and unified in God, who is love."

(43:3).

"...man's nearest and dearest approach to God is by and through love, for God is love..." (50:5).

"Love is the desire to do good to others." (648:4).

"...religion is the striving to know God and to manifest love for one's fellows through service for them..." (811:5).

"...Mother love is instinctive..." (932:3).

"...Religion eventually achieves the profoundly simple realization of an all-powerful love, the love which sweeps irresistibly through the human soul when awakened to the conception of the limitless affection of the Universal Father for the sons of the universe..." (986:3).

"In physical life the senses tell of the existence of things; mind discovers the reality of meanings; but the spiritual experience reveals to the individual the true values of life. These high levels of human living are attained in the supreme love of God and in the unselfish love of man. If you love your fellow men, you must have discovered their values..." (1098:1).

"...It is not so important to love all men today as it is that each day you learn to love one more human being..." (1098:3).

"...true religion is a living love, a life of service..." (1100:7).

"...The new loyalties of enlarged spiritual vision create new levels of love and devotion, of service and fellowship; and all this enhanced social outlook produces an enlarged consciousness of the Fatherhood of God and the brotherhood of man." (1101:3).

"The pursuit of knowledge constitutes science; the search for wisdom is philosophy; the love of God is religion; the hunger for truth is a revelation..." (1122:8).

"A good and noble man may be consummately in love with his wife but utterly unable to pass a satisfactory written examination on the psychology of marital love. Another man, having little or no love for his spouse, might pass such an examination most acceptably. The imperfection of the lover's insight into the true nature of the beloved does not in the least invalidate either the reality or sincerity of his love." (1140:3).

"...Through truth man attains beauty and by spiritual love ascends to goodness." (1142:1).

Luminous Body "Term sometimes used by occultists as a synonym for the astral body." (Drury, 2002, 189).

Luminous Energy Body "We all possess a Luminous Energy Field that surrounds our physical body and informs our body in the same way that the energy fields of a magnet organize iron filings on a piece of glass. Our Luminous Energy Field has existed since before the beginning of time. It was one with the un-manifest light of Creation, and it will endure throughout infinity. It dwells outside of time but manifests in time by creating new physical bodies, lifetime after lifetime." (Villoldo, 2000, 42-43).

"Indian and Tibetan mystics who documented the existence of the Luminous Energy Filed thousands of years ago described it as an aura or halo around the physical body..." (Ibid, 43).

"The Luminous Energy Field has four layers extending outward from the body. They are: 1. Causal (the Spirit); 2. Psychic (also known as etheric--the soul); 3. Mental-emotional (the mind); and 4. Physical (the body)." (Ibid, 45).

"Each layer stores a different quality of energy. The outermost layer stocks the energy that fuels the physical body. The layer beneath stores the energies that sustain our mental and emotional stamina. Underneath this layer are the refined psychic energies, and closest to the skin is the finest energy of all, our spiritual reserves. The mystical literature refers to these layers as 'subtle bodies.' In reality, they are not separate from each other, in the same way that the colors of rainbow are not disconnected but rather dissolve into one another." (Ibid, 45-46).

"The Luminous Energy Field contains an archive of all of our personal and ancestral memories, of all early-life trauma, and even of painful wounds from former lifetimes. These records or imprints are stored in full color and intensity of emotion. Imprints are like dormant computer programs that when activated compel us toward behaviors, relationships, accidents, and illnesses that parody the initial wounding. Our personal history indeed repeats itself. Imprints of physical trauma are stored in the outermost layer of the Luminous Energy Field. Emotional imprints are stored in the second layer, soul imprints in the third, and spiritual imprints in the fourth and deepest layer. Imprints in the Luminous Energy predispose us to follow certain pathways in life. They orchestrate the incidents, experiences, and people we attract to ourselves. Imprints propel us to re-create painful dramas and heartbreaking encounters, yet ultimately guide us toward situations wherein we can heal our ancient soul wounds." (Ibid, 46).

M

MACHO "Massive Compact Halo Object. These are dark stars, planets, asteroids, and such which are hard to detect by optical telescopes and may make up a portion of dark matter. The latest data indicates that the bulk of dark matter is non-baryonic and is not made of MACHOs." (Kaku, 2005, 393).

Macrocosm and microcosm "From the Gk. *makros kosmos*, 'great world', and *mikros kosmos*, 'little world', the concept that people and the world are a copy in miniature of God's universe. This view was advocated by the theologian Origen and taken up by such Renaissance occultists as Paracelsus and Henry Cornelius Agrippa. Similarly, in the medieval Kabbalah, the primordial or archetypal man, Adam Kadmon, is regarded as reflecting the image of God the Father, and thereby provides the necessary link between humankind and the Creator of the universe." (Drury, 2002, 192).

Magnetosphere "The region around any planetary body like Earth where the magnetic field of that sphere is strong enough to have a measurable effect on the interplanetary gases forming a driven hydro-magnetic system. On Earth these dynamics are controlled by the input solar-wind energy through magnetic field merging." (Hurtak, 1977, 588).

Manas "(Skt., 'mind'). In Skt. literature, the mind, the coordinating organ of intelligence, thought, understanding, perception, and will. In Vedic times manas meant the individual spirit and the basis of speech (vac). In the Upanisadic period manas is variously treated: sometimes it is closely associated with speech and breath as a triple entity, sometimes considered more as the intermediate link between the Self, atman, and the senses. *Katha Upanisad* pictures manas as the bridle and reins by which the intellect (buddhi), as the driver of the chariot, guides the horses of the senses." (*The Oxford Dictionary of World Religions*, 1997).

"In Buddhist psychology, manas is the rational or intellectual faculty of the mind. Manas has both an active and a passive function: in its passive mode it is responsible for the reception, ordering, and interpretation of data received through the five senses, its operation being triggered off by the input of sense-data. The manner in which manas performs this function is the result of conditioning and habit and can be modified through the exercise of self-awareness. In its active mode manas is responsible for the production of feelings and wishes. In the Pali canon it is said to be synonymous with citta and vijnana." (Ibid).

"Skt. term meaning 'mind'. It can refer to the mind at any stage or level. For example, buddhi-manas is the higher mind, or self, while kama-manas is the lower or personal mind. Because, in Hindu mysticism, there is in reality only one consciousness or Mind, which underlies all creation and manifestation, manas is sometimes equated with mahat--the First Principle, from which all else comes forth." (Drury, 2002, 203).

Manipura "Literally lustrous gem; name of the third chakra located at the solar plexus." (Judith, 1999, 417).

Mantra "Literally 'tool of thought'; denotes a sacred word, phrase, or sound, repeated internally or externally as a tool in meditation and ritual." (Judith, 1999, 417).

"1 Sacred syllables: a contracted form of the Dharanis (Skt.: syllable as prayers) for mental and spiritual expansion. The mantra gives the energy of the divinity and his attributes. 2 A set of sound patterns and thought-forms which can code consciousness into the consciousness of Light. 3 The mantras are holy energy forms of meditation which are used to charge the body with the powers and rapture of the Divine Mind. The greater the thought-form, the greater the mantra in opening the mind for the real disclosure of knowledge. The mantras should be expressive of the Names of the Deity..." (Hurtak, 1977, 588--589).

"(Skt., 'instrument of thought'; Chin., *chou*; Jap., *ju*; Korean, *chu*). A verse, syllable, or series of syllables believed to be of divine origin, used in a ritual or meditative context in Indian religions. Mantras are used for the propitiation of the gods, the attainment of power (siddha), and identification with a deity or the absolute, which leads to liberation from samsara. First appearing in the Vedic Samhitas (and millennium BCE), mantras take on a central role in sectarian Hinduism, and Buddhist and Hindu Tantrism, especially in the Buddhist Mantrayana school (7th/8th centuries CE)." (*The Oxford Dictionary of World Religions*, 1997).

Mantra Yoga "The practice of mantra repetition (*japa*) as a means of liberation (*moksa*), especially in Tantrism. By this, the *sadhaka's* consciousness is transformed from the level of gross sound (*vaikhari*) through levels of subtle sound (*madhyama* and *pasyanti*) to the absolute, the un-manifest origin of sound (*Sabdabrahman* or *Nadabrahman*). This process takes place within the body. *Pranayama* and the *yoni bandha asama* (covering the nostrils, eyes, and ears with the hands) block the outer senses and consciousness enters the *susumna nadi*, conceived as raising the Kundalini. Subtle sound is heard by an inner ear which pulls the consciousness up to its source through the various levels, to merge with the Sabdabrahman." (*The Oxford Dictionary of World Religions*, 1997).

Many Worlds interpretation "Interpretation of quantum mechanics in which all potentialities embodied by a probability

126

wave are realized in separate universes." (Greene, 2004, 539).

Many Worlds Theory "The quantum theory which states that all possible quantum universes can exist simultaneously. It solves the Schrodinger cat problem by stating that the universe splits at each quantum juncture, and hence the cat is alive in one universe but dead in another. Recently, an increasing number of physicists have voiced their support for the many-worlds theory." (Kaku, 2005, 393).

Marijuana see Cannabis.

Marriage "1 the formal union of a man and a woman, typically as recognized by law, by which they become husband and wife. 2 a combination of two or more elements." (*The Concise Oxford Dictionary*, 1999).

I believe marriage should be looked upon as the sacred union of two souls for life; for the purpose of co-creating children; to unselfishly comingle one's mind, body, and spirit for the betterment of one's spouse and family.

Marriage and divorce "Marriage is the union between at least two people (in polygamy it may be more), in which commitment is made and responsibility undertaken. It is recognized and controlled in society, because of its obvious relation to the procreation and nurture of the next generation. Because of the profound consequences of the institution of marriage (yielding experience including, but going far beyond, the pleasure of sexual satisfaction), marriage is a frequent metaphor in religions for union with God. But it is recognized that not all marriages are realized in relation to the goals, however described. Divorce is regarded in general as at least a matter of regret, more often as a matter of defeat and fault. The facilities for divorce therefore differ between religions." (*The Oxford Dictionary of World Religions*, 1997).

"(Christianity) Marriage, in the words of the *Book of Common Prayer*, 'is an honorable estate, instituted of God in the time of man's innocency [Genesis 1 and 2], signifying unto us the mystical union that is betwixt Christ and his Church [Ephesians 5. 21 ff.]; which holy estate Christ adorned and beautified with his presence, and first miracle that he wrought, at Cana of Galilee [John 2. 1-12]'. The causes of marriage are three (for the procreation of children and their nurture, for a remedy against sin and to avoid fornication, and for the mutual society, help, and comfort that the one ought to have of the other, both in prosperity and adversity). In the *Alternative Service Book*, the order of the three is inverted (and the second expressed positively), a revision which reflects changing understandings of the nature of marriage, and which is also the order of the Eastern Orthodox. In Roman Catholic understanding, marriage is a sacrament which creates a *vinculum*, an unbreakable (metaphysical) bond; it can only be brought to an end by a recognition, on various specific grounds, that it never happened in the first place, i.e. by annulment. Among other Christians, there is a more serious wrestling with the vision of Jesus Christ that marriage recreates the lost and disturbed conditions of the Garden of Eden: In those circumstances, any setting apart or divorce is to go against the intended conditions of creation. But what if those circumstances do not obtain? Jesus is reported to have allowed the possibility of the ending of a marriage if it had indeed already 'ended' through *porneia* (Matthew 19:3, 9), though no exception is recorded in Mark 10:2-12. What is also not recorded is what Jesus would have said to a woman who had been divorced and abandoned by her husband: Would he, as a matter of principle, have said that she could never be married again" Uncertainty about the texts has led to a divergence of practice among Christians, some allowing remarriage after divorce (with a previous partner still living) in some circumstances, while others do not. The Eastern Orthodox position, which allows divorce and remarriage in some circumstances, is summarized in *Marriage, Divorce and the Church* (Root Report, 1971), which was followed by a second report, *Marriage and the Church's Task* (1978); together, they offer a survey of the Christian understanding of marriage, starting from the human fact of marriage." (Ibid).

"(Buddhism) In the long process which leads eventually to enlightenment, the Buddha espoused the wisdom of addressing teaching and practice to the levels attained by different people (*upaya-kausalya*). In this perspective, marriage properly undertaken is a legitimate step, even though sexuality will be transcended in due course. In the *Sigalovada Sutta*, the Buddha laid out the responsibilities of lay Buddhists which embrace the duties involved in a householder's life. Paramount (and one of the Five Precepts, *sila*) is the avoidance of sexual impropriety. If a marriage fails, there may be a contribution of karma to the failure, but in any case the dismantling of the marriage must attempt to avoid hurt to either of those involved." (Ibid).

"The function of marriage in evolution is the insurance of race survival, not merely the realization of personal happiness; self-maintenance and self-perpetuation are the real objects of the home. Self-gratification is incidental and not essential except as an incentive insuring sex association. Nature demands survival, but the arts of civilization continue to increase the pleasures of marriage and the satisfaction of family life." (*The Urantia Book*, 1955, 765:6).

"...Polygamy is the survival of the female-slavery element in marriage. Monogamy is the slave-free ideal of the matchless association of one man and one woman in the exquisite enterprise of home building, offspring rearing, mutual culture, and self-improvement." (781:1).

"There always have been and always will be two distinct realms of marriage: the mores, the laws regulating the external aspects of mating, and the otherwise secret and personal relations of men and women. Always has the individual been rebellious against the sex regulations imposed by society; and this is the reason for this agelong sex problem: Self-maintenance is individual but is carried on by the group; self-perpetuation is social but is secured by individual impulse." (915:5).

"The mores, when respected, have ample power to restrain and control the sex urge, as has been shown among all races. Marriage standards have always been a true indicator of the current power of the mores and the functional integrity of the civil government. But the early sex and mating mores were a mass of inconsistent and crude regulations. Parents, children, relatives, and society all had conflicting interests in the marriage regulations. But in spite of all this, those races which exalted and practiced marriage naturally evolved to higher levels and survived in increased numbers." (915:6).

"Marriage has always been closely linked with both property and religion. Property has been the stabilizer of marriage; religion, the moralizer." (917:4).

"...the institution of marriage...progressed steadily from the loose and promiscuous matings of the herd through many variations and adaptions, even to the appearance of those marriage standards which eventually culminated in the realization of pair matings, the union of one man and one woman to establish a home of the highest social order." (922:1).

"...marriage functions in two directions:" (922:4).

"1. In the regulation of personal sex relations." (922:5).

"2. In the regulation of descent, inheritance, succession, and social order, this being its older and original function." (922:6).

"The family, which grows out of marriage, is itself a stabilizer of the marriage institution together with the property mores. Other potent factors in marriage stability are pride, vanity, chivalry, duty, and religious convictions. But while marriages may be approved or disapproved on high, they are hardly made in heaven. The human family is a distinctly human institution, an evolutionary development. Marriage is an institution of society, not a department of the church. True, religion should mightily influence it but should not undertake exclusively to control and regulate it." (922:7).

"Primitive marriage was primarily industrial; and even in modern times it is often a social or business affair. Through the influence of the mixture of Andite stock and as a result of the mores of advancing civilization, marriage is slowly becoming mutual, romantic, parental, poetical, affectionate, ethical, and even idealistic. Selection and so-called romantic love, however, were at a minimum in primitive mating. During early times husband and wife were not much together; they did not even eat together very often. But among the ancients, personal affection was not strongly linked to sex attraction; they became fond of one another largely because of living and working together." (922:8).

"In the early history of marriage the unmarried women belonged to the men of the tribe. Later on, a woman had only one husband at a time. This practice of *one-man-at-a-time* was the first step away from the promiscuity of the herd. While a woman was allowed but one man, her husband could sever such temporary relationships at will. But these loosely regulated associations were the first step toward living pairwise in distinction to living herdwise. In this stage of marriage development children usually belonged to the mother." (925:7).

"The next step in mating evolution was the *group marriage*. This communal phase of marriage had to intervene in the unfolding of family life because the marriage more were not yet strong enough to make pair associations permanent. The brother and sister marriages belonged to this group; five brothers of one family would marry five sisters of another. All over the world the looser forms of communal marriage gradually evolved into various types of group marriage. And these group associations were largely regulated by the totem mores. Family life slowly and surely developed because sex and marriage regulation favored the survival of the tribe itself by insuring the survival of larger numbers of children." (925:8).

"Group marriage gradually gave way before the emerging practices of polygamy--polygyny and polyandry--among the more advanced tribes. But polyandry was never general, being usually limited to queens and rich women; furthermore, it was customarily a family affair, one wife for several brothers. Caste and economic restrictions sometimes made it necessary for several men to content themselves with one wife. Even then, the woman would marry only one, the others being loosely tolerated as 'uncles' of the joint progeny." (926:1).

"The Jewish custom requiring that man consort with his deceased brother's widow for the purpose of 'raising up seed for his brother,' was the custom of more than half the ancient world. This was a relic of the time when marriage was a family affair rather than an individual association." (926:2).

"The institution of polygyny recognized, at various times, four sorts of wives:" (926:3).

"1. The ceremonial or legal wives." (926:4).

"2. Wives of affection and permission." (926:5).

"3. Concubines, contractual wives." (926:6).

"4. Slave wives." (926:7).

"True polygyny, where all the wives are of equal status and all the children equal, has been very rare..." (926:8).

"The status wife was not necessarily the love wife; in early times she usually was not. The love wife, or sweetheart, did not appear until the races were considerably advanced, more particularly after the blending of the evolutionary tribes with the Nodites and Adamites." (926:9).

"The taboo wife--one wife of legal status--created the concubine mores. Under these mores a man might have only one wife, but he could maintain sex relations with any number of concubines. Concubines were the stepping stone to monogamy, the first move away from frank polygyny. The concubines of the Jews, Romans, and Chinese were very frequently the handmaidens of the wife..." (926:10).

"The olden taboos on sex relations with a pregnant or nursing wife tended greatly to foster polygyny. Primitive women aged very early because of frequent childbearing coupled with hard work..." (926:11).

"The number of wives was only limited by the ability of the man to provide for them. Wealthy and able men wanted large numbers of children, and since the infant mortality was very high, it required an assembly of wives to recruit a large family. Many of these plural wives were mere laborers, slave wives." (926:12).

"Human customs evolve, but very slowly. The purpose of a

131

harem was to build up a strong and numerous body of blood kin for the support of the throne..." (927:1).

"Monogamy is monopoly; it is good for those who attain this desirable state, but it tends to work a biologic hardship on those who are not so fortunate. But quite regardless of the effect on the individual, monogamy is decidedly best for the children." (927:2).

"The earliest monogamy was due to force of circumstances, poverty. Monogamy is cultural and societal, artificial and unnatural, that is, unnatural to evolutionary man. It was wholly natural to the purer Nodites and Adamites and has been of great cultural value to all advanced races." (927:3).

"...the Greeks and the Romans favored monogamous marriage. Ancestor worship has always fostered monogamy, as has the Christian error of regarding marriage as a sacrament...By the time of Michael's advent on Urantia practically all of the civilized world had attained the level of theoretical monogamy. But this passive monogamy did not mean that mankind had become habituated to the practice of real pair marriage." (927:4).

"While pursuing the monogamic goal of the ideal pair marriage, which is, after all, something of a monopolistic sex association, society must not overlook the unenviable situation of those unfortunate men and women who fail to find a place in this new and improved social order, even when having done their best to co-operate with, and enter into, its requirements. Failure to gain mates in the social arena of competition may be due to insurmountable difficulties or multitudinous restrictions which the current mores have imposed. Truly, monogamy is ideal for those who are in, but it must inevitably work great hardship on those who are left out in the cold of solitary existence." (927:5).

"Always have the unfortunate few had to suffer that the majority might advance under the developing mores of evolving civilization; but always should the favored majority look with kindness and consideration on their less fortunate fellows who must pay the price of failure to attain membership in the ranks of those ideal sex partnerships which afford the satisfaction of all biologic urges under the sanction of the highest mores of advancing social evolution." (927:6).

"Monogamy always has been, now is, and forever will be the idealistic goal of human sex evolution. This ideal of true pair marriage entails self-denial, and therefore does it so often fail just because one or both of the contracting parties are deficient in that acme of all human virtues, rugged self-control." (927:7).

"Pair marriage favors and fosters that intimate understanding and effective cooperation which is best for parental happiness, child welfare, and social efficiency. Marriage, which began in crude coercion, is gradually evolving into a magnificent institution of self-culture, self-control, self-expression, and self-perpetuation." (928:1).

"In the early evolution of the marital mores, marriage was a loose union which could be terminated at will, and the children always followed the mother; the mother-child bond is instinctive and has functioned regardless of the developmental stage of the mores." (928:2).

"As the mores evolved, certain tribes developed two forms of marriage: the ordinary, which permitted divorce, and the priest marriage, which did not allow for separation. The inauguration of wife purchase and wife dowry, by introducing a property penalty for marriage failure, did much to lessen separation. And, indeed, many modern unions are stabilized by this ancient property factor." (928:4).

"The social pressure of community standing and property privileges has always been potent in the maintenance of the marriage taboos and mores. Down through the ages marriage has made steady progress and stands on advanced ground in the modern world, notwithstanding that it is threateningly assailed by widespread dissatisfaction among those peoples where individual choice--a new liberty--figures most largely. While these upheavals of adjustment appear among the more progressive races as a result of suddenly accelerated social evolution, among the less advanced people marriage continues to thrive and slowly improve under the guidance of the older mores." (928:5).

"The new and sudden substitution of the more ideal but extremely individualistic love motive in marriage for the older and long-established property motive, has unavoidably caused the marriage institution to become temporarily unstable. Man's marriage motives have always far transcended actual marriage morals, and in the nineteenth and twentieth centuries the Occidental ideal of marriage has suddenly far outrun the self-centered and but partially controlled sex impulses of the races. The presence of large numbers of unmarried persons in any society indicates the temporary breakdown or the transition of the mores." (928:6).

"The real test of marriage, all down through the ages, has been that continuous intimacy which is inescapable in all family life.

133

Two pampered and spoiled youths, educated to expect every indulgence and full gratification of vanity and ego, can hardly hope to make a great success of marriage and home building--a life-long partnership of self-effacement, compromise, devotion, and unselfish dedication to child culture." (928:7).

"The high degree of imagination and fantastic romance entering into courtship is largely responsible for the increasing divorce tendencies among modern Occidental people, all of which is further complicated by woman's greater personal freedom and increased economic liberty. Easy divorce, when the result of lack of self-control or failure of normal personality adjustment, only leads directly back to those crude societal stages from which man has emerged so recently and as the result of so much personal anguish and racial suffering." (929:1).

"But just so long as society fails to properly educate children and youths, so long as the social order fails to provide adequate premarital training, and so long as unwise and immature youthful idealism is to be the arbiter of the entrance upon marriage, just so long will divorce remain prevalent. And in so far as the social group falls short of providing marriage preparation for youths, to that extent must divorce function as the social safety valve which prevents still worse situations during the ages of the rapid growth of the evolving mores." (929:2).

"The ancients seem to have regarded marriage just about as seriously as some present-day people do. And it does not appear that many of the hasty and unsuccessful marriages of modern times are much of an improvement over the ancient practices of qualifying young men and women for mating. The great inconsistency of modern society is to exalt love and to idealize marriage while disapproving of the fullest examination of both." (929:3).

"Marriage which culminates in the home is indeed man's exalted institution, but it is essentially human; it should never have been called a sacrament. The Sethite priests made marriage a religious ritual; but for thousands of years after Eden, mating continued as a purely social and civil institution." (929:4).

"The likening of human association to divine associations is most unfortunate. The union of husband and wife in the marriage-home relationship is a material function of the mortals of the evolutionary worlds…" (929:5).

"Marriage always has been and still is man's supreme dream of temporal ideality. Though this beautiful dream is seldom realized in

134

its entirety, it endures as a glorious ideal, ever luring progressing mankind on to greater strivings for human happiness..." (930:2).

"The ideals of marriage have made great progress in recent times; among some people woman enjoy practically equal rights...In concept, at least, the family is becoming a loyal partnership for rearing offspring, accompanied by sexual fidelity. But even this newer version of marriage need not presume to swing so far to the extreme as to confer mutual monopoly of all personality and individuality. Marriage is not just an individualistic ideal; it is the evolving social partnership of a man and a woman, existing and functioning under the current mores, restricted by the taboos, and enforced by the laws and regulations of society." (930:4).

Matrix "A collection of grids, appearing as stacked upon one another. The grids are hierarchical in nature, providing a structure for the gradual transition of energy-information from one zone of parameters to another. The size, dimensions or lateral extent of the grid cell and overall grid may vary. The size and dimensions of the matrix itself will vary. Most matrices will be recognized as a subset of a larger grid-matrix system, and that one in turn will be a portion of an even larger parent system...The matrices of creation are essentially holographic in nature; each cell being whole and complete unto itself, as well as part of an even larger whole. Within each single cell lives all of the information for the entire pattern to repeat itself again, and within each cell of that pattern the repetition continues." (Braden, 1993, 193).

Matter "That which has traditionally been contrasted with form or with mind. In the philosophy of materialism, matter is the substance and basis of all reality, and is usually conceived of in the spirit of atomism. In Newtonian physics, matter, distinguished by mass and extension, was contrasted with energy. According to relativity theory, mass and energy are mutually transformable, and material systems are now regarded as forms of energy." (Sheldrake, 1995, 369).

"...Organized energy which is subject to linear gravity except as it is modified by motion and conditioned by mind." (*The Urantia Book*, 1955, 140:6).

Maxwell's Equation "The fundamental equations for light, first written down by James Clerk Maxwell in the 1860s. These equations show that electric and magnetic fields can turn into each other. Maxwell showed that these fields turn into each other in a wavelike motion, creating an electromagnetic field that travels at the speed of light. Maxwell then made the bold conjecture that this was light." (Kaku, 2005, 393).

Mechanics "In its broad, traditional sense, the body of practical and theoretical knowledge concerned with the invention and construction of machines, the explanation of their operation, and the calculation of their efficiency. In physics, the study of the behavior of matter under the action of force. In the present century, Newtonian mechanics has been substantially modified by relativity theory and has been replaced by quantum mechanics as a method of interpreting physical phenomena occurring on a very small scale." (Sheldrake, 1995, 369-370).

Mechanistic theory "The theory that all physical phenomena can be explained mechanically (see Mechanics), without reference to goals or purposive designs (cf. Teleology). The central metaphor is the machine. In the 17th cent., the universe was conceived of as a vast machine, designed, made, and set running by God and governed by his eternal laws. By the late 19th cent., it was commonly regarded as an eternal machine which was slowly running down. In biology, the mechanistic theory states that living organisms are nothing but inanimate machines or mechanical systems: all the phenomena of life can in principle be understood in terms of mechanical models and can ultimately be explained in terms of physics and chemistry." (Sheldrake, 1995, 370).

Meditation "(n.) 1 the action or practice of meditating. 2 a discourse expressing considered thoughts on a subject." (*The Concise Oxford Dictionary*, 1999).

"Choose a quiet and uplifted place to do your meditation practice. Sit cross-legged on a meditation cushion, or, if that's difficult, sit on a straight-backed chair with your feet flat on the floor, without leaning against the back of the chair." (McLeod, 2014, 3).

"Place your attention lightly on your out-breath, while remaining aware of the environment around you. Be with each breath as the air goes out through your mouth and nostrils and dissolves into the space around you. At the end of each out-breath, simply rest until the next breath goes out. For a more focused meditation, you can follow both the out-breaths and in-breaths." (Ibid).

"At the end of your meditation session, bring calm, mindfulness, and openness into the rest of your day." (Ibid).

It is best to do your meditation practice first thing in the morning. Get out of bed, splash water on your face, brush your teeth, put on comfortable clothes (or stay in your sleeping clothes), and immediately sit on your cushion. Start your practice before you have your coffee, turn on the computer, before you activate your day and realize you don't have time for this. Burn a stick of incense to time yourself. Decide in advance to sit for twenty to thirty minutes, or a bit more if you can do it. (Fischer, 2014, 10).

"Try this for two weeks, taking a day or so off each week..." (Ibid).

"...There is no doing it wrong or right...The point is to avoid falling into the trap of defining *meditation* too narrowly, and then judging yourself based on that definition , and so sabotaging yourself..." (Ibid, 12).

"...First, you must make your mind calm. Where there is knowing, there is no need to think..." (Chah, 2014, 27).

"...To meditate, you have to resolve that now is the time for training the mind and nothing else. Don't let the mind shoot off to the left or to the right, to the front or behind, above or below. At that time our only duty is to practice mindfulness of breathing. Fix your attention at the crown of the head and move it down through the body to the tips of the feet, and then back up to the head. Pass your awareness down through the body, observing with wisdom. We do this to gain an initial understanding of the way the body is. Then begin the *meditation*, remembering that your sole duty is to observe the inhalations and exhalations. Don't force the breath to be any longer or shorter than normal, just allow it to continue easily. Let it flow evenly, letting go with each in-breath and out-breath." (Ibid).

"Although you are letting go, there should still be awareness. You must maintain this awareness, allowing the breath to enter and leave comfortably. Maintain the resolve that at this time you have no other duties or responsibilities. Thoughts about what will happen or what you will see during a *meditation* may arise from time to time, but once they arise just let them cease by themselves; don't be unduly concerned with them." (Ibid, 27-28).

"During the *meditation* there is no need to pay attention to sense impressions. Whenever the mind is affected by sense contact, wherever there is a feeling or sensation in the mind, just let it go...Maintain the awareness of the breath entering and leaving. Don't create suffering over the breath being too long or too short, but simply observe it without trying to control it in any way...the mind will gradually lay things down and come to rest, the breath becoming lighter and lighter until it becomes so faint that it seems like it's not there at all. Both the body and the mind will feel light and energized. All that will remain will be a one-pointed knowing. The mind has reached a state of calm." (Ibid, 28).

"When there is total knowing, a continuous and unbroken awareness at each and every moment, this is called presence of mind…" (Ibid, 29).

"There must be both *sati* and *sampajanna*. Sati is mindfulness and sampajanna is self-awareness. Right now you are clearly aware of the breath. This exercise of watching the breath helps sati and sampajanna develop together. They share the work…when there is sati and sampajanna, then *panna* (wisdom) will arise at the same place to help out. Then all three of them support one another." (Ibid, 30).

"You must give up all the thinking, the inner dialogue, and the doubting. Don't get caught up in these things during the *meditation*. In the end all that will remain in the mind in its purest form are sati, sampajanna, and panna. Whenever these weaken, doubts will arise, but try to abandon those doubts immediately, leaving only sati, sampajanna, and panna. Try to develop sati like this until it can be maintained at all times. Then you understand sati, sampajanna, and panna thoroughly." (Ibid).

"Focusing the attention at this point you will see sati, sampajanna, *samadhi* (mental concentration), and panna together…All that should remain is sati, mindfulness; sampajanna, clear awareness; samadhi, the firm and unwavering mind; and panna, or consummate wisdom." (Ibid, 30-31).

"…there should be *metta* (goodwill) in your heart; in other words, the qualities of generosity, kindness, and helpfulness. These should be maintained as the foundation for mental purity…" (Ibid, 31).

"…In the Pali scriptures, giving is called *dana*, which results in happiness for others and helps to cleanse the mind of defilement. You should reflect on this and develop it in your practice." (Ibid, 31-32).

"The next constituent of practice is moral restraint (*sila*). Sila watches over and nurtures the practice in the same way as parents look after their children. Maintaining moral restraint means not only to avoid harming others but also to help and encourage them. At the very least you should maintain the five precepts, which are:" (Ibid, 32).

"1. Not only not killing or deliberately harming others, but also spreading goodwill toward all beings." (Ibid).

"2. Being honest, refraining from infringing on the rights of others--in other words, not stealing." (Ibid).

"3. Knowing moderation in sexual relations. A husband or wife should know each other's disposition, needs, and wishes, observe moderation, and know the proper bounds of sexual activity..." (Ibid).

"4. Being honest in speech. This is also a tool for eradicating defilements. You must be honest and straight, truthful and upright." (Ibid, 33).

"5. Refraining from taking intoxicants..." (Ibid).

"...let [your] wise attention, or mindfulness, open into awareness as vast and beautiful as space." (Kornfield, 2014, 70).

"*Meditation* comes alive through a growing capacity to release our habitual entanglement in the stories and plans, conflicts and worries that make up the small sense of self, and to rest in awareness. In *meditation* we do this simply by acknowledging the moment-to-moment changing conditions--the pleasure and pain, the praise and blame, the litany of ideas and expectations that arise. Without identifying with them, we can rest in the awareness itself, beyond conditions, and experience what my teacher Ajahn Chah called *jai pongsai*, our natural lightness of heart. Developing this capacity to rest in awareness nourishes *samadhi* (concentration), which stabilizes and clarifies the mind, and *prajna* (wisdom), which sees things as they are." (Ibid).

"...When we first sit down to meditate, the best strategy is to simply notice whatever state of our body and mind is present. To establish the foundation of mindfulness, the Buddha instructs his followers 'to observe whether the body and mind are distracted or steady, angry or peaceful, excited or worried, contracted or released, bound or free.' Observing what is so, we can take a few deep breaths and relax, making space for whatever situation we find." (Ibid, 70-71).

"From this ground of acceptance we can learn to use the transformative power of attention in a flexible and malleable way. Wise attention--mindfulness--can function like a zoom lens. Often it is most helpful to steady our practice with close-up attention. In this, we bring a careful attention and a very close focus to our breath or a sensation, or to the precise movement of feeling or thought. Over time we can eventually become so absorbed that subject and object disappear..." (Ibid, 71).

"But sometimes in *meditation* such close focus of attention can create an unnecessary sense of tightness and struggle. So we must find a more open way to pay attention…" (Ibid).

"Yet at times this middle level of attention does not serve our practice best. We may find ourselves caught in the grip of some repetitive though pattern or painful situation, or lost in great physical or emotional suffering. Perhaps there is chaos and noise around us. We sit and our heart is tight, our body and mind are neither relaxed nor gracious, and even the witnessing can seem tedious, forced, effortful." (Ibid, 72).

"In this circumstance we can open the lens of attention to its widest angle and let our awareness become like space or the sky…" (Ibid).

"From this broad perspective, when we sit or walk in *meditation*, we open our attention like space, letting experiences arise without any boundaries, without inside or outside. Instead of the ordinary orientation where our mind is felt to be inside our head, we can let go and experience consciousness that is not entangled in the particular conditions of sight, sound, and feelings, but consciousness that is independent of changing conditions--the unconditioned. Ajahn Jumnien, A Thai forest elder, speaks of this form of practice as *Maha Vipassana*, resting in pure awareness itself, timeless and unborn. For the meditator, this is not an ideal or a distant experience. It is always immediate, ever present, liberating; it becomes the resting place of the wise heart." (Ibid).

"Fully absorbed, graciously witnessing, or open and spacious…Awareness is infinitely malleable, and it is important not to fixate on any one form as best…some traditions teach that losing the self and dissolving into a breath or absorbing into an experience is the optimal form of attention. Other traditions erroneously believe that resting in the widest angle, the open consciousness of space, is the highest teaching. Still others say that the middle ground--an ordinary, free, and relaxed awareness of whatever arise here and now, 'nothing special'--is the highest attainment. Yet in its true nature awareness cannot be limited. Consciousness itself is both large and small, particular and universal. At different times our practice will require that we embrace all these perspectives." (Ibid, 72-73).

"Every form of genuine awareness is liberating. Each moment we release entanglement and identification is selfless and free…" (Ibid, 73).

"…awareness illuminates the ungraspable nature of the universe. It returns the heart and mind to its birthright, naturally luminous and free." (Ibid).

140

"...Awareness in space can be an excellent way to begin practice because it initiates the sitting period with the flavor of wakeful ease and spacious letting go. Or it can be used after a period of focused attention." (Ibid, 74).

"Whenever you begin, sit comfortably and at ease. Let your body be at rest and your breathing be natural. Close your eyes. Take several full breaths and let each release gently. Allow yourself to be still." (Ibid).

"Now shift awareness away from the breath. Begin to listen to the play of sounds around you. Notice those that are loud and soft, far and near. Just listen. Notice how all sounds arise and vanish, leaving no trace. Listen for a time in a relaxed, open way." (Ibid).

"As you listen, let yourself sense or imagine that your mind is not limited to your head. Sense that your mind is expanding to be like the sky--open, clean, vast like space. There is no inside or outside. Let the awareness of your mind extend in every direction like the sky." (Ibid).

"Now the sounds you hear will arise and pass away in the open space of your own mind. Relax in this openness and just listen. Let the sounds that come and go, whether far or near, be like clouds in the vast sky of your own awareness. The play of sounds moves through the sky, appearing and disappearing without resistance." (Ibid).

"As you rest in this open awareness, notice how thoughts and images also arise and vanish like sounds. Let the thoughts and unpleasant thoughts, pictures, words, and feelings move unrestricted in the space of mind. Problems, possibilities, joys, and sorrows come and go like clouds in the clear sky of mind." (Ibid).

"After a time, let this spacious awareness notice the body. Become aware of how the sensation of breath and body float and change in the same open sky of awareness. The breath breathes itself; it moves like a breeze..." (Ibid).

"Let the breath move like a breeze. Rest in this openness. Let sensations float and change. Allow all thoughts and images, feelings and sounds to come and go like clouds in the clear open space of awareness." (Ibid, 74).

"Finally, pay attention to the awareness itself. Notice how the open space of awareness is naturally clear, transparent, timeless, and without conflict--allowing all things, but not limited by them." (Ibid).

Developing Insight

"...an understanding of interconnection comes, in Buddhist

141

practice, from awareness of the three characteristics of experience, also known as the three marks of existence. The first is *impermanence*...The second is *suffering*, which he described as the result of 'the mind unable to accommodate its experience.'" (Boorstein, 2014, 80-81).

"...the third characteristic, *emptiness*--the insight that there is no enduring self that separates anything from anything else..." (Ibid, 81).

"Everything has a life cycle, with beauty in every part of it, and the passing of any part of it evokes a response, either of relief or nostalgia..." (Ibid).

"When I first began to teach, I would explain the four truth this way:" (Ibid, 82).

"Life is challenging because everything is always changing and we continually need to adjust to new circumstances." (Ibid).

"Adding struggle to challenge creates suffering. Pain is inevitable but suffering is optional." (Ibid).

"Peace is possible. In the middle of a complicated life, the mind can remain at ease." (Ibid, 83).

"The path for developing this kind of mind involves attention to ethical behavior, to disciplining the habits of mind through meditation, and to ardent intention." (Ibid).

"...the third noble truth, the truth of liberation is possible..." (Ibid).

"In years since, the understanding that everything anyone does is a result of karma--of causes and effects--has helped to keep me from labeling people as good or bad. Circumstances and behavior can change, of course, but at any given time no one can be other than the sum of all of their contingent causes. A student in a class discussion about this topic once said, 'When people ask me, 'How are you?' I always answer, 'I couldn't be better. Because, I couldn't!' It's true. We couldn't, any of us, be better. In our most out-of-sorts days, we couldn't be better. If we could, we would. Suffering happens, but no 'one' decides to suffer." (Ibid, 84).

Walking Meditation

"...walk quietly and take each gentle step with reverence...If we walk like that, then every step will be grounding, every step will be nourishing." (Hanh, 2014, 86).

"...Go slowly. Mindfulness lights our way..." (Ibid).

"...be grounded...walk and breath in such a way that you can connect with your body deeply." (Ibid, 87).

"Walking meditation unites our body and our mind. We

combine our breathing with our steps. When we breathe in, we may take two or three steps. When we breathe out, we may take three, four, or five steps. We pay attention to what is comfortable for our body." (Ibid).

"Our breathing has the function of helping our body and mind to calm down. As we walk, we can say, *Breathing in, I calm my body. Breathing out, I bring peace into my body.* Calming the breath calms the body and reduces any pain and tension." (Ibid).

"...Our body and our mind are two aspects of the same reality. If we remove our mind from our body, our body is dead..." (Ibid, 88).

"Walking meditation is first and foremost a practice to bring body and mind together peacefully. No matter what we do, the place to start is to calm down, because when our mind and our body have calmed down, we see more clearly. When we see our anger or sadness clearly, it dissipates. We begin to feel more compassion for ourselves and others. We can only feel this when body and mind are united." (Ibid).

"I think of the earth as a bodhisattva, a great and compassionate being. A bodhisattva is a being who has awakening, understanding, and love. Any living being who has awakened, peace, understanding, and love can be called a bodhisattva, but a bodhisattva doesn't have to be a human being...A bodhisattva is not something that is up in the clouds far away from us. Bodhisattvas are all around us. A young person who has love, who has freshness, who has understanding, who offers us a lot of happiness, is a bodhisattva..." (Ibid, 88-89).

"We are made of body and mind. Our body can radiate the energy of peace and compassion. Our mind also has energy. The energy of the mind can be powerful. If the energy of the mind is filled with fear and anger, it can be very destructive. But if we sit mindfully, if we walk mindfully and reverently on the earth, we will generate the energies of mindfulness, of peace, and of compassion in both body and mind. This kind of energy can heal and transform." (Ibid, 92).

"When you walk uphill or downhill, the number of steps per breath will change. Always follow the needs of your lungs. You may notice that your exhalation is longer than you inhalation. You might find that you take three steps during your in-breath and four steps during your out-breath, or two steps, then three steps..." (Ibid, 93).

"Don't forget to practice smiling. Your half-smile will bring calm and delight to your steps and your breath, and help sustain your attention. After practicing for half an hour or an hour, you will find that your breath, your steps, your counting, and your half-smile all blend together in a marvelous balance of mindfulness." (Ibid, 94).

Membrane "An extended surface, in any dimensions. A zero-brane is a point particle. A one-brane is a string. A two-brane is a membrane. Membranes are an essential feature of M-theory. Strings can be viewed as membranes with one dimension compactified." (Kaku, 2005, 393).

Meme "A term coined by Richard Dawkins, who defines it as 'a unit of cultural inheritance, hypothesized as analogous to the particular gene and as naturally selected by virtue of its 'phenotypic' consequences on its own survival and replication in the cultural environment." (Sheldrake, 1995, 370).

Memory "The capacity for remembering, recalling, recollecting, or recognizing. From the mechanistic point of view, animal and human memory depend on material memory traces within the nervous system. From the point of view of the hypothesis of formative causation, memory in its various forms, both conscious and unconscious, is due to morphic resonance." (Sheldrake, 1995, 370).

Mendelian inheritance "Inheritance by means of pairs of discrete hereditary factors, now identified with genes. One member of each pair comes from each parent. The genes may blend in their efforts on the body, but they do not themselves blend and are passed on intact to future generations." (Sheldrake, 1995, 370).

Mental Body "Theosophical concept of an inner body, or aspect of the personality, consisting of thoughts and mental impressions. This body, which is said to possess its own degree of consciousness, may be projected onto the astral plane, where it brings consciousness to the imaginal world of the 'subconscious' mind. The mental body is capable of both abstract and concrete conceptualization." (Drury, 2002, 211).

Meridian "In acupuncture, the channels which carry ch'i, or life energy, to different parts of the body. There are twelve principal meridians..." (Drury, 2002, 212).

Messenger particle "Smallest 'packet' or 'bundle' of a force, which communicates the forces' influence." (Greene, 2004, 530).

Microwave background radiation "The radiation from the glowing of the hot early universe; now so red-shifted that it appears not as light but as microwaves (radio waves with a wavelength of a

144

few centimeters)." (Hawking, 2001, 205).

"The remnant of the original radiation from the big bang, with a temperature of about 2.7 degrees K. Tiny deviations in this background radiation give scientists valuable data that can verify or rule out many cosmological theories." (Kaku, 2005, 393).

Mind "In Cartesian dualism, the conscious thinking mind is distinct from the material body; the mind is non-material. Materialists derive the mind from the physical activity of the brain. Depth psychologists point out that the conscious mind is associated with a much broader mental system, the unconscious mind. In the view of Jung, the unconscious mind is not merely individual but collective. On the hypothesis of formative causation, mental activity, conscious and unconscious, takes place within and through mental fields, which like other kinds of morphic fields contain a kind of in-built memory." (Sheldrake, 1995, 370)

"One's individual faculties of consciousness, awareness, and thought. Occultists regard the mind as a lower aspect of the self and maintain that in an altered state of consciousness--for example, in an out-of-body experience--the mind can be 'projected' outside the body and experience a new range of perceptions. Occultists and mystics also believe that the mind may be altered to become more 'sensitive', so that it is receptive to psi phenomena (the various manifestations of extrasensory perception)." (Drury, 2002, 215).

"Mind. The thinking, perceiving, and feeling mechanism of the human organism. The total conscious and unconscious experience. The intelligence associated with the emotional life reaching upward through worship and wisdom to the spirit level." (*The Urantia Book*, 1955, 8:8).

"*Mind* is a phenomenon connoting the presence-activity of living ministry in addition to varied energy systems; and this is true on all levels of intelligence. In personality, mind ever intervenes between spirit and matter..." (9:10).

"In the inner experience of man, *mind* is joined to matter. Such material-linked minds cannot survive mortal death. Such material-linked minds cannot survive mortal death. The technique of survival is embraced in those adjustments of the human will and those transformations in the mortal *mind* whereby such a God-conscious intellect gradually becomes spirit taught and eventually spirit led. This evolution of the human *mind* from matter association to spirit union results in the transmutation of the potentially spirit phases of the mortal *mind* into the morontia realities of the immortal soul. Mortal *mind* subservient to matter is destined to become increasingly material and consequently to suffer eventual personality extinction; *mind* yielded to spirit is destined to become increasingly spiritual and ultimately to achieve oneness with the surviving and guiding divine spirit and in this way to attain survival and eternity of personality existence." (26:1).

"The infinity of the perfection of God is such that it eternally constitutes him mystery. And the greatest of all the unfathomable mysteries of God is the phenomenon of the divine indwelling of mortal minds. The manner in which the Universal Father sojourns with the creatures of time is the most profound of all universe mysteries; the divine presence in the *mind* of man is the mystery of mysteries." (26:3).

"...Man's *mind* can only perceive the *mind* phenomena of other minds, be they human or superhuman. If man's personality can experience the universe, there is a divine *mind* and an actual personality somewhere concealed in that universe." (30:6).

"...Everything divine which the human *mind* grasps and the human soul acquires is an experiential attainment; it is a reality of personal experience and is therefore a unique possession in contrast to the inherent goodness and righteousness of the inerrant personalities of Havona." (52:2).

"...The source of the streams of universe life and of the cosmic *mind* must be above the levels of their manifestation. The human *mind* cannot be consistently explained in terms of the lower orders of existence. Man's *mind* can be truly comprehended only by recognizing the reality of higher orders of thought and purposive will. Man as a moral being is inexplicable unless the reality of the Universal Father is acknowledged." (53:1).

"Eternal survival of personality is wholly dependent on the choosing of the mortal *mind*, whose decisions determine the survival potential of the immortal soul. When the *mind* believes God and the soul knows God, and when, with the fostering Adjuster, they all desire God, then is survival assured..." (69:8).

"The ability of mortal parents to procreate is not predicated on their educational, cultural, social, or economic status. The union of the parental factors under natural conditions is quite sufficient to initiate offspring. A human *mind* discerning right and wrong and possessing the capacity to worship God, in union with a divine Adjuster, is all that is required in that mortal to initiate and foster the production of his immortal soul of survival qualities if such a spirit-endowed individual seeks God and sincerely desires to become like him, honestly elects to do the will of the Father in heaven." (70:1).

"*Mind* transmutes the values of spirit into the meanings of intellect; volition has power to bring the meanings of *mind* to fruit in both the material and spiritual domains..." (102:6).

"*Mind.* Organized energy which is subject to linear gravity except as it is modified by motion and conditioned by *mind.*" (140:7).

"...*Mind*, matter, and spirit are equally real, but they are not of equal value to personality in the attainment of divinity..." (140:11).

"...in death, both *mind* (identity) and spirit survive while the body does not..." (141:1).

"Mortal man has a spirit nucleus. The *mind* is a personal-energy system existing around a divine spirit nucleus and functioning in a material environment. Such a living relationship of personal *mind* and spirit constitutes the universe potential of eternal personality..." (142:1).

"Material *mind* is the arena in which human personalities live, are self-conscious, make decisions, choose God or forsake him, eternalize or destroy themselves." (1216:4).

"Material evolution has provided you with a life machine...But into your hands, subject to your own decisions, has been given *mind*, and it is by mind that you live or die. It is within this mind and with this mind that you make those moral decisions which enable you to achieve Adjuster-likeness, and that is God-likeness." (1216:5).

Mind-1 "The linkage capsule between the divine language systems and the language systems of the mind-body complex. The 'housing of the wetware' or perceptual apparatus for the mind-2 reality of higher intelligence. Enoch said, 'The mind is localized in consciousness; consciousness is not localized in the mind.' Here the mind receives 'images' from an infinite number of mind-2s that comprise levels of the quanta Universal Mind." (Hurtak, 1977, 593).

Mind-2 "A second world of consciousness development, preceding the world of physical form. A second world of 'advanced intelligence' as an Overself governor connecting the planetary mind-body complex with the functions of the Universal Mind. Mind-2 works considerably faster than mind-1 and interconnects with numerous entities, within the greater universe." (Hurtak, 1997, 593).

Mindfulness is a way of paying attention on purpose to both

147

external and internal stimuli.

"Mindfulness (Pali, *sati*; Skt., *smrti*; also translated as awareness) is a spiritual or psychological faculty (*indriya*) that, according to the teaching of the Buddha, is of great importance in the path of enlightenment. It is one of the seven factors of enlightenment. 'Correct' or 'right' mindfulness (Pali: *samma-sati*, Skt. *samyak-smrti*) is the seventh element of the noble eightfold path." ("Mindfulness," *Wikipedia*).

"Enlightenment (*bodhi*) is a state of being in which greed, hatred and delusion (Pali: *moha*) have been overcome, abandoned and are absent from the mind. Mindfulness, which, among other things, is an attentive awareness of the reality of things (especially of the present moment) is an antidote to delusion and is considered as such a 'power' (Pali, *bala*). This faculty becomes a power in particular when it is coupled with clear comprehension of whatever is taking place." (Ibid).

"The Buddha advocated that one should establish mindfulness (*satipatthana*) in one's day-to-day life, maintaining as much as possible a calm awareness of one's body, feelings, mind, and dharmas. The practice of mindfulness supports analysis resulting in the arising of wisdom (Pali: *panna*, Skt.: *prajna*). A key innovative teaching of the Buddha was that meditative stabilization must be combined with liberating discernment." (Ibid).

"The *Satipatthana Sutta* (Skt.: *Smrtyupasthana Sutra*) is an early text dealing with mindfulness." (Ibid).

"Mindfulness practice, inherited from the Buddhist tradition, is being employed in psychology to alleviate a variety of mental and physical conditions, including obsessive-compulsive disorder, anxiety, and in the prevention of relapse in depression and drug addiction." (Ibid).

"Mindfulness is a basic approach to the spiritual journey that is common to all traditions of Buddhism…" (Rinpoche, 2014, 35).

"…According to the buddhadharma, spirituality means relating with the working basis of one's existence, which is one's state of mind." (Ibid, 36).

"Spirituality is based on mind. In Buddhism, mind is what distinguishes sentient beings from rocks or trees or bodies of water. That which possesses discriminating awareness, that which possesses a sense of duality--which grasps or rejects something external--that is mind…The traditional Tibetan phrase defining mind means precisely that: 'That which can think of the other, the projection, is mind.'" (Ibid, 36-37).

148

"Mind...contains perception--perception that is very uncomplicated, very basic, very precise. Mind develops its particular nature as that perception begins to linger on something other than oneself. Mind makes the fact of perceiving something else stand for the existence of oneself..." (Ibid, 37).

"This mind is our working basis for the practice of meditation and the development of awareness...Mind also includes what are known as emotions, which are the highlights of mental states." (Ibid).

"Mindfulness of body, the first foundation of mindfulness, is connected with the need for a sense of being, a sense of groundedness..." (Ibid, 39).

"According to the tradition, the body we think we have is what is known as psychosomatic body. It is largely based on projections and concepts of body. This psychosomatic body contrasts with the enlightened person's sense of body...This sense of body is free form conceptualizations. It is just simple and straightforward. There is a direct relationship with the earth." (Ibid).

"Mindfulness of body brings this all-pervasive mind-imitating-body activity into the practice of meditation..." (Ibid).

"Mindfulness of body is connected with the earth. It is an openness that has a base, a foundation. A quality of expansive awareness develops through mindfulness of body--a sense of being settled and of therefore being able to afford to open out." (Ibid, 40).

"...The second foundation of mindfulness is the mindfulness of life, or survival." (Ibid, 41).

"...Mindfulness of life is based on touch and go. You focus your attention on the object of awareness, but then, in the same moment, you disown that awareness and go on. What is needed here is some sense of confidence--confidence that you do not have to securely own your mind, but that you can tune in to its process spontaneously." (Ibid).

"...Mindfulness becomes a basic acknowledgment of existing..." (Ibid).

"...mindfulness brings clarity, skill, and intelligence. You are here; you are living; let it be that way--that is mindfulness..." (Ibid, 43).

"The next foundation of mindfulness is mindfulness of effort..." (Ibid).

"The traditional Buddhist analogy for right effort is the walk of an elephant or tortoise. The elephant moves along surely, unstoppably, with great dignity. Like the worm, it is not excitable, but unlike the worm, it has a panoramic view of the ground it is treading on. Though it is serious and slow, because of the elephant's ability to survey the ground there is a sense of playfulness and intelligence in its movement." (Ibid).

"There is a kind of technique...here that is extremely effective and useful...in daily life...The way of coming back is through what we might call the abstract watcher. This watcher is just simple self-consciousness, without aim or goal." (Ibid).

"When we encounter anything, the first flash that takes place is the bare sense of duality..." (Ibid, 45).

"Instead of condemning this self-consciousness as dualistic, we take advantage of this tendency in our psychological system and use it as the basis of the mindfulness of effort..." (Ibid).

"...effort becomes self-existing. It stands on its own two feet, so to speak, rather than needing another effort to trigger it off." (Ibid, 45-46).

"This kind of effort is extremely important. The sudden flash is a key to all Buddhist meditation, from the level of basic mindfulness to the highest levels of tantra. Such mindfulness of effort could definitely be considered the most important aspect of mindfulness practice. Mindfulness of body creates the general setting; it brings meditation into the psychosomatic setup of one's life. Mindfulness of life makes meditation practice personal and intimate. Mindfulness of effort makes meditation workable: it connects the foundations of mindfulness to the path, to the spiritual journey..." (Ibid, 46).

"...Mindfulness of effort cannot be deliberately manufactured...There must be a background of discipline which sets the tone of the sitting practice...So it is extremely important to have respect for the practice, a sense of appreciation, and a willingness to work hard." (Ibid).

"Often mindfulness is referred to as watchfulness...Mindfulness means being watchful, rather than watching something. This implies a process of intelligent alertness, rather than the mechanical business of simply observing what happens." (Ibid, 47).

"Particularly the fourth foundation--mindfulness of mind--has qualities of an aroused intelligence operating. The intelligence of the fourth foundation is a sense of light-handedness..." (Ibid).

"Mindfulness of mind suggests a sense of presence and a

sense of accuracy in terms of being there." (Ibid, 48).

"...Mindfulness is the act as well as the experience, happening at the same time." (Ibid, 50).

Molecule "A chemical unit. The smallest amount of a chemical substance that is capable of independent existence. Each kind of molecule has a characteristic atomic composition, a specific structure, and specific physical and chemical properties." (Sheldrake, 1995, 371).

Moral "(adj.) 2 concerned with the principles of right and wrong behavior and the goodness or badness of human character. 2 adhering to the code of behavior that is considered right or acceptable. (n.) 1 a lesson that can be derived from a story or experience. 2 (**morals**) standards of behavior, or principles of right and wrong." (*The Concise Oxford Dictionary*, 1999).

"Some degree of *moral* affinity and spiritual harmony is essential to friendship between two persons; a loving personality can hardly reveal himself to a loveless person. Even to approach the knowing of a divine personality, all of man's personality endowments must be wholly consecrated to the effort; halfhearted, partial devotion will be unavailing." (*The Urantia Book*, 1955, 30:4).

"...Man's physical environment entails the battle for existence; the social surroundings necessitate ethical adjustments; the *moral* situations require the making of choices in the highest realms of reason; the spiritual experience (having realizing God) demands that man find him and sincerely strive to like him." (68:4).

"*Moral* conduct is always an antecedent of evolved religion and a part of even revealed religion, but never the whole of religious experience. Social service is the result of moral thinking and religious living..." (68:7).

"...scientific, *moral*, and spiritual insights, these cosmic responses, are innate in the cosmic mind, which endows all will creatures. The experience of living never fails to develop these three cosmic intuitions; they are constitutive in the self-consciousness of reflective thinking..." (192:5).

"In the local universe mind bestowals, these three insights of the cosmic mind constitute the a priori assumptions which make it possible for man to function as a rational and self-conscious personality in the realms of science, philosophy, and religion. Stated otherwise, the recognition of the reality of these three manifestations of the Infinite is by a cosmic technique of self-realization. Matter-energy is recognized by the mathematical logic of the senses; mind-reason intuitively knows its *moral* duty; spirit-faith (worship) is the religion of the reality of spiritual experience. These three basis factors in reflective thinking may be unified and coordinated in personality development, or they may become disproportionate and virtually unrelated in their respective functions. But when they become unified, they produce a strong character consisting in the correlation of a factual science, a *moral* philosophy, and a genuine religious experience. And it is these three cosmic intuitions that give objective validity, reality, to man's experience in and with things, meanings, and values." (192:6).

"Intelligence alone cannot explain the *moral* nature. Morality, virtue, is indigenous to human personality. *Moral* intuition, the realization of duty, is a component of human mind endowment and is associated with the other inalienables of human nature: scientific curiosity and spiritual insight..." (192:8).

"...The highest *moral* choice is the choice of the highest possible value--in any sphere, in all of them--this is to choose to do the will of God..." (435:7).

"Goodness is the mental recognition of the relative values of the diverse levels of divine perfection. The recognition of goodness implies a mind of *moral* status, a personal mind with ability to discriminate between good and evil. But the possession of goodness, greatness, is the measure of real divinity attainment." (647:3).

"...The free will of man is supreme in *moral* affairs..." (753:2).

"...Sin enormously retards intellectual development, *moral* growth, social progress, and mass spiritual attainment. But it does not prevent the highest spiritual achievement by any individual who chooses to know God and sincerely do his divine will." (761:5).

"A *moral* society should aim to preserve the self-respect of its citizenry and afford every normal individual adequate opportunity for self-realization..." (803:9).

"...Women, however, have always been the *moral* standard-bearer and the spiritual leaders of mankind..." (938:8).

"...The mores (religious, *moral*, and ethical), together with property, pride, and chivalry, stabilize the institutions of marriage and family..." (939:6).

"...'*Moral* self-consciousness is true human self-realization and constitutes the foundation of the human soul, and the soul is that part of man which represents the potential survival value of human experience. *Moral* choice and spiritual attainment, the ability to know God and the urge to be like him, are the characteristics of the soul. The soul of man cannot exist apart from *moral* thinking

152

and spiritual activity. A stagnant soul is a dying soul. But the soul of man is distinct from the divine spirit which dwells within the mind. The divine spirit arrives simultaneously with the first *moral* activity of the human mind, and that is the occasion of the birth of the soul." (1478:4).

"'The saving or losing of a soul has to do with whether or not the *moral* consciousness attains survival status through eternal alliance with its associated immortal spirit endowment. Salvation is the spiritualization of the self-realization of the *moral* consciousness, which thereby becomes possessed of survival value. All forms of soul conflict consist in the lack of harmony between the *moral*, or spiritual, self-consciousness and the purely intellectual self-consciousness.'" (1478:5).

"A human mind, built up solely out of the consciousness of physical sensations, could never attain spiritual levels; this kind of material mind would be utterly lacking in a sense of *moral* values and would be without a guiding sense of spiritual dominance which is so essential to achieving harmonious personality unity in time, and which is inseparable from personality survival in eternity." (1480:2).

"...*Moral* convictions based on spiritual enlightenment and rooted in human experience are just as real and certain as mathematical deductions based on physical observations, but on another and higher level." (2077:8).

"...There is great need for the teaching of *moral* discipline in the place of so much self-gratification..." (2086:3).

Moral intuition "...Moral intuition, the realization of duty, is a component of human mind endowment and is associated with the other inalienables of human nature: scientific curiosity and spiritual insight..." (*The Urantia Book*, 1955, 192:8).

Morality "(n.) 1 principles concerning the distinction between right and wrong or good and bad behavior; a system of values and moral principles. 2 the extent to which an action is right or wrong." (*The Concise Oxford Dictionary*, 1999).

"*Morality* has its origin in the reason of self-consciousness; it is superanimal but wholly evolutionary. Human evolution embraces in its unfolding all endowments antecedent to the bestowal of the Adjusters and to the pouring out of the Spirit of Truth. But the attainment of levels of *morality* does not deliver man from the real struggles of mortal living..." (*The Urantia* Book, 1955, 68:4).

"...*Morality* does not biologically lead to the higher spiritual levels of religious experience..." (68:7).

153

"...*Morality*, virtue, is indigenous to human personality..." (192:8).

"*Morality* can never be advanced by law or by force. It is personal and freewill matter and must be disseminated by the contagion of the contract of morally fragrant persons with those who are less morally responsive, but who are also in some measure desirous of doing the Father's will." (193:8).

"Family life is the progenitor of true *morality*, the ancestor of the consciousness of loyalty to duty. The enforced associations of family life stabilize personality and stimulate its growth through the compulsion of necessitous adjustment to other and diverse personalities..." (942:1).

"All men recognize the *morality* of this universal human urge to be unselfish and altruistic..." (1134:1).

"Joyful acceptance of cosmic citizenship--honest recognition of your progressive obligations to the Supreme Being, awareness of the interdependence of evolutionary man and evolving Deity. This is the birth of cosmic *morality* and the dawning realization of universal duty." (1206:8).

"The temporal relation of man to the Supreme is the foundation for cosmic *morality*, the universal sensitivity to, and acceptance of, duty. This is a *morality* which transcends the temporal sense of relative right and wrong; it is a *morality* directly predicated on the self-conscious creature's appreciation of experiential obligation to experiential Deity..." (1284:4).

"*Morality* is the essential pre-existent soil of personal God-consciousness, the personal realization of the Adjuster's inner presence, but such *morality* is not the source of religious experience and the resultant spiritual insight. The moral nature is superanimal but sub-spiritual. *Morality* is equivalent to the recognition of duty, the realization of the existence of right and wrong. The moral zone intervenes between the animal and the human types of mind as morontia functions between the material and the spiritual spheres of personality attainment." (2096:1).

"*Morality* is not necessarily spiritual; it may be wholly and purely human, albeit real religion enhances all moral values, makes them more meaningful. *Morality* without religion fails to reveal ultimate goodness, and it also fails to provide for the survival of even its own moral values. Religion provides for the enhancement, glorification, and assured survival of everything *morality* recognizes and approves." (2096:3).

Morph "change smoothly and gradually from one image to

154

another using computer animation techniques; an image processed in this way." (*The Concise Oxford Dictionary*, 1999).

Morphic field "A field within and around a morphic unit which organizes its characteristic structure and pattern of activity. Morphic fields underlie the form and behavior of holons or morphic units at all levels of complexity. The term *morphic field* includes morphogenetic, behavioral, social, cultural, and mental fields. Morphic fields are shaped and stabilized by morphic resonance from previous similar morphic units, which were under the influence of fields of the same kind. They consequently contain a kind of cumulative memory and tend to become increasingly habitual." (Sheldrake, 1995, 371).

Morphic resonance "A supposed paranormal influence by which a pattern of events or behavior can facilitate subsequent occurrences of similar patterns." (*The Concise Oxford Dictionary*, 1999).

"The influence of previous structures of activity on subsequent similar structures of activity organized by morphic fields. Through morphic resonance, formative causal influences pass through or across both space and time, and these influences are assumed not to fall off with distance in space or time, but they come only from the past. The greater the degree of similarity, the greater the influence of morphic resonance. In general, morphic units closely resemble themselves in the past and are subject to self-resonance from their own past states." (Sheldrake, 1995, 371).

Morphic unit "A unit of form or organization, such as an atom, molecule, crystal, cell, plant, animal, pattern of instinctive behavior, social group, element of culture, ecosystem, planet, planetary system, or galaxy. Morphic units are organized in nested hierarchies of units within units: a crystal, for example, contains molecules, which contain atoms, which contain electrons and nuclei, which contain nuclear particles, which contain quarks." (Sheldrake, 1995, 371).

Morphogenesis "1 (Biology) the origin and development of morphological characteristics. 2 (Geology) the formation of land forms or other structures." (*The Concise Oxford Dictionary*, 1999).

"The coming into being of form." (Sheldrake, 1995, 371).

Morphogenetic fields "Fields that play a causal role in morphogenesis. This term, first proposed in the 1920s, is now widely used by developmental biologists, but the nature of morphogenetic fields has remained obscure. On the hypothesis of formative causation, they are regarded as morphic fields stabilized

155

by morphic resonance." (Sheldrake, 1995, 371).

Mother "(n.) 1 a woman in relation to a child or children to whom she has given birth; a woman who has care of a child through adoption; a female animal in relation to its offspring. 2 (**Mother**) (especially as a title or form of address) the head of a female religious community. 3 (informal) an extreme example or very large specimen: *the mother of all traffic jams*. (v.) 1 bring up (a child) with care and affection. 2 look after kindly and protectively, sometimes excessively so. 3 (dated) give birth to." (*The Concise Oxford Dictionary*, 1999).

"No ascending mortal can escape the experience of rearing children--their own or others--either on the material worlds or subsequently on the finaliter world or on Jerusem. Fathers must pass through this essential experience just as certainly as *mothers*. It is an unfortunate and mistaken notion of modern peoples on Urantia that child culture is largely the task of mothers. Children need fathers as well as mothers, and fathers need this parental experience as much as do mothers." (*The Urantia* Book, 1955, 531:4).

Motherly "(adj.) of, resembling, or characteristic of a mother, especially in being caring, protective, and kind." (*The Concise Oxford Dictionary*, 1999).

M-theory "A theory that unites all five string theories, as well as supergravity, within a single theoretical framework, but which is not yet fully understood." (Hawking, 2001, 205).

"The most advanced version of string theory. M-theory exists in eleven-dimensional hyperspace, where two-branes and five-branes can exist. There are five ways in which M-theory can be reduced down to ten dimensions, thereby giving us the five known superstring theories, which are now revealed to be the same theory. The full equations governing M-theory are totally unknown." (Kaku, 2005, 394).

"Currently incomplete theory unifying all five versions of string theory; a fully quantum mechanical theory of all forces and all matter." (Greene, 2004, 539).

Muladhara "Chakra One, base of the spine, element Earth. It means root support." (Judith, 1999, 417).

"In Kundalini Yoga, the chakra or energy center at the base of the spine where the kundalini serpent energy lies 'coiled', ready to be awakened..." (Drury, 2002, 220).

Multiply Connected Space "A space in which a lasso or loop cannot be continuously shrunk down to a point. For example, a loop that winds around the surface of a doughnut hole cannot be contracted to a point, hence a doughnut is multiply connected. Wormholes are examples of multiply connected spaces, since a lasso cannot be contracted around the throat of a wormhole." (Kaku, 2005, 394).

Multiverse "Multiple universes. Once considered highly speculative, today the concept of the multiverse is considered essential to understanding the early universe. There are several forms of the multiverse which are all intimately related. Any quantum theory has a multiverse of quantum states. Applied to the universe, it means that there must be an infinite number of parallel universes which have decohered from each other. Inflation theory introduces the multiverse to explain the process of how inflation started and then stopped. String theory introduces the multiverse because of its large number of possible solutions. In M-theory, these universes may actually collide with each other. On philosophical grounds, one introduces the multiverse to explain the anthropic principle." (Kaku, 2005, 394).

Muon "A subatomic particle identical to the electron but with a much larger mass. It belongs to the second redundant generation of particles found in the Standard Model." (Kaku, 2005, 394).

Mutation "A sudden change. Mutations are observed in the phenotypes of organisms, and can generally be traced to changes in the genetic material. The term *mutation* is now generally taken to mean a random change in a gene." (Sheldrake, 1995, 371).

N

Nadi "(Skt., 'channel' or 'vein'). A channel of the subtle body (*suksma sarira*) connecting the chakras, along which life-energy (*prana*) flows to regulate bodily functions. There are said to be 72,000 nadis, though some texts, such as the *Siva Samhita* (2.13), say that there are 350,000. There are innumerable minor nadis (*upanadi*). The *susumna* (the Buddhist *avadhuti*) is the most important, rising from the base of the spine to the *brahmarandra* ('hole of Brahma') and the *sahasrara padma* at the top of the head. Within the *susumna* are three other nadis, the *vajra*, the *citrini*, and the *brahma*. The *susumna* is red, associated with *tamas*, the *vajra* is lustrous, associated with *rasa*, and the *citrini* is pale, associated with *sattva*. The *ida* and *pingala* (the Buddhist *lanana* and *rasana*) flank the susumna on the left and right. They either run parallel to it or are entwined about it in a spiral movement. Opening at the nostrils, they meet the susumna at the *ajni* and *muladhara* chakras. The *kanda* is the root of all nadis, commonly place at the *muladhara*." (*The*

Oxford Dictionary of World Religions, 1997).

"...the chakras are connected by a non-physical channel running straight up the center of the body called the sushumna. Two alternate channels control the yin and yang energies, Ida and Pingala, twisting in figure-eight patterns around each chakra and running alongside the sushumna. These channels are among thousands of subtle energy channels called nadis, Skt. for 'flowing waters.' Ida and Pingala represent the luna and solar aspects, respectively." (Judith, 1999, 113-114).

Nadis "Channels of psychic energy in the subtle body. The root, *nad*, means motion or flow." (Judith, 1999, 417).

Nadisuddhi "In yoga, the purification of the nadis, or energy channels, by means of conjoined breathing and mental exercises." (Drury, 2002, 225).

Naked singularity "A spacetime singularity, not surrounded by a black hole, which is visible to a distant observer." (Hawking, 2001, 205).

Nature "1 the phenomena of the physical world collectively, including plants, animals, and the landscape, as opposed to humans or human creations; the physical force regarded as causing and regulating these phenomena; *archaic* a living thing's vital functions or needs. 2 the basic or inherent features, qualities, or character of a person or thing; inborn or hereditary characteristics as an influence on or determinant of personality. Often contrasted with **nurture**. (*archaic*) a person of a specified character." (*The Concise Oxford Dictionary*, 1999).

"Traditionally personified as Mother Nature. The creative and controlling power operating in the physical world, and the immediate cause of all phenomena within it. Or the inherent and inseparable combination of qualities essentially pertaining to anything and giving it its fundamental character. Or the inherent power or impulse by which the activity of living organisms is directed or controlled. From the conventional point of view of science, nature is made up of matter, fields, and energy and is governed by the laws of nature, usually thought to be eternal." (Sheldrake, 1995, 371-372).

Nature Spirits "Popular name for a deva or elemental. Occultists regard Nature-spirits as energy-beings who sustain Nature and personify the life processes in plants, flowers, and trees..." (Drury, 2002, 227).

Nature Worship "The worship of life-sustaining forces of Nature personified by the cycles of the seasons, which inevitably result in the rebirth of spring and new life. Nature worship relates also to fertility and sexuality and is usually associated with deities of the Earth and moon..." (Drury, 2002, 227).

Near-Death Experience (NDE) "State of consciousness experienced by hospital patients who have been declared clinically dead, but who have subsequently revived. The near-death experience is often characterized by the out-of-body experience, visions of spiritual beings, and the sensation of traveling through a tunnel towards a profound and serene light. There are certain parallels between this experience and trance techniques developed by native shamans." (Drury, 2002, 227-228).

Negative Energy "Energy that is less than zero. Matter has positive energy, gravity has negative energy, and the two can cancel out in many cosmological models. The quantum theory allows for a different kind of negative energy, due to the Casimir effect and other effects, which can be used to drive a wormhole. Negative energy is useful in creating and stabilizing wormholes." (Kaku, 2005, 394).

Neo-Darwinism "(Biology) of or relating to the modern version of Darwin's theory of evolution by natural selection, incorporating the findings of genetics." (*The Concise Oxford Dictionary*, 1999).

"The modern version of the Darwinian theory of evolution by natural selection. It differs from Darwin's theory in that it denies the possibility of Lamarckian inheritance; heredity is explained in terms of genes passed on by Mendelian inheritance. Genes mutate at random, and the proportions of alternative versions of genes, or alleles, within a population are influenced by natural selection. In its most extreme form, Neo-Darwinism reduces evolution to changes of gene frequencies in populations." (Sheldrake, 1995, 372).

Neutrino "A charge-less species of particle subject only to the weak force." (Hawking, 2001, 205).

"A ghostly, almost massless subatomic particle. Neutrinos react very weakly with other particles and may penetrate several light-years of lead without ever interacting with anything. They are emitted in copious quantities from supernovae. The number of neutrinos is so large that they heat up the gas surrounding the collapsing star, thereby creating the explosion of the supernova." (Kaku, 2005, 394).

Neutron "An uncharged particle, very similar to the proton, which accounts for roughly half the particles in an atomic nucleus.

159

Composed of three quarks (2 down, 1 up)." (Hawking, 2001, 205).

"A neutral subatomic particle which, along with the proton, makes up the nuclei of atoms." (Kaku, 2005, 395).

Neutron Star "A collapsed star consisting of a solid mass of neutrons. It is usually about 10 to 15 miles across. When it spins, it releases energy in an irregular manner, creating a pulsar. It is the remnant of a supernova. If the neutron star is quite large, about 3 solar masses, it might collapse into a black hole." (Kaku, 2005, 395).

Newton's laws of motion "Laws describing the motion of bodies based on the conception of absolute space and time. These held sway until Einstein's discovery of special relativity." (Hawking, 2001, 205).

Newton's universal theory of gravity "The theory that the strength of the attraction between two bodies depends on the mass and separation of the bodies; it is proportional to the product of their masses and inversely proportional to the square of the distance between them." (Hawking, 2001, 205-6).

No boundary condition "The idea that the universe is finite but has no boundary in imaginary time." (Hawking, 2001, 206).

Noetic "(Origin C17: from Gk. *noetikos*, from *noetos* 'intellectual', from *noein* 'perceive'). Of or relating to mental activity or the intellect." (*The Oxford Dictionary of World Religions*, 1997).

Noetic Sciences "A multidisciplinary field that brings objective scientific tools and techniques together with subjective inner knowing to study the full range of human experiences." ("Noetic Sciences," Institute of Noetic Sciences).

Noosphere "The noosphere--literally, 'mind-sphere' or Earth's mental sheath, above and discontinuous with the biosphere--is a word coined by Pierre Teilhard de Chardin and a concept jointly agreed upon in Paris, 1926, by Edouard Le Roy, French philosopher and student of Henri Bergson; Jesuit paleontologist Pierre Teilhard de Chardin; and Russian geochemist Vladimir Vernadsky. At the root of the primary definition of 'noosphere' is a dual perception: that life on Earth is a web of unity constituting a whole system known as the biosphere; and that the mind or self-reflective consciousness of life--the noosphere, Earth's thinking layer-constitutes a unity that is presently discontinuous but coexistent with the entire system of life on Earth, including its inorganic support systems. A third critical premise arising from the first two is that the noosphere defines the inevitable next stage of terrestrial evolution, which will subsume

160

and transform the biosphere, while making the noosphere continuous with the biosphere." (Arguelles, 2011, 178).

North "In Western ceremonial magic, the direction associated with the element Earth. It is said to be ruled by the archangel Uriel." (Drury, 2002, 234).

Nuclear fission "The process by which a nucleus breaks down into two or more smaller nuclei, releasing energy." (Hawking, 2001, 206).

Nuclear fusion "The process by which two nuclei collide and join to form a larger, heavier nucleus." (Hawking, 2001, 206).

Nucleosynethesis "The creation of higher nuclei from hydrogen, starting from the big bang. In this way, one can obtain the relative abundance of all the elements found in nature. This is one of the three 'proofs' of the big bang. The higher elements are cooked in the center of stars. The elements beyond iron are cooked in a supernova explosion." (Kaku, 2005, 395).

Nucleus "The central part of an atom, consisting only of protons and neutrons held together by the strong force." (Hawking, 2001, 206).

"The tiny core of an atom, consisting of protons and neutrons, which is roughly 10^{-13} cm across. The number of protons in a nucleus determines the number of electrons in the shell surrounding the nucleus, which in turn determines the chemical properties of the atom." (Kaku, 2005, 395).

O

Observable universe "Part of universe within our cosmic horizon; part of universe close enough to that light it emitted can have reached us by today; part of universe we can see." (Greene, 2004, 539).

Omega "The parameter that measures the average density of matter in the universe. If Lambda = 0, and Omega is less than 1, then the universe will expand forever into a big freeze. If Omega is greater than 1, then there is enough matter to reverse the expansion into a big crunch. If Omega equals 1, then the universe is flat." (Kaku, 2005, 395).

Ontology "The branch of metaphysics concerned with the nature of being." (*The Concise Oxford Dictionary*, 1999).

Open strings "Filaments of energy in string theory, in the shape of snippets." (Greene, 2004, 539).

Out-of-Body Experience (OBE) "An experience, either spontaneous or induced, in which one's center of consciousness seems to be in a spatial location outside of one's physical body."

161

(Tart, 1997, 224).

P

Padma "Lotus; sometimes used as an alternate name for the chakras." (Judith, 1999, 417).

Para- "(Origin from Gk. *para* 'beside, beyond'). (prefix) 1 beside; adjacent to: *parathyroid*. 2 beyond or distinct from, but analogous to: *paramilitary*. 3 (Chemistry) denoting substitution at diametrically opposite carbon atoms in a benzene ring: *paradichloro-benzene*." (*The Concise Oxford Dictionary*, 1999).

"(Skt., 'supreme, highest'). Found in conjunction with many Hindu words to express the superlative state--e.g. *para-bhakti*. Unless some special sense is created, the meaning will be carried within the basic word, and will not be listed separately." (*The Oxford Dictionary of World Religions*, 1997).

"Prefix meaning 'beyond' or 'beside'. It may be joined to certain scientific words to suggest the study of that which is beyond the normal confines of that discipline (e.g. *parapsychology*). It is sometimes combined with the names of deities." (Drury, 2002, 245).

Paradigm "1 (technical) a typical example, pattern, or model of something. 2 a world view underlying the theories and methodology of a scientific subject. 3 (Linguistics) a set of items that form mutually exclusive choices in particular syntactic roles. Often contrasted with syntagm. 4 (Grammar) a table of all the inflected forms of a word." (*The Concise Oxford Dictionary*, 1999).

"An example or pattern. In the sense of T. S. Kuhn (1970), scientific paradigms are general ways of seeing the world shared by members of a scientific community, and they provide models of acceptable ways in which problems can be solved." (Sheldrake, 1995, 372).

Paradigm shift "A fundamental change in approach or underlying assumptions." (*The Concise Oxford Dictionary*, 1999).

Paradox "1 a seemingly absurd or self-contradictory statement or proposition that may in fact be true; an apparently sound statement or proposition which leads to a logically unacceptable conclusion." (*The Concise Oxford Dictionary*, 1999).

Parallel lives "Concurrent incarnation when the soul is split between more than one embodiment." (Backman, 2009, 232).

Paranormal "Term for any phenomenon that in one or more respects exceeds the limits of what is deemed physically possible according to current scientific assumptions." (Tart, 1997, 224).

Parapsychology "The scientific study of paranormal

162

phenomena. This includes mental telepathy, precognition, extrasensory perception, psychokinesis, and the out--of--body experience." (Drury, 2002, 246).

"The scientific study of certain paranormal or ostensibly paranormal phenomena, in particular, ESP and PK." (Tart, 1997, 224).

Parent

Parenting

Particle accelerator "A machine that can accelerate moving charged particles, increasing their energy." (Hawking, 2001, 206).

P-brane "A brane with p dimensions." (Hawking, 2001, 206).

"Ingredient of string/M-theory with p-spatial dimensions." (Greene, 2004, 539).

Past Life "Soul embodiment prior to current time." (Backman, 2009, 232).

Past-Life Experiences "This is probably the most fascinating and controversial group of transpersonal phenomena. Past incarnation memories resemble in many ways ancestral, racial, and collective experiences. However, they are usually dramatic and are associated with an intense emotional charge of a negative or positive quality. Their essential experiential characteristic is a convinced sense of remembering something that happened once before to the same entity, to the same unity of consciousness. The person participating in these dramatic sequences maintains a sense of individuality and personal identity, but experiences themselves in another form, at another place and time, and in another context." (Grof, 1988, 84).

"This sense of reliving something that one has seen before (*deja vu*) and experienced before (*deja vecu*) in a previous incarnation is basic and cannot be analyzed any further. It is comparable to the ability to distinguish in everyday life our memories of events that actually happened from our dreams, fantasies, and daydreams. It would be difficult to convince a person who is relating to us a memory of something that happened last week that the event involved did not really occur and that it is just a figment of his or her imagination. Past incarnation memories have a similar subjective quality of authenticity and reality." (Ibid).

"Biological birth thus seems to represent something like a transformation station, where the intangible 'morphogenetic fields' of the karmic record (referred to as the 'akashic record' in the spiritual literature) enter the bio-psychological life of the individual." (Ibid, 86).

163

"The opening of the realm of past life incarnation experiences is sometimes preceded by or associated with complex insights and instructions communicated by nonverbal means. In this way, the individual is introduced to the understanding that the law of karma is an important part of the cosmic order mandatory for all sentient beings. On the basis of this new comprehension, he or she accepts responsibility for the deeds in previous lifetimes that at the time are still covered by amnesia. In addition to this general information, such insights can include details of the mechanisms involved in the cycles of rebirth and the necessary strategies for attaining liberation from karmic bonds." (Ibid).

"To reach a complete resolution of a karmic pattern or bond, the individual has to experience fully all the painful emotions and physical sensations involved in a destructive past life incarnation scene. In addition, it is necessary to transcend the event emotionally, ethically, philosophically, and spiritually, to rise above it entirely, and to forgive and be forgiven. Such a full liberation from a karmic pattern and the bondage involved is typically associated with a sense of paramount accomplishment and triumph that is beyond any rational comprehension. When it occurs, it is associated with an overwhelming feeling that one has waited for this moment and worked for the achievement of this goal for centuries. At this point, nothing in the world seems more important that to free oneself from karmic bondage." (Ibid, 96-87).

"This is typically associated with an ecstatic rapture and feelings of overwhelming bliss. In some instances, the individual can see a rapid replay of his or her karmic history and have clear insights as to how this pattern repeated itself in different variations through ages and has contaminated life time after life time. Several people have reported in this context the experience of something like a cleansing, a 'karmic hurricane,' or a 'cyclone' blowing through their past and tearing their karmic bonds in all the situations that involve the pattern that they just resolved." (Ibid, 87).

"It seems clear that the past incarnation phenomena observed in deep experiential psychotherapy, in meditation, and in spontaneous episodes of non-ordinary states of consciousness are identical with those that are responsible for the fact that the belief in reincarnation is so widespread and universal. The concept of karma and reincarnation represents a cornerstone of Hinduism, Buddhism, Jainism, Sikhism, Zoroastrianism, the Tibetan Vajrayana Buddhism, and Taoism. Similar ideas can be found in such geographically, historically, and culturally diverse groups as various

164

African tribes, American Indians, pre-Columbian cultures, the Polynesian Kaunas, practitioners of the Brazilian *umbanda*, the Gauls, and the Druids. In ancient Greece, several important schools of thought subscribed to it, among these were the Pythagoreans, the Orphics, and the Platonists. This doctrine was also adopted by the Essenes, the Pharisees, the Karaites, and other Jewish and semi-Jewish groups, and it formed an important part of the Kabbalistic theology of medieval Judaism. It was also held by the Neo-Platonists and Gnostics and in modern times by the Theosophists, Anthroposophists, and certain Spiritualists." (Ibid, 87-88).

"It is not very well known that concepts similar to reincarnation and karma existed also among the early Christians. According to St. Jerome (CE 340-420), reincarnation was given an esoteric interpretation that was communicated to a selected elite. The most famous Christian thinker speculating about the pre-existence of souls and world cycles was Origen (CE 186-253), one of the greatest Church Fathers of all times. In his writings, particularly in the book *On First Principles* (*De Principiis*) (Origenes Adamanteus, 1973), he expressed his opinion that certain scriptural passages cold only be explained in the light of reincarnation. His teachings were condemned by the Second Council of Constantinople, convened by the Emperor Justinian in CE 553, and became a heretical doctrine. The Constantinople Council decreed 'If anyone assert the fabulous pre-existence of souls and shall submit to the monstrous doctrine that follows from it, let him be anathema.' However, some scholars believe that they can detect traces of the teachings in the writings of St. Augustine, St. Gregory, and even St. Francis of Assisi." (Ibid, 88).

"In addition to the universality of the concept of reincarnation, it is important to emphasize that past life reincarnation experiences occur in experiential sessions without any programming and often despite the disbelief of the therapist and client." (Ibid).

"In several instances, subjects who had not been familiar with the concept of karma and reincarnation not only experienced dramatic past life memories, but also gained complex and detailed insights into various specific aspects of this doctrine, identical with those found in various spiritual systems and occult literature." (Ibid).

Past Life Regression "Technique, used by some practitioners of hypnosis, in which subjects are regressed beyond their point of birth into alleged earlier incarnations...." (Drury, 2002, 247).

Past Life Soul Regression "Regression hypnotherapy to re-experience past lives." (Backman, 2009, 232).

Peak Experiences "Term used by the psychologist Abraham Maslow (1908-1970) to describe experiences of sudden and profound joy, ecstasy, and illumination. Maslow associated them with insights of perfection and wonderment. In his book *Motivation and Personality* (1970), he described the highest peaks as those 'feelings of limitless horizons opening up to the vision, the feeling of being simultaneously more powerful and also more helpless than one ever was before, the feeling of great ecstasy and wonder and awe, the loss of placing in time and space...' With the growth of literature in the human potential movement and the transpersonal movement, Maslow's term has become generally synonymous with 'mystical experience'." (Drury, 2002, 247).

Perennial Philosophy "Phrase coined by the German philosopher Gottfried Leibniz (1646-1716) and summarized by Aldous Huxley as 'the metaphysic that recognizes a divine Reality substantial to the world of things and lives and minds; the psychology that finds in the soul something similar to, or even identical with, divine Reality; the ethic that places man's final end in the knowledge of the immanent and transcendent Ground of all being...' Huxley's book *The Perennial Philosophy*--one of his major works of non-fiction--was published in 1946." (Drury, 2002, 248).

Person "(Origin ME: from OFr. *persone*, from L. *persona* 'actor's mask, character in a play', later 'human being'). (n.) (pl. **people** [in most general contexts] or **persons** [chiefly in official and formal contexts]) 1 a human being regarded as an individual. 2 an individual characterized by a preference or liking for a specified thing: *she is not a cat person*. 3 an individual's body: *concealed on his person*. 4 a character in a play or story. 5 (Grammar) a category used in the classification of pronouns, possessive determiners, and verb forms, according to whether they indicate the speaker (**first person**), the addressee (**second person**), or a third party (**third person**). 6 (Christian Theology) each of the three modes of being of God, namely the Father, the Son, and the Holy Ghost [currently called Holy Spirit]." (*The Concise Oxford Dictionary*, 1999).

Persona "1 the aspect of a person's character that is presented to or perceived by others. Compare with Anima. 2 a role or character adopted by an author or actor." (*The Concise Oxford Dictionary*, 1999).

Personality "1 the combination of characteristics or qualities that form an individual's distinctive character. 2 the qualities that make someone interesting or popular. 3 a celebrity." (*The Concise Oxford Dictionary*, 1999).

"Personality has to do with individual differences among people in behavior pattern, cognition and emotion..." ("Personality," *Wikipedia*).

"Personality is usually broken into components called the Big Five, which are: openness to experience, conscientiousness, extroversion, agreeableness, and neuroticism (or emotionality). These components are generally stable over time and appear to be attributable to a person's genetics rather than the effects of one's environment." (Ibid).

"Some research has investigated whether the relationship between happiness and extraversion seen in adults can also be seen in children. The implications of these findings can help identify children that are more likely to experience episodes of depression and develop types of treatment that such children are likely to respond to. In both children and adults, research shows that genetics, as opposed to environmental factors, exert a greater influence on happiness levels. Personality is not believed to become stable until approximately the age of thirty, and personality constructs in children are referred to as temperament. Temperament is regarded as the precursor to personality. Whereas McCrae and Costa's Big Five Model assesses personality traits in adults, the EAS model is used to assess temperament in children. This model measures levels of emotionality, activity, sociability and shyness in children. The EAS model is believed to be the equivalent of the Big Five model in adults. Findings show that high degrees of sociability and low degrees of shyness are equivalent to adult extroversion, and also correlate with higher levels of life satisfaction in children." (Ibid).

"Another interesting finding has been the link found between acting extroverted and positive affect. Extroverted behaviors include acting talkative, assertive, adventurous and outgoing. For the purposes of this study, positive affect is defined as experiences of happy and enjoyable emotions. This study investigated the effects of acting in a way that is counter to a person's dispositional nature. In other words, the study focused on the benefits and drawbacks of introverts (people who are shy, socially inhibited and non-aggressive) acting extroverted, and of extroverts acting introverted. After acting extroverted, introverts' experience of

167

positive affect increased whereas extroverts seemed to experience lower levels of positive affect and suffered from the phenomenon of ego depletion. Ego depletion, or cognitive fatigue, is the use of one's energy to overtly act in a way that is contrary to one's inner disposition. When a person acts in a contrary fashion, he diverts most, if not all, (cognitive) energy toward regulating this foreign style of behavior and attitudes. Because all available energy is being used to maintain this contrary behavior, the result is an inability to use any energy to make important or difficult decisions, plan for the future, control or regulate emotions, or perform effectively on other cognitive tasks." (Ibid).

"One question that has been posed is why extroverts tend to be happier than introverts. Two types of explanations attempt to account for this difference: instrumental theories and temperamental theories. The instrumental theory suggests that extraverts end up making choices that place them in more positive situations and they also react more strongly than introverts to positive situations. The temperamental theory suggests that extroverts have a disposition that generally leads them to experience a higher degree of positive affect. In their study of extroversion, Lucas and Baird found no statistically significant support for the instrumental theory but did, however, find that extraverts generally experience a higher level of positive affect." (Ibid).

"Research has also been conducted to uncover some of the mediators that are responsible for the correlation between extroversion and happiness. Self-esteem and self-efficacy are two such mediators. Self-efficacy has been found to be related to the personality traits of extroversion and subjective well-being. Self-efficacy is one's belief about abilities to perform up to personal standards, the ability to produced desired results, and the feeling of having some ability to make important life decisions. However, the relationship between extroversion (and neuroticism) and subjective happiness is only partially mediated by self-efficacy. This implies that there are most likely other factors that mediate the relationship between subjective happiness and personality traits. Another such factor may be self-esteem. Individuals with a greater degree of confidence about themselves and their abilities seem to have both higher degrees of subjective well-being and higher levels of extroversion." (Ibid).

"Other research has examined the phenomenon of mood maintenance as another possible mediator. Mood maintenance, the ability to maintain one's average level of happiness in the face of an ambiguous situation (meaning a situation that has the potential to engender either positive or negative emotions in different individuals), has been found to be a stronger force in extroverts. This means that the happiness levels of extroverted individuals are less susceptible to the influence of external events. Another implication of this finding is that extroverts' positive moods last longer than those of introverts." (Ibid).

"*Personality* is a level of deified reality and ranges from the mortal and midwayer level of the higher mind activation of worship and wisdom up through the morontial and spiritual to the attainment of finality status. That is the evolutionary ascent of mortal- and kindred-creature *personality*, but there are numerous other orders of universe *personality*." (*The Urantia Book*, 8:1).

"Reality is subject to universal expansion, *personality* to infinite diversification, and both are capable of well-nigh unlimited Deity coordination and eternal stabilization..." (8:2).

"On attained experiential levels all *personality* orders or values are associable and even cocreational. Even God and man can coexist in a unified *personality*, as is so exquisitely demonstrated in the present status of Christ Michael--Son of Man and Son of God." (8:3).

"All subinfinite orders and phases of *personality* are associative attainables and are potentially cocreational. The prepersonal, the personal, and the superpersonal are all linked together by mutual potential of coordinate attainment, progressive achievement, and cocreational capacity...*Personality* is never spontaneous; it is the gift of the Paradise Father. *Personality* is superimposed upon energy, and it is associated only with living energy systems; identity can be associated with non-living energy patterns." (8:4).

"The Universal Father is the secret of the reality of *personality*, the bestowal of *personality*, and the destiny of *personality*..." (8:5).

"These qualities of universal reality are manifest in Urantian human experience on the following levels:" (8:6).

"1. *Body*. The material or physical organism of man. The living electro-chemical mechanism of animal nature and origin." (8:7).

"2. *Mind*. The thinking, perceiving, and feeling mechanism of the human organism. The total conscious and unconscious experience. The intelligence associated with the emotional life reaching upward through worship and wisdom to the spirit level." (8:8).

3. *Spirit*. The divine spirit that indwells the mind of man--The

Thought Adjuster. This immortal spirit is prepersonal--not a *personality*, though destined to become a part of the *personality* of the surviving mortal creature." (8:9).

"4. *Soul.* The soul of man is an experiential acquirement. As a mortal creature chooses to 'do the will of the Father in heaven,' so the indwelling spirit becomes the father of a *new reality* in human experience. The mortal and material mind is the mother of this same emerging reality. The substance of this new reality is neither material nor spiritual--it is *morontial.* This is the emerging and immortal soul which is destined to survive mortal death and begin the Paradise ascension." (8:10).

"*Personality.* The *personality* of mortal man is neither body, mind, nor spirit; neither is it the soul. *Personality* is the one changeless reality in an otherwise ever-changing creature experience; and it unifies all other associated factors of individuality. The *personality* is the unique bestowal which the Universal Father makes upon the living and associated energies of matter, mind, and spirit, and which survives with the survival of the morontial soul." (9:1).

"...In *personality*, mind ever intervenes between spirit and matter; therefore is the universe illuminated by three kinds of light: material light, intellectual insight, and spirit luminosity." (9:10).

"Eternal survival of *personality* is wholly dependent on the choosing of the mortal mind, whose decisions determine the survival potential of the immortal soul. When the mind believes God and the soul knows God, and when, with the fostering adjuster, they all desire God, then is survival assured. Limitations of intellect, curtailment of education, deprivation of culture, impoverishment of social status, even inferiority of the human standards of morality resulting from the unfortunate lack of educational, cultural, and social advantages, cannot invalidate the presence of the divine spirit in such unfortunate and humanly handicapped but believing individuals. The indwelling of the Mystery Monitor constitutes the inception and insures the possibility of the potential of growth and survival of the immortal soul." (69:8).

Perturbation Theory "The process by which physicists solve quantum theories by summing over an infinite number of small corrections. Almost all the work in string theory is done via string perturbation theory, but some of the most interesting problems lie beyond the reach of perturbation theory, such as supersymmetry breaking. Thus, we need non-perturbative methods to solve string theory, which at the present time do not really exist in any systematic fashion." (Kaku, 2005, 395).

Phase transition "Qualitative change in a physical system when its temperature is varied through a sufficiently wide range." (Greene, 2004, 539).

Phenology "the study of cyclic and seasonal natural phenomena, especially in relation to climate and plant and animal life." (*The Concise Oxford Dictionary*, 1999).

Phenomenalism "(Philosophy) the doctrine that human knowledge is confined to the appearances presented to the senses." (*The Concise Oxford Dictionary*, 1999).

Phenomenology "(Philosophy) 1 the science of phenomena as distinct from that of the nature of being. 2 an approach that concentrates on the study of consciousness and the objects of direct experiences." (*The Concise Oxford Dictionary*, 1999).

Phenotype "(Biology) the observable characteristics of an individual resulting from the interaction of its genotype with the environment." (*The Concise Oxford Dictionary*, 1999).

"The actual appearance of an organism; its manifested attributes. Contrasted with the genotype, which is the particular genetic material the organism has inherited from its parents." (Sheldrake, 1995, 372).

Photon "A quantum of light; the smallest packet of the electromagnetic field." (Hawking, 2001, 206).

"A particle or quantum of light. The photon was first proposed by Einstein to explain the photoelectric effect, i.e., the fact that shining light on a metal results in the ejection of electrons." (Kaku, 2005, 395).

"Messenger particle of the electromagnetic force; a 'bundle' of light." (Greene, 2004, 539).

Photoelectric effect "The way in which certain metals give off electrons when light falls on them." (Hawking, 2001, 206).

Pineal Gland "Small vascular, conical body situated behind the third ventricle of the brain. It has no known anatomical function, but is often described by mystics and occultists as the gland of extrasensory perception: the so-called third eye." (Drury, 2002, 251).

Pingala "One of the three major nadis, representing the male or solar energy. Related to the Yamuna river, its color is red." (Judith, 1999, 417).

"In Kundalini Yoga, the positively charged solar current that circles around the central axis of the nervous system, sushumna. It counterbalances the negatively charged lunar current known as ida." (Drury, 2002, 251).

"...the chakras are connected by a non-physical channel running straight up the center of the body called the sushumna. Two alternate channels control the yin and yang energies, Ida and Pingala, twisting in figure-eight patterns around each chakra and running alongside the sushumna. These channels are among thousands of subtle energy channels called nadis, Sanskrit for 'flowing waters.' Ida and Pingala represent the luna and solar aspects, respectively." (Judith, 1999, 113-114).

PK "In parapsychology, shorthand for psychokinesis." (Drury, 2002, 252).

Planck energy "10^{19} billion electron volts. This might be the energy scale of the big bang, where all the forces were unified into a single superforce." (Kaku, 2005, 395).

Planck length "About 10^{-35} centimeters. The size of a typical string in string theory." (Hawking, 2001, 206).

"10^{-33} cm. This is the scale found at the big bang in which the gravitational force was as strong as the other forces. At this scale, space-time becomes 'foamy' with tiny bubbles and wormholes appearing and disappearing into the vacuum." (Kaku, 2005, 396).

Planck time "About 10^{-43} seconds; time it takes light to travel the distance of the Planck length." (Hawking, 2001, 206).

Planck's constant "The cornerstone of the uncertainty principle--the product of the uncertainty in position and velocity must be greater than Planck's constant. It is represented by the symbol $\hbar$." (Hawking, 2001, 206).

Planck's quantum principle "The idea that electromagnetic waves (e.g. light) can be emitted and absorbed only in discrete quanta." (Hawking, 2001, 206).

Platonism "The philosophy of Plato or his followers, especially that relating to Plato's theory of 'ideas' or 'forms', in which abstract entities ('universals') are contrasted with their objects ('particulars') in the material world; the theory that numbers or other abstract objects are objective, timeless entities, independent of the physical world and of the symbols used to represent them." (*The Concise Oxford Dictionary*, 1999).

"The philosophical tradition that, following Plato, postulates the existence of an autonomous realm of Ideas or Forms or essences existing outside space and time and independently of manifestations of the in the phenomenal world." (Sheldrake, 1995, 372).

Pneuma "Gk. word for 'air', 'breath', and 'spirit', closely associated with Life itself." (Drury, 2002, 253).

Pneumocatharsis "Intense breathing." (Grof, 1988, 170).

"It has been known for centuries that it is possible to induce profound changes of consciousness by techniques which involve breathing. The procedures that have been used for this purpose by various ancient and non-Western cultures cover a very wide range from drastic interferences with breathing to subtle and sophisticated exercises of the various spiritual traditions. Thus the original form of baptism as it was practiced by the Essenes involved forced submersion of the initiate under water, which typically brought the individual close to death by suffocation. This drastic procedure thus induced a convincing experience of death and rebirth...Profound changes in consciousness can be induced by both extremes in the breathing rate--hyperventilation and prolonged withholding of breath--or a combination of both. Sophisticated and advanced methods of this kind can be found in the ancient Indian science of breath, or pranayama." (Ibid).

"Specific techniques involving intense breathing or withholding of breath are also part of various exercises in Kundalini Yoga, Siddha Yoga, the Tibetan Vajrayana, Sufi practice, Burmese Buddhist and Taoist meditation, and many others. More subtle techniques which emphasize special awareness in relation to breathing rather than changes of the respiratory dynamics have a prominent place in Soto Zen Buddhism, and in certain Taoist and Christian practices..." (Ibid).

"We have ourselves experimented, particularly in the context of our month--long seminars at the Esalen Institute in Big Sur, California, with various techniques involving breathing: some of these came from the spiritual traditions, others from the experiential psychotherapies of humanistic psychology. Of all these methods, we have opted for simple increase of the rate of breathing. We have concluded that a specific technique of breathing is less important than the fact that the client is breathing faster and more efficiently than usual, and with full concentration on and awareness of the inner process. It is a general strategy in holotropic therapy to trust the intrinsic wisdom of the body. The clients should therefore be encouraged to listen to the inner clues from their organism, rather than to follow any specific conceptual scheme." (Ibid, 170-171).

"We have been able to confirm repeatedly Wilhelm Reich's observation that psychological resistances and defenses use the

173

mechanism of restricting the breathing. Respiration has a special position among the physiological functions of the body. It is an autonomous function, but it can also be easily influenced by volition. Increase of the rate and of the depth of breathing typically loosens the psychological defenses and leads to release and emergence of the unconscious (and superconscious) material. Unless one have witnessed or experienced this process personally, it is difficult to believe on theoretical grounds alone the power and efficacy of this technique." (Ibid, 171).

I have experimented with some "intense breathing" techniques and experienced some incredible results. (See Kelley, 2013, 38-40).

Positivist approach "The idea that a scientific theory is a mathematical model that describes and codifies the observations we make." (Hawking, 2001, 206).

Positron "The positively charged antiparticle of the electron." (Hawking, 2001, 206).

Potential energy "Energy stored in a field or object." (Greene, 2004, 539).

Potential energy bowl "Shape describing the energy a field contains for a given field value; technically called the field's potential energy." (Greene, 2004, 539).

Power Animal "In shamanism, a creature which appears on the spirit journey of the soul while the shaman is in a state of trance. The power animal usually resembles an actual species but man sometimes be a mythical or imaginary creature. It is invariably regarded as a personification of magical power and may be summoned in rituals and ceremonies." (Drury, 2002, 254).

Powers of Ten "Shorthand notation used by scientists to denote very large or very small numbers. Thus, 10^n means 1 followed by n zeroes. A thousand is therefore 10^3. Also, 10^{-n} means the inverse of 10^n--that is, 000...001, where there are n-1 zeroes. A thousandth is therefore 10^{-3} or 0.001." (Kaku, 2005, 396).

Prana "(Skt., 'breadth'). In Hinduism, the vital force which differentiates the living from the dead. By the breath from his mouth, Prajapati created the gods. In *Atharva Veda*, Prana is personified, and one hymn is addressed to him. There are five different 'life-winds', i.e. types of pranas, of which the first, prana itself, the essential characteristic of breath as life-bestowing, was eventually identified with Brahman present as atman: 'He is your atman, which is in all things' (*Brhadaranyaka Upanisad* 3.4.1). The cultivation of prana-control is an important part of yoga." (*The*

Oxford Dictionary of World Religions, 1997).

"The breath of life, first unit, the five life winds (the pranas), the moving force of the universe." (Judith, 1999, 418).

Pranayama "The practice of controlling or exercising the breath for the purposes of purification and spiritual illumination." (Judith, 1999, 418).

"(Skt.) Breath (*prana*) control in yoga; the fourth limb of Patanjali's eight-limbed (*astanga*) or *raja yoga*. In the *Yoga Sutra* (2.49) Patanjali defines it as the 'cutting off (*viccheda*) of the flow of inhalation and exhalation' which is achieved after the attaining of 'posture' (*asana*) and prepares the mind for concentration (*dharana*). The yogin makes his breathing rhythmical and slower by equalizing the three moments of breath, namely inhalation (*puraka*), exhalation (*recaka*), and retention (*kumbhaka*). Eventually the breath ceases altogether or becomes so minimal as to be undetectable. Due to the connection between breath (*prana*) and consciousness (*citta*), it is thought that through arresting the breath the yogin is thereby arresting and calming consciousness and so achieving one-pointed (*ekagrata*) concentration." (*The Oxford Dictionary of World Religions*, 1997).

"Hatha Yoga texts connect pranayama with the physiology of the subtle body (*suksma-sarira, linga-sarira*). The yogin should breath in through the right nostril, thought to be the entrance to the *ida nadi*, and out through the left, thought to be the entrance to the *pingala nadi*. This practice results in perspiration and trembling. Through constant practice the nadis are purified and the yogin achieves the ability to hear inner sound (*nada*)." (Ibid).

Precognition "A form of ESP involving awareness of some future event that cannot be deduced from normally known data in the present." (Tart, 1997, 225).

Protein "(Origin C19: from Fr. *proteine*, Ger. *Protein*, from Gk. *proteios* 'primary'). Any of a class of nitrogenous organic compounds forming structural components of body tissues and constituting an important part of the diet." (*The Concise Oxford Dictionary*, 1999).

"A complex organic molecule composed of many amino acids linked together in chains, called polypeptide chains. The sequence of amino acids is specified by the sequence of nucleotides in the DNA of genes. There may be one or more such chains in a protein, and the chains are folded up into characteristic three-dimensional configurations. Proteins are found in all living organisms, and there are many different kinds of protein molecule.

Many proteins are enzymes, the catalysts of biochemical reactions; others play a variety of structural and other roles." (Sheldrake, 1995, 372-373).

Proton "A positively charged particle, very similar to the neutron, that accounts for roughly half the mass of an atomic nucleus. It is made of three quarks (2 up and 1 down)." (Hawking, 2001, 206).

"A positively charged subatomic particle which, along with neutrons, makes up the nuclei of atoms. They are stable, but GUT theory predicts that they may decay over a long period of time." (Kaku, 2005, 396).

PSI "A general term used either as a noun or adjective to identify ESP or PK." (Tart, 1997, 225).

Psyche "Gk. word for 'mind', 'consciousness', 'spirit', and 'soul'--originally used to denote the state of being alive, and the life-force itself. It is used in modern psychology to mean the mental faculties, encompassing both the conscious and unconscious mind." (Drury, 2002, 258).

Psychokinesis (PK) "Paranormal action; the influence of mind on a physical system that cannot be entirely accounted for by the mediation of any known physical energy." (Tart, 1997, 225).

"In parapsychology, the paranormal ability to move [or bend] physical objects through the powers of the mind..." (Drury, 2002, 259).

Pulsar "A rotating neutron star. Because it is irregular, it resembles a rotating lighthouse beacon, giving the appearance of a blinking star." (Kaku, 2005, 396).

Pythagoreanism "The belief that the universe is somehow essentially mathematical. Its fundamental mathematical reality transcends space and time. Closely akin to Platonism." (Sheldrake, 1995, 373).

Q

Qigong "The term qigong refers to a set of practices integrated into traditional Chinese exercise, meditation, and healing practices. The practices are tied together by the belief in *qi* (also known as chi or *ki*), the universal energy existing throughout the cosmos. In psychic circles, *qi* is usually identified with prana, spirit, and other names for cosmic energy. In traditional Chinese healing practices, such as acupuncture, *qi* is pictured as flowing through the body along a number of invisible channels called meridians. Disease is the result of blockages of the normal energy flow through the body." (Melton, 2008, 261).

176

"Qigong has both its esoteric side, known only to a few master practitioner-teachers, and a practical side, as demonstrated in the popular practices in which the public engaged. Qigong masters traditionally hoarded their knowledge and passed it on orally to a few successors. The role of qigong radically changed after the Chinese revolution. The Maoist government suppressed the Taoist and Buddhist centers and monasteries from which most qigong teachings were generated and oversaw the destruction of numerous qigong texts. As a result, some teachers fled to southeast Asia and the west, and some of the texts began to be published." (Ibid).

"The height of suppression of traditional practices in China, viewed by many as superstitious practices, occurred during the decade of the cultural revolution that began in 1966. In the aftermath, Chinese leadership began a reevaluation of traditional culture, one result of which was the encouragement of qigong. A national association of qigong groups emerged and the practice flourished. At the same time, several teachers established themselves in the west." (Ibid).

"Qigong reemerged as a secular practice, though some connection to Taoism and Buddhism, which were also reemerging at the same time, continued. The teachings about qi as the underlying cause of qigong's value helped the practice retain some of its religious connections. It also led to the appearance of parapsychologists in China who carried out a number of experiments attempting to scientifically verify the existence of qi." (Ibid).

"One effect of the re-emergence of qigong was the founding of a number of new groups, which were more or less attached with the national qigong association, to perpetuate its practice. One such group, called Falun Gong, was founded in the 1990s by Master Li Hongzhi. It ties the practice of to a variety of traditional Buddhist ideas, but as a total set of teachings it was a new religious movement in which qigong practice was an essential tool leading to enlightenment. Li left China in 1996 and now resides in the United States." (Ibid, 261, 263).

"Falun Gong claimed millions of practitioners inside China by the end of the 1990s. It also came under attack. It was independent of the national association and was advocating a new religious teaching independent of the state-approved China Buddhist Association at its temples. After a newspaper criticized Falun Gong on April 25, 1999, some 10,000 members engaged in a silent

177

protest at Tiananmen Square in front of the government buildings in Beijing. This demonstration, which came as a surprise to government security forces, had a completely opposite effect than that desired by the organization. Rather than stopping the actions against it, Falun Gong became a major target of government suppression. The Chinese government moved to destroy the organization, and inside China it has largely succeeded in suppressing it. Numerous adherents were jailed and all public activity outlawed. The organization was declared an evil cult." (Ibid, 263).

"By 1999 Falun Gong had nevertheless spread to a number of countries outside China, and adherents have organized an international campaign to call attention to the suppression of the movement inside China. It has negatively branded the government for violating human and religious rights, as well as for engaging in the torture and killing of its members. The Chinese government has retaliated by charging the movement with denying members proper medical care and thus causing the death of many people. While justifying its actions within China, the government's charges have found little support outside the country." (Ibid).

Quanta "The vibratory patterns of light may be considered as pulsed waves created by discrete bursts of energy. Modern researchers recognize these bursts of energy as quanta, (brief, rapid pulses of light) and study this phenomenon as the science of quantum physics." (Braden, 1993, 194).

Quantum "(pl., **quanta**) The indivisible unit in which waves may be absorbed or emitted." (Hawking, 2001, 206).

Quantum chromodynamics "Quantum mechanical theory of the strong nuclear force." (Greene, 2004, 540).

Quantum fluctuation "Tiny variations from the classical theory of Newton or Einstein, due to the uncertainty principle. The universe itself may have started out as a quantum fluctuation in nothing (hyperspace). Quantum fluctuations in the big bang give us the galactic clusters of today. The problem with quantum gravity, which has prevented a unified field theory for many decades, is that the quantum fluctuations of gravity theory are infinite, which is nonsense. So far, only string theory can banish these infinite quantum fluctuations of gravity." (Kaku, 2005, 396).

"The unavoidable, rapid variations in the value of a field on small scales, arising from quantum uncertainty." (Greene, 2004, 540).

Quantum foam "Tiny, foam-like distortions of space-time at the level of the Planck length. If we could peer into the fabric of space-time at the Planck length, we would see tiny bubbles and wormholes, with a foam-kike appearance." (Kaku, 2005, 396).

Quantum gravity "A theory that merges quantum mechanics with general relativity." (Hawking, 2001, 206).

"A form of gravity that obeys the quantum principle. When gravity is quantized, we find a packet of gravity, which is called the graviton. Usually, when gravity is quantized, we find its quantum fluctuations are infinite, which renders the theory useless. At present, string theory is the only candidate which can remove these infinities." (Kaku, 2005, 396).

Quantum leap "A sudden change in the state of an object that is not allowed classically. Electrons inside an atom make quantum leaps between orbits, releasing or absorbing light in the process. The universe might have made a quantum leap from nothing to our present-day universe." (Kaku, 2005, 396).

"1 A sudden change in the energy state of a subject, accompanied by the emission or absorption of a quantum of radiant energy in another spectrum. 2 Rapid 'god realization' enabling Man to freely commingle with other worlds of intelligence." (Hurtak, 1977, 600).

Quantum mechanics "The physical laws that govern the realm of the very small, such as atoms, protons, and the like; developed from Planck's quantum principle and Heisenberg's uncertainty principle." (Hawking, 2001, 206).

"The complete quantum theory proposed in 1925, which replaced the 'old quantum theory' of Planck and Einstein. Unlike the old quantum theory, which was a hybrid of old classical concepts and newer quantum ideas, quantum mechanics is based on wave equations and the uncertainty principle and represents a significant break from classical physics. No deviations from quantum mechanics has ever been found in the laboratory. Its most advanced version today is called quantum field theory, which combines special relativity and quantum mechanics. A fully quantum mechanical theory of gravity, however, is exceedingly difficult." (Kaku, 2005, 396-397).

"Theory, developed in the 1920s and 1930s, for describing the realm of atoms and subatomic particles." (Greene, 2004, 540).

Quantum Theory "The theory of subatomic physics. It is one of the most successful theories of all time. Quantum theory plus relativity together make up the sum total of all physical knowledge at a fundamental level. Roughly speaking, the quantum

179

theory is based on three principles: (1) energy is found in discrete packets called quanta; (2) matter is based on point particles but the probability of finding them is given by a wave, which obeys the Schrodinger wave equation; (3) a measurement is necessary to collapse the wave and determine the final state of an object. The postulates of the quantum theory are the reverse of the postulates of general relativity, which is deterministic and based on smooth surfaces. Combining relativity and the quantum theory is one of the greatest problems facing physics today." (Kaku, 2005, 397).

Quark "A charged elementary particle that feels the strong force. Quarks come in six 'flavors': up, down, strange, charmed, bottom, and top, and each flavor in three 'colors': red, green, and blue." (Hawking, 2001, 206).

"A subatomic particle that makes up the proton and neutron. Three quarks make up a proton or neutron, and a quark and antiquark pair make up a meson. Quarks in turn are part of the Standard Model." (Kaku, 2005, 397).

Quasar "Quasi-stellar object. They are huge galaxies that were formed shortly after the big bang. They have huge black holes at their center. The fact that we do not see quasars today was one way to disprove the steady state theory, which says that the universe today is similar to the universe billions of years ago." (Kaku, 2005, 397).

R

Radiation "The energy transmitted by waves or particles through space or some other medium." (Hawking, 2001, 207).

Radioactivity "The spontaneous breakdown of one type of atomic nucleus into another." (Hawking, 2001, 207).

Raja Yoga "System of 'royal' yoga based on the Sutras of Patanjali. Raja Yoga has eight branches, each of which is referred to an *anga*, or 'limb'. Together the eight limbs create a unity of thought and purpose and allow the practitioner to find union with Brahman. The eight angas are: *yama* (ethical restraints), *niyama* (moral observances); *asana* (meditation posture); *pranayama* (control of the breath); *pratyahara* (mastery of senses); *dharana* (mental concentration); *dhyana* (meditation); and *samadhi* (attainment of cosmic consciousness)." (Drury, 2002, 264).

Rajas "The guna associated with raw energy, the mover, the changer, the fiery guna." (Judith, 1999, 418).

Reality "...as comprehended by finite beings, is partial, relative, and shadowy..." (*The Urantia Book*, 1955, 5:19).

"Reality differentially actualizes on diverse universe levels;

180

reality originates in and by the infinite volition of the Universal Father and is realizable in three primal phases on many different levels of universe actualization:" (6:6).

"1. *Undeified reality* ranges from the energy domains of the non-personal to the reality realms of the non-personalizable values of universal existence, even to the presence of the Unqualified Absolute." (6:7).

"2. *Deified reality* embraces all of infinite Deity potentials ranging upward through all realms of personality from the lowest finite to the highest infinite, thus encompassing the domain of all that which is personalizable and more--even to the presence of the Deity Absolute." (7:1).

"3. *Inter-associated reality.* Universe reality is supposedly either deified or undeified, but to sub-deified beings there exists a vast domain of inter-associated reality, potential and actualizing, which is difficult of identification. Much of this coordinate reality is embraced within the realms of the Universal Absolute." (7:2).

"This is the primal concept of original reality: The Father initiates and maintains Reality..." (7:3).

"From the viewpoint of time and space, reality is further divisible as:" (7:4).

"1. *Actual and Potential.* Realities existing in fullness of expression in contrast to those which carry undisclosed capacity for growth. The Eternal Son is an absolute spiritual actuality; mortal man is vary largely an unrealized spiritual potentiality." (7:5).

"2. *Absolute and Subabsolute.* Absolute realities are eternity existences. Subabsolute realities are projected on two levels: Absonites--realities which are relative with respect to both time and eternity. Finites--realities which are projected in space and are actualized in time." (7:6).

"3. *Existential and Experiential.* Paradise Deity is existential, but the emerging Supreme and Ultimate are experiential." (7:7).

"4. *Personal and Impersonal.* Deity expansion, personality expression, and universe evolution are forever conditioned by the Father's freewill act which forever separated the mind-spirit personal meanings and values of actuality and potentiality centering in the Eternal Son from those things which center and inhere in the eternal Isle of Paradise." (7:8).

Red Giant "A star that burns helium. After a star like our Sun exhausts its hydrogen fuel, it begins to expand and form a helium-burning red giant star. This means that Earth will ultimately die in fire when our Sun becomes a red giant, about 5 billion years from

181

now." (Kaku, 2005, 397).

Red shift "The reddening of radiation emitted by an object that is moving away from an observer, caused by the Doppler effect." (Hawking, 2001, 207).

"The reddening or decrease in frequency of light from distant galaxies due to the Doppler effect, indicating that they are moving away from us. The redshift can also take place via the expansion of empty space, as in the expanding universe." (Kaku, 2005, 397).

Reductionism "The doctrine that more complex phenomena can be reduced to less complex." (Sheldrake, 1995, 373).

Regression Hypnotherapy "Hypnotic trance used to guide the client into an altered state of consciousness to access memories of past experience." (Backman, 2009, 232).

"Rebirth of the soul in another body." (Backman, 2009, 232).

"The idea that there is survival after death and rebirth; that there is a continuity of some essence of us that transmigrates from one birth to the next." (Goswami, 2001, 264).

"The belief that one's identity survives physical death and may be reborn in different physical bodies, in a succession of future lives. Belief in reincarnation is commonly associated with the concept of spiritual evolution. In Hinduism, the karma earned in the present lifetime has direct bearing on the subsequent incarnation. Reincarnation is an important part of Hindu and Buddhist belief, and has also been central in the Western mystery tradition. Many influential thinkers, including Pythagoras, Plato, Plotinus, Hegel, Emerson, and William James have embraced it; and it is an accepted teaching among most adherents of modern Theosophy, spiritualism, and occultism. The most impressive evidence for the reality of reincarnation is contained in *Twenty Cases Suggestive of Reincarnation* (1995) by Dr. Ian Stevenson, of the School of Medicine at the University of Virginia. Dr. Stevenson specializes in cases involving verifiable reincarnation memories in young children." (Drury, 2002, 267).

"The concept of life after death has had as many interpretations as there are religions. There was not a philosopher of any notoriety who did not hold to the doctrine of metempsychosis, as taught by the Brahmans, Buddhists, and later by the Pythagoreans, in its esoteric sense, whether he expressed it more or less intelligibly. Origen and Clement Alexandrinus, Synesius and Chalcidius, all believed in it; and the Gnostics, who are unhesitatingly proclaimed by history as a body of the most refined, learned, and enlightened men, were all believers in

182

metempsychosis. These philosophers held with the Hindus that God had infused into matter a portion of his own Divine Spirit, which animates and moves every particle. They taught that men have two souls of separate and quite different natures: the one perishable--the astral soul, or the inner, fluidic body--the other incorruptible and immortal--the *augoeides*, or portion of the Divine Spirit; that the mortal or astral soul perishes at each gradual change at the threshold of every new sphere, becoming with every transmigration more purified. The astral man, intangible and invisible as he might be to our mortal, earthly senses, is still constituted of matter, though sublimated." (Blavatsky, 1972, 6).

"Reincarnation is one component of the concept of life after death and the immortal soul; it is the belief that one's soul continues for eternity, that one soul is fused into or reborn into a new physical body, repeatedly over many lifetimes. This concept also incorporates the belief that the soul reappears in another form after death, i.e., continues in the spirit world in-between lives. It is interesting that two thirds of the world knows about reincarnation yet it has been played down or not spoken of officially in Catholicism for a long time." (Milanovich and McCune, 1997, 53).

"Most references of reincarnation were taken out of the Bible at the Second Council of Constantinople in CE 553." (Stone, 1994, 73).

Philo Judeaus "...believed in the transmigration of souls and believed that, upon death, the souls are reborn again in new bodies." (Bunick, 1998, 157).

Flavius Josephus (CE 37-93) wrote in "...*Antiquity of Jews* (Book 18, Chapters 1-2), that of the three sects of the Judaic religion, the Sadducees did not know if the soul lived after death, but the Essenes and Pharisees believed that it did. He wrote, 'The Pharisees believe that their souls have an immortal vigor in them and that the virtuous shall have the power to revive and live again.'" (Ibid).

Josephus also wrote in "*Jewish War Book 3* (chapter 8, 5), 'The bodies of men are indeed mortal and are created out of corruptible matter, but the soul is ever immortal. Do ye not remember that all pure spirits when they depart out of this life obtain a most holy place in heaven, and they are again sent into pure bodies, while the souls of those who have committed self-destruction are doomed to a region in the darkness." (Ibid, 157-158).

Justin Martyr (CE 100-165), "a great early Christian teacher... wrote in his *Dialogue with Trypho*, of the souls inhabiting more than

183

one human body, and upon being reborn again, not remembering its previous experiences." (Ibid, 158).

Origen (CE 185-254), another brilliant scholar and "the greatest teacher of Christianity, wrote Souls are introduced into a body according to what it deserves in former actions...Every soul comes into this world strengthened by the victories or weakened by the defeats of his previous life." (Ibid).

"...This idea of *reincarnation* originated in the observance of hereditary and trait resemblance of offspring to ancestors. The custom of naming children after grandparents and other ancestors was due to [the] belief in *reincarnation*. Some later-day races believed that man died from three to seven times..." (*The Urantia Book*, 1955, 953:5).

"There was, throughout all these regions, a lingering belief in *reincarnation*. The older Jewish teachers, together with Plato, Philo, and many of the Essenes, tolerated the theory that men may reap in one incarnation what they have sown in a previous existence; thus in one life they were believed to be expiating the sins committed in preceding lives. The Master found it difficult to make men believe that their souls had not had previous existences." (1811:5).

"...The human soul (personality) of man survives mortal death by identity association with this indwelling spark of divinity, which is immortal, and which functions to perpetuate the human personality upon a continuing and higher level of progressive universe existence. The concealed seed of the human soul is an immortal spirit. The second generation of the soul is the first of a succession of personality manifestations of spiritual and progressing existences, terminating only when this divine entity attains the source of its existence, the personal source of the all existence, God, the Universal Father." (1459:6).

Dr. Brian Weiss, M.D., has "...regressed more than two thousand patients to perinatal, in-utero, or past-life memories. [He has] already written three books about these experiences, and the books have been translated into nearly thirty languages." (Weiss, 2000, 2).

"Because [his] work deals with the themes of reincarnation, past-life regression therapy, and the reunion of soul mates, [he has] become the unofficial dean of reincarnation...I believe we do reincarnate until we learn our lessons and graduate...there is considerable historical and clinical evidence that reincarnation is a reality." (Ibid).

"...each of us possesses a soul that exists after the death of the physical body and that it returns time and time again to other bodies in a progressive effort to reach a higher plane..." (Weiss, 2004, 7-8).

Relationist "Perspective holding that all motion is relative and space is not absolute." (Greene, 2004, 540).

Relativity "The theory of Einstein, both special and general. The first theory is concerned with light and flat, four-dimensional space-time. It is based on the principle that the speed of light is constant in all inertial frames. The second theory deals with gravity and curved space. It is based on the principle that gravitating and accelerating frames are indistinguishable. The combination of relativity with quantum theory represents the sum total of all physical knowledge." (Kaku, 2005, 397-398).

Relativity, General "Einstein's theory of gravity; invokes curvature of space and time." (Greene, 2004, 538).

Relativity, Special See Special Relativity.

REM Periods "In psychology, periods of rapid eye movements (REMs), which are accompanied by dreaming." (Drury, 2002, 267).

Resonance "An exchange of energy between two or more systems of energy. The exchange is two-way, allowing each system to become a point of reference for the other..." (Braden, 1993, 194).

Rhine, Dr. Joseph Banks (1895-1980). Distinguished American psychical researcher who co-founded the Parapsychology Laboratory at Duke University in 1935 with Dr. William McDougall. Rhine was its Director until 1965, when he retired . He is often referred to as the father of parapsychology--a term he invented--for he put research into mental telepathy, clairvoyance, precognition, and psychokinesis onto a systematic, scientific basis. He made use of Zenar cards in his extrasensory perception (ESP) tests, and over many years performed a number of experiments that seemed to indicate the presence of psi phenomena at a level greater than could be expected through chance. After his retirement, Dr. Rhine continued to research ESP and held summer schools dealing with the subject. He was the author of many books in the field, including *Extrasensory Perception* (1935), *The Reach of the Mind* (1947), *New World of Mind* (1953), and *Parapsychology, Frontier Science of the Mind* (1957)." (Drury, 2002, 268).

Ring, Kenneth (b.1935) American psychologist and researcher who is internationally regarded as one of the leading authorities on the near-death experience. Ring received his Ph.D.

from the University of Minnesota and has served as an editorial advisor for *ReVision*, a leading journal in transpersonal psychology. His main contribution to consciousness research has been in the field of near-death studies, and he is credited with producing the first scientific investigation of this phenomenon, the results of which were published in his first book *Life at Death* (1980). Since then he has produced several other important publications on this topic, including *Heading Toward Omega*, *The Omega Project*, *Lessons from the Light* and a co-authored book titled *Mindsight* which describes the near-death experiences of blind people." (Drury, 2002, 269).

Rotational invariance, rotational symmetry "Characteristic of a physical system, or of a theoretical law, of being unaffected by a rotation." (Greene, 2004, 540).

S

Sahasrara "Literally, thousandfold, the name of the seventh or crown chakra." (Judith, 1999, 418).

"(Skt., 'thousand'). The lotus (*padma*) or circle (chakra) which exists at or above the crown of the head, at the top of the susumna nadi in the Tantric esoteric anatomy of the subtle body. It is the place where Siva and Sakti are united enjoying perpetual bliss. The guru is also thought to dwell there, at one with the divine. The sahasrara is envisaged as lotus, a symbol of purity, with innumerable petals on which are inscribed the letters of the Sanskrit alphabet and all their possible combinations. In the center of the lotus is the nectar of immortality (*amrta*). The sahasrara is attained through the yoga of Kundalini." (*The Oxford Dictionary of World Religions*, 1997).

Scalar Potential "A quality of energy described as having not been dispersed or dissipated. Scalar energy may be thought of as energy that is fully enabled and waiting to be used; a potential force available for activation. Upon activation, the potential becomes 'real,' or a vector quantity, that may be measured as magnitude and direction." (Braden, 1993, 195).

Schrodinger equation "Equation governing the evolution of the wave function in quantum theory." (Hawking, 2001, 207).

Schrodinger's cat paradox "The paradox that asks if a cat can be dead and alive at the same time. According to the quantum theory, a cat in a box may be dead and alive simultaneously, at least until we make an observation, which sounds absurd. We must add the wave function of a cat in all possible states (dead, alive, running, sleeping, eating, and so forth) until a measurement is made. There are two main ways to resolve the paradox, either

186

assuming that consciousness determines existence or assuming an infinite number of parallel worlds." (Kaku, 2005, 398).

Schwarzschild radius "The radius of the event horizon, or the point of no return for a black hole. For the Sun, the Schwarzschild radius is roughly two miles. Once a star is compressed to within its event horizon, it collapses into a black hole." (Kaku, 2005, 398).

Scientific determinism "A clockwork conception of the universe in which complete knowledge of the state of the universe enables the complete state to be predicted at earlier or future times; suggested by Laplace." (Hawking, 2001, 207).

Second law of thermodynamics "The law stating that entropy always increases and can never decrease." (Hawking, 2001, 207).

"Law that says that, on average, the entropy of a physical system will tend to rise from any given moment." (Greene, 2004, 540).

Sensation Body "Term used by occultists to describe the etheric body, which they believe provides awareness through the senses when united with the physical body." (Drury, 2002, 280).

Serpent "The serpent is an archetypal symbol throughout the world representing enlightenment, immortality, and a path to the Gods..." (Judith, 1999, 37).

Shaman "Shamanism is not a religion per se, but a system of ecstatic and therapeutic methods whose purpose is to obtain contact with the parallel yet invisible universe of the spirits and win its support in dealing with human affairs. Shamanism is present in the religions of all continents and at all levels of culture; yet its center is central and northern Asia." (Eliade, Couliano, and Wiesner, 2000, 214).

"A sorcerer, magician or spirit-healer who is able to enter a trance state under will and who serves as an intermediary between people and the realm of gods and spirits. Shamans make use of drums, ritual objects, and ceremonial costume in identifying with the gods; and they often enter a state of trance in order to undertake a journey of the soul. The purpose of this spirit-journey is to recover stolen spirits or to seek information from the deities relating to the availability of food and the likely outcome of the hunt. Associated with hunter-gatherer societies, the shaman may be distinguished from the spirit-medium, who is possessed in trance but does not control the experience; and also from the priest, who conducts rituals but does not necessarily enter a state of trance."

(Drury, 2002, 283).

"Inspired, ecstatic, and charismatic individuals, male and female, with the power to control spirits, often by incarnating them, and able to make journeys out of the body, both to 'heaven' and 'hell'. The word is traced to the Tungu in Siberia (where shamanism is common), though the claim is also made (but not universally accepted) that the origin is Sanskrit *sramana*, reaching China in the form of *shamen* and Japan of *shamon*. The word is now used (towards) a wide variety of people who enter trance and ecstatic states, and make 'out of body' journeys. In so far as Tungu shamanism acts as a control on usage, the careful description of S. M. Shirokogoroff (*The Psychomental Complex of Tungus*, 1935) indicates that a potential shaman is marked out by a traumatic episode or illness. If she or he can bring the spirit causing this under control, and can demonstrate ecstatic states, then she or he is recognized as a shaman. The inducing of ecstatic states is accomplished in many ways, including exclusion of general sensory stimuli through drumming, concentration on a mirror, etc., and through tobacco, alcohol, and hallucinogens (see M. J. Harner, (ed.), *Hallucinogens and Shamanism*, 1973). The spirits involved are not regarded as inherently either good or evil: the outcome depends on context and on whether they are controlled. The shaman removes threat to an individual or community by incorporating potentially destructive spirits into his or her own body and thereby neutralizing them. The ability to make journeys to upper or (more often) lower worlds is a part of the protective role of the shaman extended from its main focus on this earth. This, as C. Blacker points out in relation to Japanese shamanism (*The Catalpa Bow*, 1975), is different from the medium (*miko*) who passes on messages from the spirits, although the two work closely together." (*The Oxford Dictionary of World Religions*, 1997).

"Intermediaries to the spirit world; originally a term given to tribal specialists, medicine men, or exorcists by the Tungus of Siberia, from which it was extended to similar individuals among Indian tribes of North America. Shamans are individuals, both men and women, who due to illness, dreams, visions, or some inborn sensitivity or need directly experience the presence of spirits, whether those of living persons, plants, animals, other environmental features, or ghosts of the dead. The dreams or visions the shamans receive give them direct experience of sacred knowledge. Shamans may also have special powers if they have recovered from illness that brought them close to death. Shamans journey from the world of the living (the physical world) to the spirit world and back. Shamans are capable of altered states of awareness; are able to travel beyond ordinary boundaries of reality; can see over great distances; can travel inward to learn the way the human body and mind work. (Hirschfelder and Molin, 2000, 265-266).

"The *shaman* was the ranking medicine man, the ceremonial fetish-man, and the focus personality for all the practices of evolutionary religion. In many groups the shaman outranked the war chief, marking the beginning of the church domination of the state. The shaman sometimes functioned as a priest and even as a priest-king. Some of the later tribes had both the earlier shaman-medicine men (seers) and the later appearing shaman-priests. And in many cases the office of shaman became hereditary." (*The Urantia Book*, 1955, 986:4).

"...the great majority of the shamans believed in the fact of their spirit possession..." (987:1).

"The shamans dressed well and usually had a number of wives; they were the original aristocracy, being exempt from all tribal restrictions..." (989:1).

Shamanic visualization "Contemporary application of traditional shamanic practice in which undertakes a 'spirit-journey' in the mind's eye, usually to the accompaniment of a monotonous and regular drum-beat. During this spirit-journey the meditator may make contact with power animals, spirit-helpers or inner guides--all of whom may assist in processes of healing or self-renewal, or in some form of magical activity." (Drury, 2002, 283).

Shamanism "Shamanism is not a religion per se, but a system of ecstatic and therapeutic methods whose purpose is to obtain contact with the parallel yet invisible universe of the spirits and win its support in dealing with human affairs. Shamanism is present in the religions of all continents and at all levels of culture; yet its center is central and northern Asia." (Eliade, Couliano, and Wiesner, 1991, 214).

Within the shamanism of the Americas there is a belief that we live in a world where the Creator is not separate from the Creation, heaven is not separate from Earth, and spirit and matter infuse each other. The shaman knows we are much more than our body, that the visible and invisible worlds permeate and suffuse each other. (Villoldo, 2000, 71).

"Pre-literate technique of gaining trance consciousness, in which the medicine-man, healer, or sorcerer undertakes a journey

189

of the soul in order to encounter the gods or spirits. The shaman may use the monotonous sound of a drum-beat to 'ride' into this trance state, and usually performs his ceremonies in darkness. Psychedelics are sometimes used to enhance the states of visionary consciousness. Shamanism is found in Siberia, North and South America, and Indonesia, and is characterized by trance states in which the shaman retains control of his experience--unlike states of spirit-possession, where the gods or spirits dominate proceedings." (Drury, 2002, 283).

Shift of the Ages "Both a time in Earth history and an experience of human consciousness. Defined by the convergence of decreasing planetary magnetics and increasing planetary frequency upon a point in time, the Shift of the Ages, or simply The Shift, represents a rare opportunity of collectively repatterning the expression of human consciousness." (Braden, 1993, 195).

"The Shift is the term applied to the process of Earth accelerating through a course of evolutionary change, with the human species linked, by choice, to the electromagnetic fields of Earth, following suit through a process of cellular change." (Ibid).

Siddha Yoga "The 'yoga of perfection'--a school of yoga formulated and developed by the late Swami Muktananda. In Siddha Yoga, according to Muktananda, the kundalini energy can be aroused in a devotee through the intervention of the guru." (Drury, 2002, 285).

"...In this [practice], a force referred to as *saktipat* ('descent of power') is said to activate the spiritual energy within the central nervous system." (*The Oxford Dictionary of World Religions*, 1997).

"Muktananda arrived in the USA at the invitation of Werner Erhard, founder of EST, in 1976 and established a center there. Today there are centers in over fifty countries and an estimated 40,000 devotees. There are few strict rules apart from daily meditation and vegetarianism." (Ibid).

Siddhi "yogic powers." (See Siddha). (*The Oxford Dictionary of World Religions*, 1997).

Siddhis "Magical powers believed attainable at certain stages of yoga practice and/or Kundalini awakening." (Judith, 1999, 418).

"In yoga, magical or mystical powers that arise in the practitioner who is advanced in the technique of self-realization, and has become a siddha (perfect master). Siddhis include levitation, the ability to increase in height, and the faculty of passing through solid objects unimpeded." (Drury, 2002, 285).

Simply Connected Space "A space in which any lasso can

be continuously shrunk to a point. Flat space is simply connected, while the surface of a doughnut or a wormhole is not." (Kaku, 2005, 398).

Singularity "A point in spacetime at which the spacetime curvature becomes infinite." (Hawking, 2001, 207).

"A state of infinity gravity. In general relativity, singularities are predicted to exist at the center of black holes and at the instant of creation, under very general conditions. They are thought to represent a breakdown of general relativity, forcing the introduction of a quantum theory of gravity." (Kaku, 2005, 398).

Singularity theorem "A theorem showing that a singularity, a point where general relativity breaks down, must exist under certain circumstances; in particular, that the universe must have started with a singularity." (Hawking, 2001, 207).

Sixth Sense "Popular term for extrasensory perception. It derives from the idea that the faculties of paranormal perception lie beyond the familiar five physical senses." (Drury, 2002, 287).

Social "1 of or relating to society or its organization; of or relating to rank and status in society: *a woman of high social standing*. 2 needing companionship; suited to living in communities. 3 relating to or designed for activities in which people meet each other for pleasure." (*The Concise Oxford Dictionary*, 1999).

Sociology "the study of the development, structure, and functioning of human society; the study of social problems." (*The Concise Oxford Dictionary*, 1999).

Solar Plexus "A large network of nerves found behind the stomach. The solar plexus is regarded in yoga as the seat of the chakra or energy center known as Manipura. According to Carlos Castaneda, it is also the source of the magical power of the shaman." (Drury, 2002, 289).

Solstice "(Origin ME: from OFr., from L. *solstitium*, from *sol* 'sun' + *stit-*, *sistere* 'stop, be stationary'). Each of the two times in the year, respectively at midsummer and midwinter, when the sun reaches its highest or lowest point in the sky at noon, marked by the longest and shortest days." (*The Concise Oxford Dictionary*, 1999).

South "In Western ceremonial magic, the direction associated with the element Fire. It is said to be ruled by the archangel Michael." (Drury, 2002, 290).

Spacetime "The union of space and time first articulated by special relativity." (Greene, 2004, 540).

Spatial dimension "Any of the three spacetime dimensions that are space-like." (Hawking, 2001, 207).

Special relativity "Einstein's theory in which space and time are not individually absolute, but instead depend upon the relative motion between distinct observers." (Greene, 2004, 540).

"Einstein's theory based on the idea that the laws of science should be the same for all observers, no matter how they are moving, in the absence of gravitational fields." (Hawking, 2001, 207).

"Einstein's 1905 theory, based on the constancy of the speed of light. Consequences include: time slows down, mass increases, and distances shrink the faster you move. Also, matter and energy are related via $E = mc^2$. One consequence of special relativity is the atomic bomb." (Kaku, 2005, 398).

Spectrum "The component frequencies that make up a wave. The visible part of the sun's spectrum can sometimes be seen as a rainbow." (Hawking, 2001, 207).

"The different colors or frequencies found within light. By analyzing the spectrum of starlight, one can determine that stars are mainly made of hydrogen and helium." (Kaku, 2005, 398).

"1 In our present system, an array of frequencies or wavelengths resulting from the dispersion of radiation. 2 A quanta range in one of the myriad levels of Light." (Hurtak, 1977, 604).

Spin "An internal property of elementary particles, related to but not identical to the everyday notion of spin." (Hawking, 2001, 207).

"Quantum mechanical property of elementary particles in which, somewhat like a top, they undergo rotational motion (they have intrinsic angular momentum)." (Greene, 2004, 540).

Spontaneous symmetry breaking "Technical name for the formation of a Higgs ocean; process by which a previously manifest symmetry is hidden or spoiled." (Greene, 2004, 540).

Standard Big Bang Theory "Theory describing a hot, expanding universe from a moment after its birth." (Greene, 2004, 537).

Standard Candle "A source of light that is standardized and the same throughout the universe, which allows scientists to calculate astronomical distances. The fainter a standard candle is, the farther away it is. Once we know the luminosity of a standard candle, we can calculate its distance. The standard candles used today are type Ia supernovae and Cepheid variables." (Kaku, 2005, 398).

Standard Model "Quantum mechanical theory composed of quantum chromodynamics and the electroweak theory; describes all matter and forces, except for gravity. Based on conception of point particles." (Greene, 2004, 540).

Standard Model of Particle Physics "A unifying theory for the three non-gravitational forces and their effects on matter." (Hawking, 2001, 207).

"The most successful quantum theory of the weak, electromagnetic, and strong interactions. It is based on the $SU(3)$ symmetry of quarks, the $SU(2)$ symmetry of electrons and neutrinos, and the $U(1)$ symmetry of light. It contains a large collection of particles: quarks, gluons, leptons, W- and Z-bosons, and Higgs particles. It cannot be the theory of everything because (a) it lacks any mention of gravity; (b) it has nineteen free parameters which have to be fixed by hand; and (c) it has three identical generations of quarks and leptons, which is redundant. The Standard Model can be absorbed into a GUT theory and eventually into string theory, but at present there is no experimental evidence for either." (Kaku, 2005, 398-399).

Star "1 a fixed luminous point in the night sky which is a large, remote incandescent body like the sun. 2 a stylized representation of a star, typically with five or more points; a star-shaped symbol indicating a category of excellence; used in names of starfishes and similar echinoderms, e.g. **cushion star**. 3 a famous or talented entertainer or sports players; an outstanding person or thing. 4 (Astrology) a planet, constellation, or configuration regarded as influencing one's fortunes or personality. (**stars**) a horoscope." (*The Concise Oxford Dictionary*, 1999).

Stationary state "A state that is not changing with time." (Hawking, 2001, 207).

Steady State Theory "The theory which states that the universe had no beginning but constantly generates new matter as it expands, keeping the same density. This theory has been discredited for various reasons, one being when the microwave background radiation was discovered. Also, it was found that quasars and galaxies have distinct evolutionary phases." (Kaku, 2005, 399).

String "A fundamental one-dimensional object in string theory that replaces the concept of structureless elementary particles. Different vibration patterns of a string give rise to elementary particles with different properties." (Hawking, 2001, 207).

String theory "A theory of physics in which particles are described as waves on strings; unites quantum mechanics and general relativity. Also known as superstring theory." (Hawking, 2001, 207).

"The theory based on tiny vibrating strings, such that each mode of vibration corresponds to a subatomic particle. It is the only theory that can combine gravity with the quantum theory, making it the leading candidate for a theory of everything. It is only mathematically self-consistent in ten dimensions. Its latest version is called M-theory, which is defined in eleven dimensions." (Kaku, 2005, 399).

Strong force "The strongest of the four fundamental forces, with the shortest range of all. It holds quarks together to form protons and neutrons and these particles together to form the atomic nucleus." (Hawking, 2001, 207).

Strong nuclear force "The force that binds the nucleus together. It is one of the four fundamental forces. Physicists use Quantum Chromodynamics to describe the strong interactions, based on quarks and gluons with $SU(3)$ symmetry." (Kaku, 2005, 399).

"Force of nature that influences quarks; holds quarks together inside protons and neutrons." (Greene, 2004, 540).

Subatomic particles "1 This term is applied to all particles of less than atomic mass, i.e., the elementary particles (boson, proton, neutron, electron, positron, neutrino, meson, and photons), alpha-particles, deuterons, as well as the antineutron, antineutrino, antiproton, etc., according to the *Keys of Enoch*. 2 Sub-nuclear family of particles including upsilon, tau and ze'on, etc., particles which define the immediate physical universe as a subset of the super-electron universe of Metatron." (Hurtak, 1977, 605-606).

Subconscious "In modern analytic psychology, that part of the mind which lies below the threshold of consciousness. It can be tapped using the techniques of guided imagery, hypnosis, automatic writing, automatic painting and drawing, and random association, and may be the origin of many of the phenomena reported spiritualistic seances." (Drury, 2002, 295).

Subliminal "That which is below the threshold of consciousness." (Drury, 2002, 295).

Subtle Body "(Skt., *linga sarira* or *suksma sarira*). In Indian religions, a non-physical body. This latter term refers to a classification of the subtle body in accordance with the *tattvas*, namely the five *tanmatras* or subtle elements (sound, touch, form, taste, and smell) and the *antah karana* or inner instrument (comprising *buddhi*, *ahamkara*, and *manas*). A Vedantic classification,

194

however, says that the subtle body comprises seventeen parts, namely the five pranas, ten organs of action and knowledge, manas, and buddhi." (*The Oxford Dictionary of World Religions*, 1997).

"In occultism, the etheric body, or 'subtle' counterpart of the physical body." (Drury, 2002, 295).

"Every energy system includes energy bodies beyond the chakras, some so numerous it is hard to count them all. In the classical Hindu system, there are three basic energy bodies, which interface with five sheaths, or *koshas*, that relate to the different levels of reality." (Dale, 2009, 281).

"The Taittiriya Upanishad describes five bodies or sheaths called *koshas* that 'cover' or contain our higher consciousness. The koshas are contained within three bodies of incarnation: subtle energy bodies that govern different levels of development and the koshas." (Ibid).

"The koshas constitute layers, or veils, that originate with the material body and transcend to the ethereal realm..." (Ibid).

"There are three bodies of incarnation (*sariras*) that correlate with the koshas. These are: 1 the gross body (*sthula sarira*), or physical body, which is composed of the five elements; 2 the subtle body (*suksma sarira*) that holds the chakras and the nadis; and 3 the causal body (*karana sarira*), the vehicle for our soul." (Dale, 2009, 282).

Subtle Planes "In Theosophy, mysticism, and occultism, the 'inner' or 'higher' planes of being, which are regarded as more 'subtle' than the plane of physical reality. In many cosmologies, the subtle planes are expressed as emanations from the Godhead (the 'grossest' and the furthest removed from the Spirit, being the level of the everyday world)." (Drury, 2002, 295).

Supergravity "A set of theories unifying general relativity and supersymmetry." (Hawking, 2001, 208).

Superior Planets "In astrology, those planets which lie outside Earth's orbit: Mars, Jupiter, Saturn, Uranus, Neptune, and Pluto." (Drury, 2002, 296).

Supernova "An exploding star. They are so energetic that they can sometimes outshine a galaxy. There are several types of supernovae, the most interesting being the type Ia supernova. They all can be used as standard candles to measure galactic distances. Type Ia supernovae are caused when an aging white dwarf star steals matter from its companion and is pushed beyond the Chandrasekhar limit, causing it to suddenly collapse and then blow up." (Kaku, 2005, 399).

Superstring theory "Theory in which fundamental ingredients are one-dimensional loops (closed strings) or snippets (open strings) of vibrating energy, which unites general relativity and quantum mechanics; incorporates supersymmetry." (Greene, 2004, 540).

Supersymmetry "A principle that relates the properties of particles of different spin." (Hawking, 2001, 208).

"The symmetry that interchanges fermions and bosons. This symmetry solves the hierarchy problem, and it also helps to eliminate any remaining divergencies within superstring theory. It means that all the particles in the Standard Model must have partners, called sparticles, which have so far never been seen in the laboratory. Supersymmetry in principle can unify all the particles of the universe into a single object." (Kaku, 2005, 399).

"A symmetry in which laws are unchanged when particles with a whole number amount of spin (force particle) are interchanged with particles that have half of a whole number amount of spin (matter particles)." (Greene, 2004, 540).

Sushumna "The central vertical nadi that connects all the chakras. To have a full Kundalini awakening, the energy must travel up the sushumna." (Judith, 1999, 419).

"In yoga, the primary nadi or energy channel in the body, corresponding with the spinal column. It is the only nadi that connects all the chakras, and is therefore regarded as the channel through which the kundalini is raised. Sushumna culminates in the supreme chakra, Sahasrara." (Drury, 2002, 297).

"...the chakras are connected by a non-physical channel running straight up the center of the body called the sushumna. Two alternate channels control the yin and yang energies, Ida and Pingala, twisting in figure-eight patterns around each chakra and running alongside the sushumna. These channels are among thousands of subtle energy channels called nadis, Sanskrit for 'flowing waters.' Ida and Pingala represent the luna and solar aspects, respectively." (Judith, 1999, 113-114).

"The central vertical nadi that connects all the chakras. To have a full Kundalini awakening, the energy must travel up the sushumna." (Ibid, 419).

Svadhisthana "The name for the second chakra, located in the abdomen and genital area. Early on the name meant 'to drink in sweetness,' from the root *svadha*, to relish, or sweeten. Later interpretations ascribe it to the root *svad*, meaning one's own, giving this chakra the name of 'one's own place.' Both are pertinent

196

to describing the second chakra." (Judith, 1999, 419).

"In yoga, the chakra located below the navel in the sacral region." (Drury, 2002, 297).

Symbiosis "(Origin C19: mod. Lat., from Gk. *sumbioun* 'live together', from *sumbios* 'companion'). (Biology) an interaction between two different organisms living in close physical association, especially to the advantage of both." (*The Concise Oxford Dictionary*, 1999).

Symmetry "the quality of being made up of exactly similar parts facing each other or around an axis; correct or pleasing proportion of parts; similarity or exact correspondence. (Physics & Mathematics) the property of being unchanged by a given operation or process." (*The Concise Oxford Dictionary*, 1999).

"A reshuffling or rearrangement of an object that leaves it invariant, or the same. Snowflakes are invariant under a rotation of a multiple of 60 degrees. Circles are invariant under a rotation of any angle. The quark model remains invariant under a reshuffling of the three quarks, giving $SU(3)$ symmetry. Strings are invariant under supersymmetry and also under conformal deformations of its surface. Symmetry is crucial in physics because it helps to eliminate many of the divergences found in quantum theory." (Kaku, 2005, 399-400).

Symmetry Breaking "The breaking of a symmetry found in the quantum theory. It is thought that the universe was in perfect symmetry before the big bang. Since then, the universe has cooled and aged, and hence the four fundamental forces and their symmetries have broken down. Today, the universe is horribly broken, with all the forces split off from each other." (Kaku, 2005, 400).

Synapse "(Origin C19: from Gk. *sunapsis*, from *sun-* 'together' + *hapsis* 'joining', from *haptein* 'to join'). A gap between two nerve cells, across which impulses pass by diffusion of a neurotransmitter." (*The Concise Oxford Dictionary*, 1999).

"An area of functional contact between nerve cells or between nerve cells and effectors such as muscle cells." (Sheldrake, 1995, 373).

Synchronicity "Term used by the Swiss psychoanalyst Carl Jung to describe 'meaningful coincidences'. In Jung's view, it was not uncommon for symbols of the unconscious mind to coincide in dreams or mystical experiences with events occurring in the waking world of physical reality. Jung believed that synchronicity provided a rationale for astrology and some forms of divination,

197

such as the *I Ching*." (Drury, 2002, 299).

Synchronous "1 existing or occurring at the same time. 2 of or denoting a satellite which revolves in its orbit in exactly the same time as the primary body rotates on its axis." (*The Concise Oxford Dictionary*, 1999).

Synergy "Interaction or cooperation of two or more organizations, substances, or other agents to produce a combined effect greater than the sum of their separate effects." (*The Concise Oxford Dictionary*, 1999).

Synthesis "1 the combination of components to form a connected whole. Often contrasted with **analysis**. 2 the production of chemical compounds by reaction from simpler materials. 3 (in Hegelian philosophy) the final stage in the process of dialectical reasoning, in which a new idea resolves the conflict between thesis and antithesis. 4 (Grammar) the process of making compound and derivative words." (*The Concise Oxford Dictionary*, 1999).

System "1. *The System*. The basic unit of the supergovernment consists of about one thousand inhabited and inhabitable worlds. Blazing suns, cold worlds, planets too near the suns, and other spheres not suitable for creature habitation are not included in this group. These one thousand worlds adapted to support life are called a system, but in the younger systems only a comparatively small number of these worlds may be inhabited. Each inhabited planet is presided over by a Planetary Prince, and each local system has an architectural sphere as its headquarters and is ruled by a System Sovereign." (*The Urantia Book*, 1955, 166:2).

Systems Theory "A form of holism concerned with the organization and properties of 'systems' at all levels of complexity. Much of the early inspiration for this approach came from an attempt to establish parallels between physiological systems in biology and social systems in the social sciences. The systems approach has been deeply influenced by cybernetics. The central metaphor in much systems thinking is the self-regulating machine." (Sheldrake, 1995, 373).

T

Tart, Charles T. "(b.1937) Internationally respected for his scientific research into trance, dreams, out-of-body experience, and extrasensory perception. Professor Tart is one of the number of contemporary scientists (others include Dr. Stanislav Grof and Dr. John Lilly), who have sought to close the gulf between science and mysticism. Tart has investigated the apparent astral projection faculties of Ingo Swann and Robert Monroe and has called for the recognition of 'state-specific sciences' (i.e. scientific systems that recognize the existence of different states of consciousness, each with their distinct types of 'reality'). Tart has written and compiled several important books, including *Altered States of Consciousness* (1969), *States of Consciousness* (1975), and *Transpersonal Psychologies* (1975)." (Drury, 2002, 301).

Telepathy "The paranormal acquisition of information about the thoughts, feelings, or activity of another conscious being." (Tart, 1997, 227).

"In parapsychology, the apparent ability of two people to communicate on a mind-to-mind basis, without recourse to speech or other normal channels of communication. Mental telepathy is one of the best-known and most widely accepted faculties of extrasensory perception." (Drury, 2002, 302).

Thanatos "(in Freudian theory) the death instinct. Often contrasted with Eros." (*The Concise Oxford Dictionary*, 1999).

Thermodynamics "The study of the relationship between energy, work, heat, and entropy in a dynamical physical system." (Hawking, 2001, 208).

"The physics of heat. There are three laws of thermodynamics: 1. The total amount of matter and energy is conserved; 2. Total entropy always increases; and 3. You cannot reach absolute zero. Thermodynamics is essential to understanding how the universe might die." (Kaku, 2005, 400).

Theta Brain-Wave State "An altered state of consciousness demonstrated by intuitive, superconsciousness, and out-of-body awareness; brain-wave activity of 4-8 Hz." (Backman, 20009, 233).

Third Eye "(Skt. '*Ajna*'). 1 It is associated with the pineal gland which is considered a rudimentary eye. The awakening of this chakra constitutes the beginning of the spiritual journey to oneness, the beginning of cosmic consciousness. As it develops, it joins with the chakras directly above it as a stem and flower. The turaya or pathway of the third eye should not be confused with the multitude of eyes of self-realized beings, nor with the higher Crown Chakra (*sahasrara*), the Thousand-petaled Lotus, associated with the eighth and ninth chakras of the higher self, and ninth through twelfth chakras of the Overself. 2 The chakra center connected with the intellect and the receiving of information." (Hurtak, 1977, 607).

"Expression made popular by the mystical author Lobsang Rampa, whose book *The Third Eye* was an international bestseller. The third eye is the sixth of the seven chakras in Kundalini Yoga, and is located between and slightly above the eyebrows, as the

199

center of the forehead. It is sometimes linked to the pineal gland, which is regarded by occultists as the seat of psychic and paranormal powers." (Drury, 2002, 306-307).

Thought "Thought may be considered as an energy of scalar potential, the directional seed of an expression of energy that may or may not materialize as a real or vector event. A virtual assembling of your experience, thought provides the guidance system, the direction, for where the energy of your attention may be directed." (Braden, 1993, 195).

Time "(n.) 1 the indefinite continued progress of existence and events in the past, present, and future, regarded as a whole. 2 a point of time as measured in hours and minutes past midnight or noon; the favorable or appropriate moment to do something: *it was time to go*. (**a time**) an indefinite period: *he worked for a time as a gardener*. (also **times**) a more or less definite portion of time characterized by particular events or circumstances: *Victorian times*. (**one's time**) a period regarded as characteristic of a particular stage of one's life; the length of time taken to run a race or complete an activity. (informal) a prison sentence; an apprenticeship. 3 (Brit.) The moment at which the opening hours of a public house end. (Baseball & American Football) a moment at which play stops temporarily within a game. 4 time as allotted, available, or used: *a waste of time*. 5 the normal rate of pay for time spent working: *they are paid time and a half*. 6 an instance of something happening or being done: *the nurse came in four times a day*. 7 (**times**) (following a number) expressing multiplication. 8 the rhythmic pattern or tempo of a piece of music. 8 the rhythmic pattern or tempo of a piece of music. (v.) 1 arrange a time for; perform at a particular time. 2 measure the time taken by. 3 (**time something out**) Computing (of a computer or a program) cancel an operation automatically because a predefined interval of time has passed. 4 (**times**) (informal) multiply (a number)." (*The Concise Oxford Dictionary*, 1999).

Time dilation "A feature of special relativity predicting that the flow of time will slow for an observer in motion, or in the presence of a strong gravitational field." (Hawking, 2001, 208).

Time loop "Another name for a closed time-like curve." (Hawking, 2001, 208).

Time-reversal symmetry "Property of the accepted laws of nature in which laws make no distinction between one direction in time and the other. From any given moment, the laws treat past and future in exactly the same way." (Greene, 2004, 541).

Time Warp "1 **Space-time warps**: Within the galaxy, the coordinates of electrical and magnetic grids connected with electromagnetic geometries around the Earth and natural time warp areas on the surface of the planet. A universal space-filling lattice. 2 **Natural time warps**: On meteorological and geological maps, points of space anomalies, forming a dodecahedral energy map of the Earth. A magnetic grid system on the planet similar to the major acupuncture points of the human body. Architectural vortices which interfere with the celestial influences so as to produce different levels of magnetic phenomena. Points at which planetary energy currents affect not only the magnetic currents of the Earth's surface, but energy layers of the Earth deep below. The major vortex over the Takla Makan area of Sinkiang is the largest configuration used by the Brotherhood of Light." (Hurtak, 1977, 608).

Trance, Hypnotic "An altered state of consciousness in which a subject's powers of concentration are mobilized, and subconscious memories and perceptions brought to the surface. Hypnotherapists relax their subjects progressively, often by using a countdown of numbers or by progressively relaxing the body limb by limb from the feet to the head. The pioneering European hypnotherapists recognized the value of the imagination for therapeutic purposes, and combined relaxation techniques with guided imagery. For example, Alfred Binet encouraged his patients to 'talk' to the visual images that arose in what he called 'provoked introspection', and Wolfgang Kretschmer described the process in 1922 as *bilderstrei-fenderken*--'thinking in the form of a movie'. For Kretschmer, hypnotic trance could be used to 'expose internal psychic problems' that presented themselves in the consciousness of the subject." (Drury, 2002, 309).

Trance, Shamanic "In pre-literate religion, a type of trance state characterized by the journey of the soul. The shaman undertakes this journey in order to obtain information, and sometimes visionary insights, from the gods of creation whose rules and taboos govern society. The shaman enters the magical dimensions in a state of sensory deprivation (usually total darkness) and often uses percussion instruments to establish a rhythm that is used to propel him on his vision-quest. Shamanic trance differs from mediumistic trance to the extent that the shaman returns with full knowledge of his visionary journey and is able to report on his encounter with the gods. The deities do not 'possess' the shaman as they do in mediumism, although in some shamanic initiations

201

the body of the shaman is transformed by the gods in order to bestow supernatural powers." (Drury, 2002, 310).

Translation invariance, translational symmetry "Property of accepted laws of nature in which the laws are applicable at any location in space." (Greene, 2004, 541).

Transpersonal "of, denoting, or dealing with states of consciousness beyond the limits of personal identity." (*The Concise Oxford Dictionary*, 1999).

"Transpersonal experiences can be defined as experiential expansion or extension of consciousness beyond the usual boundaries of the body-ego and beyond the limitations of time and space. They cover an extremely wide range of phenomena which occur on different levels of reality; in a sense, the entire spectrum of transpersonal experiences is commensurate with existence itself." (Grof, 1988, 38).

"To create a transpersonal taxonomy that would reflect in an accurate and comprehensive way the introspective date and objective observations from modern consciousness research is not an easy task. The spectrum of transpersonal experiences is not only extremely rich, ramified, and variegated, but includes levels of reality governed by laws and principles that are different from those that rule ordinary reality. Many transpersonal experiences, being ineffable, elude adequate verbal descriptions and occur on levels of reality where these very aspects that could ordinarily serve as *principia divisionis*, such as time, space, duality, and polarity, or linear causality, are transcended. The problem is further complicated by the holographic nature of consciousness and mutual interpenetration of its different levels and domain." (Ibid, 40).

Transpersonal Psychology "Name given to the so-called 'fourth force' in psychology. Transpersonal psychology follows on from 'first force' classical psychoanalytical theory; 'second force' behavioristic psychology; and 'third force' humanistic psychology. It deals with such areas of human consciousness as self-transcendence, peak experience, mystical transformation, and ultimate values. The term 'transpersonal' itself refers to that which transcends the ego, and thus implies a sympathy for mystical and paranormal topics and ideas. The term was first used in a lecture in 1967 by the psychiatrist Dr. Stanislav Grof, and became the title of the new psychological movement following a proposal by Abraham Maslow and Anthony Sutich." (Drury, 2002, 310-311).

"The Transpersonal Movement is closely associated with

202

Esalen Institute." (Ibid).

Tunneling "The process by which particles can penetrate barriers that are forbidden by Newtonian mechanics. Tunneling is the reason for radioactive alpha decay and is a by-product of the quantum theory. The universe itself may have been created by tunneling. It has been conjectured that one may be able to tunnel between universes." (Kaku, 2005, 400).

"Also called 'tunneling effect.' 1 A quantum effect that permits a particle that obeys quantum mechanical laws to traverse energy barriers that contradict classical mechanics and thermodynamics. 2 By analogy, a process that permits the crossing of barriers or the connecting of regions, that are usually considered impossible. 3 A process used for electro-fusion." (Hurtak, 1977, 609).

Type Ia Supernova "A supernova that is often used as a standard candle to measure distances. This supernova takes place in a double star system, where a white dwarf star slowly sucks matter from a companion star, pushing it over the Chandrasekhar limit of 1.4 solar masses, causing it to explode." (Kaku, 2005, 400).

U

Ultimaton "Matter-energy--for they are but diverse manifestations of the same cosmic reality, as a universe phenomenon is inherent in the Universal Father. 'In him all things consist.' Matter may appear to manifest inherent energy and to exhibit self-contained powers, but the lines of gravity involved in the energies concerned in all these physical phenomena are derived from, and are dependent on, Paradise. The *ultimaton*, the first measurable form of energy, has Paradise as its nucleus." (*The Urantia Book*, 1955, 467:4).

"...These *ultimaton* energies escape out into space, to engage in the adventure of electronic association and energy materialization, as a veritable energy blast during adolescent solar times." (465:1).

"The power centers and their associates are much concerned in the work of transmuting the *ultimaton* into the circuits and revolutions of the electron. These unique beings control and compound power by their skillful manipulation of the basic units of materialized energy, the *ultimatons*..." (473:1).

Uncertainty Principle "The principle formulated by Heisenberg that one can never be exactly sure of both the position and the velocity of a particle. The more accurately one knows the one, the less accurately one can know the other." (Hawking, 2001, 208).

203

"The principle which states that you cannot know both the location and velocity of a particle with infinite precision. The uncertainty in the position of a particle, multiplied by the uncertainty in its momentum, must be greater than or equal to Planck's constant divided by $2\prod$. The uncertainty principle is the most essential component of the quantum theory, introducing probability into the universe. Because of nanotechnology, physicists can manipulate individual atoms at will and hence test the uncertainty principle in the laboratory." (Kaku, 2005, 400).

"Property of quantum mechanics in which there is a fundamental limit on how precisely certain complementary physical features can be measured or specified." (Greene, 2004, 541).

Unified Field Theory "The theory sought by Einstein that would unify all the forces of nature into a single coherent theory. Today, the leading candidate is string theory or M-theory. Einstein originally believed that his unified field theory could absorb both relativity and the quantum theory into a higher theory that would not require probabilities. String theory, however, is a quantum theory and hence introduces probabilities." (Kaku, 2005, 400-401).

Unified theory "Any theory which describes all four forces and all of matter within a single framework." (Hawking, 2001, 208).

"A theory that describes all forces and all matter in a single theoretical structure." (Greene, 2004, 541).

Urantia The spiritual or God's name for planet Earth. (*The Urantia Book*, 1955, 1:1).

"In the minds of the mortals of Urantia--that being the name of your world..." (1:1).

"Your world, Urantia, is one of many similar planets which compromise the local universe of Nebadon. This universe, together with similar creations, makes up the superuniverse of Orvonton, from whose capital, Uversa, our commission hails. Orvonton is one of the seven evolutionary superuniverses of time and space which circle the never-beginning, never-ending creation of divine perfection--the central universe of Havona. At the heart of this eternal and central universe is the stationary Isle of Paradise, the geographic center of infinity and the dwelling place of the eternal God." (1:5).

V

Vacuum "Empty space. But empty space, according to the quantum theory, is teeming with virtual subatomic particles, which last only a fraction of a second. The vacuum is also used to describe the lowest energy of a system. The universe, it is believed, went from a state of a false vacuum to the true vacuum of today." (Kaku, 2005, 401).

"The emptiest that a region can be; the state of lowest energy." (Greene, 2004, 541).

Vacuum energy "Energy that is present even in apparently empty space. It has curious property that unlike the presence of mass, the presence of vacuum energy would cause the expansion of the universe to speed up." (Hawking, 2001, 208).

Velocity "A number describing the speed and direction of an object's motion." (Hawking, 2001, 208).

"The speed and direction of an object's motion." (Greene, 2004, 541).

Virtual Particles "In quantum mechanics, a particle that can never be directly detected, but whose existence does have measurable effects." (Hawking, 2001, 208).

"Particles that briefly dart in and out of the vacuum. They violate known conservation laws but only for a short period of time, via the uncertainty principle. The conservation laws then operate as an average in the vacuum. Virtual particles can sometimes become real particles if enough energy is added to the vacuum. On a microscope scale, these virtual particles may include wormholes and baby universes." (Kaku, 2005, 401).

Vision "In mysticism, an altered state of consciousness or peak experience, in which sacred images dominate one's perception and are accompanied by feelings of awe, mystery, and transcendence. On a less profound level, mental images and visions may appear during...session of guided imagery. Mystical visions usually have archetypal content and arise from the spiritual areas of the psyche." (Drury, 2002, 322).

Vital Force "The life-force, which resides in all living things and which, in mystical and occult traditions, is presumed to be the source of health and vitality. If the life-force is blocked from the organism, disease results and eventually death ensues. The life-force is known variously as ch'i (Taoism); ki (Japanese Buddhism); and prana (Hinduism)." (Drury, 2002, 322).

Vissuddha "Literally, purification; the name for the fifth chakra, located at the throat...Major Indian male deity, one of the major triad (Brahma, Visnu, Shiva), known as the Pervader and partner to Lakshmi." (Judith, 1999, 420).

W

W and Z particles "The messenger particles of the weak nuclear force." (Greene, 2004, 541).

Water "One of the four alchemical elements, the others being Earth, Fire, and Air. The spirits of water are known as undines and mermaids, or mermen. The three astrological signs linked to water are Cancer, Scorpio, and Pisces." (Drury, 2002, 324).

Wave function "A fundamental concept in quantum mechanics; a number at each point in space associated with a particle, determining the probability that the particle is to be found at that position." (Hawking, 2001, 208).

"A wave that accompanies every subatomic particle. It is the mathematical description of the wave probability locating the position of any particle. Schrodinger was the first to write down the equations for the wave function of an electron. In the quantum theory, matter is composed of point particles, but the probability of finding the particle is given by the wave function. Dirac later proposed a wave equation which included special relativity. Today, all of quantum physics, including string theory, is formulated in terms of these waves." (Kaku, 2005, 401).

Wave/particle duality "The concept in quantum mechanics that there is no distinction between waves and particles; particles may behave like waves and vice versa." (Hawking, 2001, 208).

Wavelength "The distance between two adjacent troughs or two adjacent peaks of a wave." (Hawking, 2001, 208).

Wave force "The second weakest of the four fundamental forces, with a very short range. It affects all matter particles, but not force-carrying particles." (Hawking, 2001, 208).

Weak nuclear force "The force within the nucleus that makes possible nuclear decay. This force is not strong enough to hold the nucleus together, hence the nucleus can fall apart. The weak force acts on leptons (electrons and neutrinos) and is carried by the W- and Z-bosons." (Kaku, 2005, 401).

"Forces of nature, acting on subatomic scales, and responsible for phenomena such as radioactive decay." (Greene, 2004, 541).

West "In Western ceremonial magic, the direction associated with the element Water. It is said to be ruled by the archangel Gabriel." (Drury, 2002, 325).

White dwarf "A star in its final stages of life, consisting of lower elements such as oxygen, lithium, carbon, and so forth. They are found after a red giant exhausts its helium fuel and collapses. Typically, they are about the size of Earth and weigh no more than 1.4 solar masses (or else they collapse)." (Kaku, 2005, 401).

Wilber, Ken "(b.1949) A practitioner of Buddhist meditation, American author and philosopher Ken Wilber is a leading transpersonal theorist and has been acclaimed by many as 'the long-sought Einstein of consciousness research'. A prolific author and former editor-in-chief of *ReVision*, Wilber has sought to develop a unified theory of consciousness, encompassing the world's great psychological, philosophical and spiritual traditions. His many books include *The Spectrum of Consciousness*; *No Boundary*; *The Holographic Paradigm*; *Sex, Ecology and Spirituality*; and *A Brief History of Everything*." (Drury, 2002, 327).

WIMP "Weakly interacting massive particle. WIMPs are conjectured to make up most of dark matter in the universe. One leading candidate for the WIMPs are the sparticles predicted by string theory." (Kaku, 2005, 401).

Wormhole "A thin tube of spacetime connecting distant regions of the universe. Wormholes may also link parallel or baby universes and could provide the possibility of time travel." (Hawking, 2001, 208).

"A passageway between two universes. Mathematicians call these spaces 'multiply connected spaces'--spaces in which a lasso may not be shrunk to a point. It is not clear if one may be able to pass through a wormhole without destabilizing it or dying in the attempt." (Kaku, 2005, 401).

"1 Spirals interconnecting the electron and sub-electron spaces as subtle units of the super-electron. 2 A singularity where the matter-energy construct is warped to yield another space-time continuum. The wormhole effects are found in any media where the rotating 'magnetic fields' propagate faster than the speed of light and which increase in proportion to distance." (Hurtak, 1977, 612).

X

Xenoglossy "A term coined in the 19th cent. by French parapsychologist Charles Richet (1850-1935) and is the ability to speak in a foreign language not previously learned by any normal process. This rare phenomenon is often confused with glossolalia, or Speaking in Tongues, the ecstatic language spoken by Pentecostals and Charismatics as they pray. Glossolalia is most commonly concerned with speaking a kind of proto-language derived from the language already spoken by individuals." (Melton, 2008, 359).

"There are a variety of reports of xenoglossy throughout history. For example, the possessed nuns at the famous convent at Loudon were said to speak several languages, which was seen as an indication of their dealings with Satan. Then, during the 19th cent.,

207

accounts of Spiritualist mediums speaking in foreign tongues while in a trance led researchers of the paranormal to investigate. John W. Edmonds (1799-1874), a prominent judge and early convert to Spiritualism, claimed in the 1850s that his daughter could converse with spirits in a variety of languages. The most-well-documented case of xenoglossy, however, concerned Swiss medium Helene Smith (1861-1929), who falsely claimed to speak the Martian language." (Ibid).

"In the 20th cent., many claims involving xenoglossy stemmed from studies into reincarnation in which a person supposedly recalled a language spoken in a previous life. The most impressive evidence for such cases was compiled by University of Virginia psychiatrist Ian Stevenson (b.1918). Typical of Stevenson's cases is that of Uttara (b.1941), a Marathi-speaking woman from India. In 1974 she began to speak Bengali after her personality was taken over by someone who called herself Sharada. Bengali was unknown to Uttara or to members of her family. Sharada claimed to have lived early in the 19th cent. Besides speaking Bengali, Sharada could also write it." (Ibid).

"Stevenson's research remains the most substantial body of evidence in support of xenoglossy to date. He has offered his research as further evidence of reincarnation, which is an important facet of many alternative religions. Critics assume that xenoglossy must have a more mundane explanation, though no one has yet produced a convincing refutation of Stevenson's work." (Ibid).

Y

Yoga "Literally, yoke; a system of philosophy and techniques designed to link mind and body, and individual self to universal or god-self. There are many forms and practices of yoga: Bhakti, Hatha, Jnana, Karma, Tantra, Mantra, Yantra, and Pranayama." (Judith, 1999, 420).

"From the Skt. *yuj*, 'to bind together', Hindu spiritual teachings and techniques related to the attainment of self-realization and union with Brahman, the supreme reality. The four main concepts underlying the Hindu spiritual tradition are karma, the law of causality which links people to the universe; maya, the illusion of the manifested world; nirvana, absolute reality beyond illusion; and yoga, as the means of gaining liberation from the senses. Because people tend to confuse feelings and thoughts with 'spirit', a means has to be found to overcome these sensory limitations. Yoga is thus a means of training to see things as they are, rather than as they seem. One of the basic techniques in yoga is

208

therefore meditation, since this turns one's consciousness towards the inner reality and finally towards transcendence in samadhi." (Drury, 2002, 334-335).

"(Skt., 'yoking', 'joining'). The means or techniques for transforming consciousness and attaining liberation (*moksa*) from karma and rebirth (*samsara*) in Indian religions. The mind (*manas*, *citta*) is thought to be constantly fluctuation, but through yoga it can be focused, one-pointedness (*ekagrata*) developed, and higher states of consciousness (*samadhi*) experienced. Such control of consciousness, which is taught by a guru, also results in the attainment of paranormal powers (*siddha*)." (*The Oxford Dictionary of World Religions*, 1997).

"It is probable (though not agreed) that yoga is of non-Vedic origin. This is indicated by seals of the Indus Valley Civilization (2500-1500 B.C.E.) depicting a horned, sometimes ithyphallic, figure sitting in a posture resembling a yoga *asana*. A further indication of non-Vedic origin is found in the Kesin hymn of the *Rg Veda* (10.136) which describes a figure resembling a yogin--long-haired, naked, silent (*muni*)--in contrast to the Vedic *rsi*. There is, however, also evidence of Vedic influence, as there is clear documentation of *tapas* in the *Rg Veda* (8.59.6), a force which is later thought to be generated by yoga. Also the *Atharva Veda* describes an Aryan group called the Vratyas who practiced austerities and breathing exercises suggestive of yogic breath-control (*pranayama*)." (Ibid).

"Techniques of meditative absorption (*dhyana, samdhi*) were developed in the Sramana tradition which constrained Jainism and Buddhism, emphasizing control of consciousness as the means of liberation. Although the early Upanishads speak of the interiorization of the sacrifice, the actual term 'yoga' and technical terms such as asana do not appear until the late Upanishads (500 B.C.E. onwards). For example, the *Svetasvatara Upanisad* (11.8-9) clearly states the idea of controlling the mind through the control of body and breath (*prana*): 'Suppressing the breaths, with controlled movement, he should breath through his nostrils with diminished breath. Let the wise man vigilantly restrain his mind as he would a chariot yoked to bad horses.' The text goes on to describe the kind of place conducive to yoga and describes the forms or visions which appear in the yogin's mind prior to the realization of Brahman. One who practices yoga achieves a transformed body, 'made in the fire of yoga', which is beyond old age, sickness, and death (*Svetasvatara Upanisad* 2.12). Yoga becomes

209

systematized into various stages. *Maitri Upanisad* (6.18-19) describes a six fold yoga comprising the stages of breath control (*pranayama*), sense-withdrawal (*pratyahara*), meditation (*dhyana*), concentration (*dharana*), contemplative inquiry (*tarka*), and absorption (*samadhi*)." (Ibid).

"Classical yoga is referred to as one of the six systems of Indian philosophy (*darsana*). Expressed in Patanjali's *Yoga Sutra* (2nd-3rd centuries C.E.) it represents a refinement of ideas and practices found in the Upanishads. Patanjali states the goal of yoga to be quite simply 'cessation of mental fluctuation' (*cittavrtti nirodha*) which results in higher levels of consciousness or absorptions (*samadhi*) and the purification of the self (atman). The *Yoga Sutra* advocates *raja* or eightfold (*astanga*) yoga which comprises the same stages as in the *Maitri Upanisad*, only adding restraint (*yama*), discipline (*niyama*), and posture (*asana*), and dropping tarka. Classical yoga is closely allied with Samkhya which provides its theoretical underpinning, though Yoga differs from Samkhya in that it is theistic, that is, it accepts God (*Isvara*) as an object of consciousness; and Patanjali uses such terms as purusa and prakrti in ways different from Samkhya." (Ibid).

"The *Bhagavad-gita* addresses yoga specifically, in that here Krishna is the object of the yogin's mediation. The *Gita* advocates there kinds of yoga, karma yoga, the performance of action without attachment to its result, jnana yoga, knowledge of God, and bhakti yoga, devotion to God (which the *Gita* evidently regards as the highest)." (Ibid).

"Yoga became associated with the theistic traditions of Vaisnavism, Saivism, and Saktism, the object of meditation becoming the deities of those traditions. During this period (900-1600 C.E.) various yoga techniques were developed along with ideas about the physiology of the subtle body (*linga/suksma sarira*)-- for example in the Yoga Upanishads. The Nath tradition developed Hatha yoga., though the latter is not confined to this one tradition. Nath texts such as the *Hathayogapradipika*, *Gheranda Samhita*, and *Siddha Siddhanta Paddhati* are syncretistic, dealing with subtle physiology, pranayama, samadhi, Kundalini yoga, siddhi, and the attaining of a divine (*divya*) or perfected body (*siddha deha*), not subject to decay and death. The yoga of Tantrism includes these ideas, but places particular emphasis on practices involving sound and vision, that is the visualization of mandalas, yantras, and deities (*devata*), mantra, and kundalini yoga. Tantrism also uses sexual intercourse (*maithuna*) as a form of yoga." (Ibid).

210

"Today yoga is an integral part of Hinduism. Important modern Hindus have advocated various kinds of yoga. For example, Aurobindo advocated a form of Tantric yoga, calling it Integral Yoga, Ramakrishna practiced bhakti yoga, and Ramana Marharshi the yoga of knowing the identity of the self and God." (Ibid).

Yoga Sutra "The text of classical yoga attributed to Patanjali and composed during the 2nd or 3rd century CE. The text comprises 195 aphorisms (*sutras*) and is divided into four sections (*pada*) on (i) *samadhi* or concentration, (ii) *sadhana* or practice, (iii) *vibhuti* or magical powers, and (iv) *kaivalya*, the condition of isolation or freedom. The *Sutra* is a systematic exposition of the theory and practice of eight-limbed (*astanga*) or raja yoga, using a highly developed technical vocabulary and assuming *Samkhya* metaphysics. There are many commentaries on the text though these may not be of the same school as Patanjali. The oldest commentary is the *Yoga Sutra-bhasya* of Vyasa (5th century) which throws light on many obscure sutras; Vacaspatimisra wrote a sub-commentary, *Tattvavaisaradi* (*c*.850-*c*.950 CE); the Saiva king Bhoja wrote a commentary, *Rajamartanda* (1000-1050); and the Persian scholar al-Biruni (11th century) translated the sutra into Arabic which may have influenced Persian mysticism. Finally Vijnanabhiksu annotated Vyasa in the *Yoga-varttika* (*c*.1550) from a Vedantic viewpoint." (*The Oxford Dictionary of World Religions*, 1997).

Yogi "(Skt., 'one who is joined'). A participant in one of the schools of Yoga. More casually, the word is used of Hindu ascetics in general." (*The Oxford Dictionary of World Religions*, 1997).

"A male practitioner of yoga." (Drury, 2002, 335).

Yogini "A female practitioner of yoga." (Drury, 2002, 335).

Yoni "Female genitalia; sometimes depicted or worshiped in the form of a chalice; counterpart to lingam worship." (Judith, 1999, 420).

Z

Z particle "A particle that is identical to the photon in all properties except mass." (Hurtak, 1977, 612).

Ze "1 Light polarization which can mediate between the body of consciousness and its divine double. 2 A divine Light projection which triggers bio-computing in the physical manifestations of Z^0." (Hurtak, 1977, 614).

Ze'on "Through-particles needed to expand, contract and do omnidirectional world with the Higher Evolution. A quanta of Light particles responsible for the basic control of combined magnetic and electrostatic fields, etc., necessary for the exchange of the paradigms controlling physical-spiritual fusion." (Hurtak, 1977, 614).

Zero Point Field (ZPF) "The amount of vibrational energy associated with matter, as the parameters defining that matter decline to zero. To an observer, the world of Zero Point appears to be very still, while the participant experiences a quantum restructuring of the very boundaries that define the experience. Earth and our bodies are preparing for the Zero Point experience of change, collectively known by the ancients as The Shift of the Ages." (Braden, 1993, 195).

Bibliography & Recommended Reading

"Akasha." *Wikipedia*. http://en.wikipedia.org/wiki/Akasha accessed June 27, 2013.

"Applied kinesiology." *Wikipedia*. http://en.wikipedia.org/wiki/Applied_kinesiology accessed April 26, 2014).

Arguelles, Jose. 1996. *The Mayan Factor: Path Beyond Technology*. Rochester, VT: Bear & Company.

_____. 2011. *Manifesto for the Noosphere: The Next Stage in the Evolution of Human Consciousness*. Berkeley, CA: Evolver Editions.

Arrien, Angeles. 1993. *The Four-Fold Way: Walking the Paths of the Warrior, Teacher, Healer, and Visionary*. San Francisco, CA: HarperSanFrancisco, a Division of HarperCollins Publishers.

Atwater, P. M. H. 2007. *The Big Book of Near-Death Experiences: The Ultimate Guide to What Happens When We Die*. Charlottesville, VA: Hampton Roads Publishing Co, Inc.

Aveni, Anthony F. 2000. *Between the Lines: The Mystery of the Giant Ground Drawings of Ancient Nasca, Peru*. Austin, TX: University of Texas Press.

Backman, Linda. 2009. *Bringing Your Soul to Life: Healing Through Past Lives and the Time Between*. Woodbury, MN: Llewellyn Publications.

Bailey, Alice A. 1934. *A Treatise on White Magic or The Way of the Disciple*. 10th ed., 1970, New York: Lucis Publishing Co.

Barrow, John D. 2011. *The Book of Universes: Exploring the Limits of the Cosmos*. New York, NY: W. W. Norton & Company.

Barnstone, Willis, and Marvin Meyer, eds. 2003. *The Gnostic Bible*. Boston, MA: Shambhala Publications, Inc.

Bateson, Gregory. 2002. *Mind and Nature: A Necessary Unity*. Cresskill, NJ: Hampton Press, Inc., and the Institute of Intercultural Studies.

Baumbach, Gerald F., et al. 1995. *Coming to the Church*. NY: William H Sadlier.

Barfield, Arthus Owen. 2010. *The Case for Anthroposophy*. Oxford, England: Barfield Press UK.

Barrett, Francis. 1989. *The Magus: A Complete System of Occult Philosophy*. 1st Carol Publishing Group edition, New York, NY: Citadel Press Book, Carol Publishing Group.

Beck, Peggy V., Anna Lee Walters, and Nia Francisco. 1977. *The Sacred Ways of Knowledge, Sources of Life*. 5th printing, redesigned 1996 edition, Tsaile, AZ: Navajo Community College Press.

Berger, Peter L. 1967. *The Sacred Canopy: Elements of a Sociological Theory of Religion*. Anchor Books 1990 edition, New York, NY: Anchor Books, a Division of Random House, Inc.

213

Bernbaum, Edwin. 1997. *Sacred Mountains of the World*. Berkeley and Los Angeles, CA: Univ. of California Press.

Bingham, Hiram. 1948. *Lost City of the Incas: The Story of Machu Picchu and Its Builders*. Reprint 1981, Westport, CT: Greenwood Press.

Blackburn, Simon. 1994. *Oxford Dictionary of Philosophy*. 2nd edition revised 2008, New York, NY: Oxford University Press.

Blakeslee, Thomas R. 1980. *The Right Brain: A New Understanding of the Unconscious Mind and Its Creative Powers*. Garden City, NY: Anchor Press/Doubleday.

Blavatsky, Helena P. 1972. *Isis Unveiled: Secrets of the Ancient Wisdom Tradition; Madame Blavatsky's First Work*. An abridgement by Michael Gomes, Quest 1997 edition, Wheaton, IL: Theosophical Pub. House.

Bohm, David. 1965. *The Special Theory of Relativity*. Routledge Classics 2006 edition, New York, NY: Routledge.

_____. 1980. *Wholeness and the Implicate Order*. Routledge Classics 2002 edition, reprint 2007, New York, NY: Routledge.

_____. 1992. *Thought as a System*. Reprint 2007, New York, NY: Routledge.

Bohm, David and F. David Peat. 1987. *Science, Order, and Creativity*. Reprint, 2007, New York, NY: Routledge.

Bohm, D. and B. J. Hiley. 1993. *The Undivided Universe: An Ontological Interpretation of Quantum Theory*. Reprint 2005, New York, NY: Routledge.

"Book of Enoch." *Wikipedia*. http://en.wikipedia.org/Book_of_enoch accessed November 11, 2011.

Boorstein, Sylvia. 2014. "Developing Insight," ," *A Beginner's Guide to Meditation: Practical Advice and Inspiration from Contemporary Buddhist Teachers*. Edited by Rod Meade Sperry. Boston, MA: Shambhala Publications, Inc.

Bourne, Edmund J. 2008. *Global Shift: How a New Worldview is Transforming Humanity*. Oakland, CA: New Harbinger Publications, Inc. and Noetic Books.

Bowker, John. 2002. *God: A Brief History*. 1st American edition, 2002, New York, NY: DK Publishing, Inc.

Braden, Gregg. 1993. *Awakening to Zero Point: The Collective Initiation*. 1997 revised edition, Bellevue, WA: Radio Bookstore Press.

_____. 1997. *Walking Between the Worlds: The Science of Compassion*. Bellevue, WA: Radio Bookstore Press.

_____. 2007. *The Divine Matrix: Bridging Time, Space, Miracles, and Belief*. Carlsbad, CA: Hay House, Inc.

_____. 2011. *Deep Truth: Igniting the Memory of Our Origin,*

214

History, Destiny, and Fate. Carlsbad, CA: Hay House, Inc.

Braud, William. 1997. "Parapsychology and Spirituality Implications and Intimations," *Body Mind Spirit: Exploring the Parapsychology of Spirituality.* Charles T. Tart, ed. Charlottesville, VA: Hampton Roads Pub. Co.

Braude, Stephen E. 1997. "Some Thoughts on Parapsychology and Religion," *Body Mind Spirit: Exploring the Parapsychology of Spirituality.* Charles T. Tart, ed. Charlottesville, VA: Hampton Roads Pub. Co.

Brennan, Barbara. 1997. *Reading Auras.* New York: Barbara Brennan School of Healing, Pamphlet.

Brennan, Barbara Ann. 1993. *Light Emerging: The Journey of Personal Healing.* New York: Bantam Books.

Bruyere, Rosalyn L. 1994. *Wheels of Light: Chakras, Auras, and the Healing Energy of the Body.* New York, NY: A Fireside Book, Simon & Schuster.

Bunick, Nick. 1998. *In God's Truth.* Charlottesville, VA: Hampton Roads Publishing Company, Inc.

Campbell, Joseph. 1949. *The Hero with a Thousand Faces.* Princeton, 3rd printing 1973, NJ: Princeton University Press.

Campbell, Joseph and Bill Moyers. 1988. *The Power of Myth.* First Anchor Books edition, July 1991, New York: Anchor Books/Doubleday, a div. of Bantam Doubleday Dell Publishing Group, Inc.

Capra, Fritjof. 1975. *The Tao of Physics: An Exploration of the Parallels Between Modern Physics and Eastern Mysticism.* 2000 edition, Boston, MA: Shambhala Publications, Inc.

_____. 1982. *The Turning Point: Sciences, Society, and the Rising Culture.* 6th printing, 1988 edition, New York, NY: Bantam Books, Simon & Schuster.

_____. 1996. *The Web of Life: A New Scientific Understanding of Living Systems.* 1st Anchor Books Trade Paperback edition, 1997, New York, NY: Anchor Books, a Division of Random House, Inc.

_____. 2002. *The Hidden Connections: Integrating the Biological, Cognitive, and Social Dimensions of Life into a Science of Sustainability.* New York, NY: Doubleday, a Division of Random House, Inc.

Chah, Ajahn. 2014. "What's What," *A Beginner's Guide to Meditation: Practical Advice and Inspiration from Contemporary Buddhist Teachers.* Edited by Rod Meade Sperry. Boston, MA: Shambhala Publications, Inc.

"Chaos Theory." *Wikipedia.* http://en.wikipedia.org/wiki/Chaos_theory accessed February 14, 2013.

Choksy, Jamsheed K. 1998. "Zoroastrianism," *How Different Religions View Death and Afterlife*. Edited by Christopher Jay Johnson and Marsha G. McGee. Philadelphia, PA: The Charles Press, Publishers, Inc.

Citro, Massimo. 2011. *The Basic Code of the Universe*. Rochester, VT: Park Street Press.

Cleary, Rev. Francis X., SJ. 1998. "Roman Catholicism," *How Different Religions View Death and Afterlife*. Edited by Christopher Jay Johnson and Marsha G. McGee. Philadelphia, PA: The Charles Press, Publishers, Inc.

Cleg, Brian. 2006. *The God Effect: Quantum Entanglement, Science's Strangest Phenomenon*. New York, NY: St. Martin's Griffin Press.

Braud, William. 2012. *Exploring the Universe: The Illustrated Guide to Cosmology*. Vivays Publishing Ltd.: http://vivays-publishing.com.

Clow, Barbara Hand. 1995. *The Pleiadian Agenda: A New Cosmology for the Age of Light*. Tera Thomas, ed. Sante Fe, NM: Bear & Co. Pub.

Cobo, Father Bernabe. 1990. *Inca Religion & Customs*. Trans. & edited Roland Hamilton. 2nd printing 1994, Austin, TX: University of Texas Press.

Coelho, Paulo. 1993. *The Alchemist*. Trans. by Alan R. Clarke, San Francisco, CA: HarperSanFrancisco, a Division of HarperCollins Publishers.

Cohen, Andrew. 2011. *Evolutionary Enlightenment: A New Path to Spiritual Awakening*. New York, NY: Select Books, Inc.

"Collective consciousness." *Wikipedia*. http://en.wikipedia.org/wiki/Cosmic_consciousness accessed January 4, 2014.

"Consciousness." The Institute of Noetic Sciences. http://noetic.org/about/what-are-noetic-sciences accessed March 16, 2014.

Cowan, Eliot. 1995. *Plant Spirit Medicine*. Newberg, OR: Swan-Raven & Co.

Coward, Harold, ed. 1997. *Life After Death in World Religions*. Maryknoll, NY: Orbis Books.

Cox, Brian and Jeff Forshaw. 2011. *The Quantum Universe (and why anything that can happen, does)*. Boston, MA: Da Capo Press, a member of the Perseus Books Group.

Cumes, Carol and Romulo Lizarraga Valencia. *Pachamama's Children*. St. Paul, MN: Llewellyn Pub., 1995.

Dalai Lama, HH, and Cutler, Howard C. 1998. *The Art of Happiness: A Handbook for Living*. New York, NY: Riverhead Books.

Dale, Cyndi. 2009. *The Subtle Body: An Encyclopedia of Your Energetic*

Anatomy. Boulder, CO: Sounds True Publishing.

Darwin, Charles. 1859. *The Origin of Species: Complete and Fully Illustrated.* Reprint 1976 edition, New York, NY: Gramercy Books, an imprint of Random House Value Publishing, a division of Random House, Inc., & Penquin Books.

_____. 1879. *The Descent of Man and Selection in Relation to Sex.* Penquin Classics, 2004 edition, New York, NY: Penquin Putnam, Inc.

Davies, Paul. 1988. *The Cosmic Blueprint: New Discoveries in Nature's Creative Ability to Order the Universe.* Templeton Foundation Press paperback 2004 edition, Philadelphia, PA: Templeton Foundation Press.

Davies, Paul and John Gribbin. 1992. *The Matter Myth: Dramatic Discoveries That Challenge Our Understanding of Physical Reality.* Simon & Schuster paperback 2007 edition, New York, NY: Simon & Schuster Paperback, a Division of Simon & Schuster.

Dawkins, Richard. 1989. *The Selfish Gene.* Scientific American Book Club, 2004. New York, NY: Oxford University Press.

Dealy, Glen Caudill. 1992. *The Latin Americans: Spirit & Ethos.* Boulder, CO: Westview Press.

Deutsch, David. 2011. *The Beginning of Infinity: Explanations that Transform the World.* New York, NY: Viking, a div. of Penguin Group (USA) Inc.

Devereux, Paul. 1992. *Earth Memory: Sacred Sites--Doorways into Earth's Mysteries.* St. Paul, MN: Llewellyn Pub.

Dowling, Leo W. and Eva S. Dowling. 1907. *The Aquarian Gospel of Jesus the Christ: The Philosophic and Practical Basis of the Religion of the Aquarian Age of the World and of the Church Universal.* Transcribed from The Book of God's Remembrance, known as The Akashic Records, by Levi. 54th printing, 2001, Marina del Rey, CA: DeVorss & Co.

Durkheim, Emile. 1912. *The Elementary Forms of Religious Life.* Translated by Carol Cosman. Introduction and abridgement by Mark S. Cladis, 2001, Oxford World Classics 2008 edition, New York, NY: Oxford University Press.

Drury, Nevill. 2002. *The Dictionary of the Esoteric.* 2004 edition, London: Watkins Publishing.

Easwaran, Eknath, trans. 1985. *The Bhagavad Gita.* Vintage Spiritual Classics 2000 edition, New York, NY: Vintage Books, Random House, Inc.

Edge, Hoyt. L. 1997. "Spirituality in the Natural and Social Worlds," *Body Mind Spirit: Exploring the Parapsychology of Spirituality.* Charles T.

Tart, ed. Charlottesville, VA: Hampton Roads Pub. Co.

Eisler, Riane. 1987. *The Chalice and The Blade: Our History, Our Future.* 1st HarperCollins Paperback 1988 edition, San Francisco, CA: HarperSanFrancisco, a Division of HarperCollins Publishers.

Eliade, Mircea. 1958. *Patterns in Comparative Religion.* Translated by Rosemary Sheed. Lincoln, NE: University of Nebraska Press, First Bison Books 1996 printing, New York, NY: Sheed & Ward.

Eliade, Mircea. 1957. *The Sacred and The Profane: The Nature of Religion.* Harcourt 1987 edition, New York, NY: Harvest Book, Harcourt, Inc.

Eliade, Mircea, Ioan P. Couliano, with Hillary S. Wiesner. 1991. *The HarperCollins Concise Guide to World Religions.* HarperCollins Paperback rpt. 2000 edition, New York, NY: HarperCollins.

Ellis, Laura. 1977. *Steps to Immortality.* Costa Mesa, CA: Manosophy, Inc.

"Etheric Body." *Wikipedia.* http://en.wikipedia.org/Energetic_body accessed 23 February 2013.

Farrer-Halls, Gill. 2000. *The Illustrated Encyclopedia of Buddhist Wisdom: A Complete Introduction to the Principles and Practices of Buddhism.* 1st Quest Books 2000 edition. Wheaton, IL: The Theosophical Publishing House & Godsfield Press.

"Family." *Wikipedia.* http://en.wikipedia.org/wiki/Family accessed May 16, 2014.

"Father." *Wikipedia.* http://en.wikipedia.org/wiki/Father accessed May 16, 2014.

Feynman, Richard. 1942. *Feynman's Thesis: A New Approach to Quantum Theory.* Laurie M. Brown, ed. *The Principle of Least Action in Quantum Mechanics.* Reprint 2006, New Jersey: World Scientific Publishing Co, Ltd.

_____. 1965. *The Character of Physical Law.* 1st MIT Press Paperback 1967 edition, Boston, MA: The MIT Press.

_____. 1985. *QED: The Strange Theory of Light and Matter.* 1st Princeton Science Library 1988 edition, Princeton, NJ: Princeton University Press.

Feynman, Richard P. and Steven Weinberg. 1987. *Elementary Particles and the Laws of Physics.* 1st Paperback 1999 edition, 10th printing 2008, New York, NY: Cambridge University Press.

Fideler, David. 1993. *Jesus Christ, Sun of God: Ancient Cosmology and Early Christian Symbolism.* Quest Books edition, Wheaton, IL: The Theosophical Publishing House.

Fischer, Norman. 2014. "Getting Started," *A Beginner's Guide to Meditation: Practical Advice and Inspiration from Contemporary Buddhist Teachers.* Edited by Rod Meade Sperry. Boston, MA: Shambhala

Publications, Inc.

Freke, Timothy and Peter Gandy. 1997. *The Hermetica: The Lost Wisdom of the Pharaohs.* 1st paperback 1999 edition, New York, NY: Jeremy P. Tarcher/Putnam, a member of Penquin Putnam, Inc.

Freud, Sigmund. 1949. *An Outline of Psycho-Analysis.* Translated by James Strachey, ed. Paperback 1989 edition, New York, NY: W. W. Norton & Company.

_____. 1961. *Civilization and Its Discontents.* Translated by James Strachey, ed. New York, NY: W. W. Norton & Company.

Gawain, Shakti. 1978. *Creative Visualization.* Mill Valley, CA: Whatever Pub.

_____. 1993. *The Path of Transformation: How Healing Ourselves Can Change the World.* Mill Valley, CA: Nataraj Pub.

Gerber, Richard. 1988. *Vibrational Medicine: New Choices for Healing Ourselves.* Santa Fe, NM: Bear and Co.

_____. 2000. *A Practical Guide to Vibrational Medicine: Energy Healing and Spiritual Transformation.* 1st Quill 2001 edition, New York, NY: HarperCollins Publishers, Inc.

George, Mike. 2000. *Discover Inner Peace: A Guide to Spiritual Well-Being.* San Francisco, CA: Chronicle Books.

Gilbert, Adrian and Maurice Cotterell. 1995. *The Mayan Prophecies: Unlocking the Secrets of a Lost Civilization.*, 1st Element Books, Ltd., 1996 edition, New York, NY: Barnes & Noble Books.

Glotzhober, Robert C. and Bradley T. Lepper. 1994. *Serpent Mound: Ohio's Enigmatic Effigy Mound.* Columbus, OH: Ohio Historical Society.

Glover, Jonathan, ed. 1976. *The Philosophy of Mind.* Reprint 1980, New York, NY: Oxford University Press.

Godwin, Malcolm. 1990. *Angels: An Endangered Species.* New York, NY: Simon and Schuster.

Gold, Peter. 1994. *Navajo & Tibetan Sacred Wisdom: The Circle of the Spirit.* Rochester, VT: Inner Traditions.

Goswami, Amit. 2001. *Physics of the Soul: The Quantum Book of Living, Dying, Reincarnation, and Immortality.* Charlottesville, VA: Hampton Roads Publishing Company, Inc.

Govindan, Marshal. 1991. *Babaji and the 18 Siddha Kriya Yoga Tradition.*4th Eastman 1996 edition, Quebec, Canada: Kriya Yoga Publications.

Grant, Campbell. 1978. *Canyon de Chelly: Its People and Rock Art.* Tucson, AZ: The University of Arizona Press.

Grattan, Brian. 1994. *Mahatma I & II: The I AM Presence.* Sedona, AZ: Light Technology Pub.

Gray, William G. 1991. *Growing The Tree Within: Patterns of the Unconscious*

Revealed by the Qabbalah. 1st Llewellyn 1991 edition, St. Paul, MN: Llewellyn Publications.

Greene, Brian R. 1999. *The Elegant Universe: Superstrings, Hidden Dimensions, and the Quest for the Ultimate Theory*. New York, NY: Vantage Books, div. of Random House, Inc.

_____. 2004. *The Fabric of the Cosmos: Space, Time, and The Texture of Reality*. 1st Vintage Books 2005 edition, New York, NY: Vintage Books, a Division of Random House, Inc.

_____. 2011. *The Hidden Reality: Parallel Universes and the Deep Laws of the Cosmos*. New York, NY; Alfred A. Knopf, a division of Random House, Inc.

Grof, Stanislav. 1985. *Beyond the Brain: Birth, Death and Transcendence in Psychotherapy*. New York, State University of New York Press.

_____. 1988. *The Adventure of Self--Discovery*. Albany, NY: State University of New York Press.

_____. 2006. *The Ultimate Journey: Consciousness and the Mystery of Death*. Ben Lomond, CA: Multidisciplinary Association for Psychedelic Studies (MAPS).

Grof, Stanislav, and Hal Zina Bennett. 1993. *The Holotropic Mind: The Three Levels of Human Consciousness and How They Shape our Lives*. New York: HarperCollins Pub.

Groom, A. 1952. *I Saw a Strange Land*. Sydney: Angus & Robertson.

Grosso, Michael. 1997. "The Parapsychology of God," *Body Mind Spirit: Exploring the Parapsychology of Spirituality*. Charles T. Tart, ed. Charlottesville, VA: Hampton Roads Pub. Co.

Guthrie, Kenneth Sylvan and David Fideler, eds. 1987. *The Pythagorean Sourcebook and Library*. Grand Rapids, MI: Phanes Press.

Haisch, Bernard. 2006. *The God Theory: Universes, Zero-Point Fields, and What's Behind It All*. San Francisco, CA: Weiser Books, Red Wheel/Weiser, LLC.

Hall, Manly P. 1928. *The Secret Teachings of All Ages: An Encyclopedic Outline of Masonic, Hermetic, Qabbalistic and Rosicrucian Symbolical Philosophy*. First Trade Paperback 2003 edition, New York, NY: Jeremy P. Tarcher/Putnam, a member of Penguin Group (USA), Inc.

Hancock, Graham. 1995. *Fingerprints of the Gods*. New York, NY: Three Rivers Press, a member of Crown Publishing Group, Random House, Inc.

Hancock, Graham and Robert Bauval. 1996. *The Message of the Sphinx: A Quest for the Hidden Legacy of Mankind*. New York, NY: Crown Publishers, Inc., a member of Group Publishing Group.

Hanh, Thich Nhat. 2014. "Getting Grounded through Walking

Meditation," *A Beginner's Guide to Meditation: Practical Advice and Inspiration from Contemporary Buddhist Teachers*. Edited by Rod Meade Sperry. Boston, MA: Shambhala Publications, Inc.

Harner, Michael. 1980. *The Way of the Shaman*. Harper & Row paperback 3rd edition, 1990, New York, NY: HarperCollins Publishers.

Hastings, Arthur C. 1997. "Channeling and Spiritual Teachings," *Body, Mind, Spirit: Exploring the Parapsychology of Spirituality*. Charles T. Tart, ed. Charlottesville, VA: Hampton Roads Publishing Company, Inc.

Hawking, Stephen. 1988. *A Brief History of Time*. 10th rev. edition, 1998, New York, NY: Bantam Books.

_____. 2001. *The Universe in a Nutshell*. New York, NY: Bantam Books.

Hawking, Stephen and Leonard Mlodinow. 2010. *The Grand Design*. New York, NY: Bantam Books.

"Heartfulness." *Wikipedia*. http://en.wikipedia.org/wiki/Heartfulness accessed April 26, 2014.

"Heaven." *Wikipedia*. http://en.wikipedia.org/wiki/Heaven accessed June 8, 2013.

Heide, Della May. 1983. *The Covenant Renewed*. 1st printing rev. 1995 edition, Los Gatos, CA: The Academy for Future Science.

Hemming, John. 1970. *The Conquest of the Incas*. New York, NY: Harvest Book, Harcourt Brace & Company.

Henderson, John S. 1981. *The World of the Ancient Maya*. 1st printing Cornell Paperbacks, 1983; 2nd edition, 1997. Ithaca, NY: Cornell University Press.

"Higgs boson." *Wikipedia*. http://en.wikipedia.org/wiki/Higgs_boson accessed November 24, 2013.

Hirschfelder, Arlene and Paulette Molin. 1992. *Encyclopedia of Native American Religions*. Updated 2000 edition, New York, NY: Checkmark Books, an imprint of Facts On File, Inc.

Holzer, Hans. 1994. *Life Beyond: Compelling Evidence for Past Lives and Existence After Death*. Chicago, IL: Contemporary Books, Aspera and Astra, Inc.

Holy Bible. 1886. New York, NY: American Bible Society.

Holy Bible: The Saint Joseph New Catholic Edition. 1962. Fine Art edition, NY: Catholic Book Pub.

Howe, Linda with Juliette Looye. 2009. *How to Read the Akashic Records: Accessing the Archive of the Soul and Its Journey*. Boulder, CO: Sounds True.

Hurtak, J. J. 1975. *An Introduction To The Keys of Enoch*. 3rd edition, 1988, 4th printing, 1994, Los Gatos, CA: The Academy For Future Science.

_____. 1977. *The Book of Knowledge: The Keys of Enoch.* 4th edition, 1996, Los Gatos, CA: The Academy of Future Science.

_____. 1983. *The Lord's Prayer: An Exposition of The Scroll of Matthew 6:9-13.*Los Gatos, CA: The Academy For Future Science.

Hurtak, James J. 1990. *Our Higher Heritage: The Significance Of The Holy Scriptures.* Los Gatos, CA: The Academy For Future Science.

Hurtak, J. J. and Desiree Hurtak. 1996. *The Five Bodies: An Explanation Of The Five Light Energy Bodies.* Los Gatos, CA: The Academy For Future Science.

Huxley, Aldous. 1945. *The Perennial Philosophy.* 1946 edition, London: Chatto & Windus.

Ingram, Julia and G. W. Hardin. 1997. *The Messengers: A True Story of Angelic Presence and the Return to the Age of Miracles.* New York: Pocket Books.

Iyengar, B. K. S. 2001. *Yoga: The Path to Holistic Health.* New York, NY: Dorling Kindersley Pub.

Jahnke, Roger. 2002. *The Healing Promise of Qi: Creating Extraordinary Wellness Through Qigong and Tai Chi.* New York, NY: Contemporary Books.

James, William. 1902. *The Varieties of Religious Experience: A Study in Human Nature.* Forgotten Books 2008 edition, http://www.forgottenbooks.org.

Jaskolski, Helmut. 1997. *The Labyrinth: Symbol of Fear, Rebirth, and Liberation.* Boston, NY: Shambhala Publications, Inc.

Jauregui, Ann. 2007. *Epiphanies: Where Science and Miracles Meet.* New York, NY: Atria Books, Beyond Words Publishing, a division of Simon & Schuster.

Jenkins, John Major. 2002. *Galactic Alignment: The Transformation of Consciousness According to Mayan, Egyptian, and Vedic Traditions.* Rochester, VT: Bear & Company, a division of Inner Traditions International.

Johnson, Christopher Jay and Marsha G. McGee, editors. 1998. *How Different Religions View Death and Afterlife.* 2nd edition, Philadelphia, PA: The Charles Press.

Jones, Marie D. 2007. *PSIence: How New Discoveries in Quantum Physics and New Science May Explain the Existence of Paranormal Phenomena.* Franklin Lakes, NJ: New Page Books, a Division of The Career Press, Inc.

Jones, Marie D. 2011. *Destiny vs. Choice: The Scientific and Spiritual Evidence Behind Fate and Free Will,* Pompton Plains, NJ: Career Press Inc., New Page Books.

Jones, Timothy. 1994. *Celebration of Angels.* Nashville, TN: Thomas

Nelson Pub.

Jordan, Michael. 1993. *Encyclopedia of the Gods: Over 2,500 Deities of the World.* New York, NY: Facts of Life, Inc.

Joy, W. Brugh. 1979. *Joy's Way. A Way for the Transformational Journey: An Introduction to the Potentials for Healing with Body Energies.* Los Angeles, CA: Jeremy P. Tarcher, Inc.

Judith, Anodea. 1987. *Wheels of Life.* 1st edition, 1994 reprint, St. Paul, MN: Llewellyn Pub.

_____. 1999. *Wheels of Life.* 2nd edition, 2000 reprint, St. Paul, MN: Llewellyn Pub.

Juergensmeyer, Mark, ed. 2003. *Global Religions, An Introduction.* New York, NY: Oxford University Press.

Juergensmeyer, Mark. 2008. *Global Rebellion: Religious Challenges to the Secular State, from Christian Militias to Al Qaeda.* Berkeley, CA: University of California Press.

Kaku, Michio. 1994. *Hyperspace: A Scientific Odyssey Through Parallel Universes, Time Warps, and the 10th Dimension.* 1st Anchor Books 1995 edition, New York, NY: Anchor Books, a Division of Random House, Inc.

_____. 2005. *Parallel Worlds: A Journey Through Creation, Higher Dimensions, and the Future of the Cosmos.* New York, NY: Doubleday, a div. of Random House.

Kalweit, Holger. 1984. *Dreamtime & Inner Space: The World of the Shaman.* Translated by Werner Wunsche, 1988, Boston, MA: Shambhala Publications, Inc.

_____. 1992. *Shamans, Healers, and Medicine Men.* Translated by Michael H. Kohn. Boston, MA: Shambhala.

Kang, K. Connie. "In survey, heaven's way up there: 78 percent of Americans believe in eternal place; most think they're deserving," *Denver Post*, October 24, 2003.

Kant, Immanuel. 1959. *Foundations of the Metaphysics of Morals.* Intro. and translated by Lewis White Beck. 22nd printing, 1981, Indianapolis, IN: Bobbs-Merrill Company, Inc.

Kelley, Craig L. 2013. *Messages from Jesus and the Transpersonal Realms: Journals of Out--of--Body Experiences, Akashic Record Readings, Past Life Regressions and Apparitions.* Charleston, SC: On-Demand Publishing, LLC.

Kerle, J. A. 1995. *Uluru, Kata, Tjuta and Watarrka.* Sydney, Australia: University of New South Wales Press.

"Kinesiology." *Wikipedia.* http://en.wikipedia.org/wiki/Kinesiology accessed April 26, 2014.

King, Peter J. 2004. *One Hundred Philosophers: The life and work of the world's greatest thinkers*. Quarto Books 2004 edition, Hauppauge, NY: Quarto, Inc., & Barron's Educational Series, Inc.

Klein, Anne C. 1998. "Buddhism," *How Different Religions View Death and Afterlife*. Christopher Jay Johnson and Marsha G. McGee, eds. 2nd edition, Philadelphia, PA: The Charles Press, Publishers, Inc.

Kornfield, Jack. 2014. "A Mind Like Sky," *A Beginner's Guide to Meditation: Practical Advice and Inspiration from Contemporary Buddhist Teachers*. Edited by Rod Meade Sperry. Boston, MA: Shambhala Publications, Inc.

Kubler-Ross, Elisabeth. 2008. *On Life after Death*. Berkeley, CA: Celestial Arts, an imprint of Ten Speed Press.

Lama Surya Das. 1997. *Awakening The Buddha Within: Eight Steps to Enlightenment; Tibetan Wisdom for the Western World*. 1st edition, 1997, New York, NY: Broadway Books, a division of Bantam Doubleday Dell Publishing Group, Inc.

Lamsa, George, trans. 1939. *Gospel Light*. 1999 edition, Covington, GA: Aramaic Bible Society, Inc.

Lanza, Robert, with Bob Berman. 2009. *Biocentrism: How Life and Consciousness are the Keys to Understanding the True Nature of the Universe*. Dallas, TX: Benbella Books, Inc.

Laszlo, Ervin. 2003. *The Connectivity Hypothesis: Foundations of an Integral Science of Quantum, Cosmos, Life, and Consciousness*. New York, NY: State University of New York Press.

_____. 2004. *Science and the Akashic Field: An Integral Theory of Everything*. Rochester, VT: Inner Traditions.

_____. 2006. *Science and the Reenchantment of the Cosmos: The Rise of the Integral Vision of Reality*. Rochester, VT: Inner Traditions.

_____. 2006. *The Chaos Point: The World at the Crossroads*. Charlottesville, VA: Hampton Roads Publishing Co., Inc.

_____. 2008. *Quantum Shift in the Global Brain: How the New Scientific Reality Can Change Us and Our World*. Rochester, VT: Inner Traditions.

_____. 2009. *The Akashic Experience: Science and the Cosmic Memory Field*. Rochester, VT: Inner Traditions.

Lawlor, Robert. 1991. *Voices of the First Day: Awakening in the Dreamtime*. Rochester, VT: Inner Traditions.

Leadbeater, C. W. 1986. *Freemasonry and Its Ancient Mystic Rites*. Gramercy Books 1998 edition, an imprint of Random House Value Publishing, div. of Random House, Inc., New York, NY: Theosophical Publishing House.

Levi. 1907. *The Aquarian Gospel of Jesus the Christ: The Philosophical and Practical Basis of the Religion of the Aquarian Age of the World and the*

Church Universal. Trans. from the Book of God's Remembrance, known as the Akashic Records, intro. by Eva S. Dowling, 1935, 1964, fifty-fourth printing, 2001, Marina del Ray, CA: DeVorss & Company Publisher.

Leviton, Richard. 2002. *The Galaxy on Earth: A Traveler's Guide to the Planet's Visionary Geography.* Charlottesville, VA: Hampton Roads Publishing Company, Inc.

Lewis, C. S. 2005. *Made for Heaven and Why on Earth it Matters.* New York, NY: HarperSanFrancisco, a Division of HarperCollins Publishers.

Lewis, C. S. 2005. *Paved with Good Intentions: A Demon's Road Map to Your Soul.* New York, NY: HarperSanFrancisco, a Division of HarperCollins Publishers.

Lewis, C. S. 2005. *What Christians Believe.* New York, NY: HarperSanFrancisco, a Division of HarperCollins Publishers.

Lewis, James R. and Evelyn Dorothy Oliver. 2002. *Angels A to Z*, Kelle S. Sisung, editor. Canton, MI: Visible Ink Press.

Lipton, Bruce. 2005. *The Biology of Belief: Unleashing the Power of Consciousness, Matter, & Miracles.* Santa Rosa, CA: Mountain of Love/Elite Books.

"List of Religious Population." *Wikipedia.* http://en.wikipedia.org/wiki/List_of_religious_populations accessed May 19, 2007.

Littleton, C. Scott, editor. 2002. *Mythology: The Illustrated Anthology of World Myth and Storytelling.* London, England: Duncan Baird Publishers.

Long, Barry. 1984. *The Origins of Man and the Universe.* Revised 1998 edition, 2001 reprint, London, England: Barry Long Books.

Lumbreras, Luis G. 1974. *The Peoples and Cultures of Ancient Peru.* Translated by Betty J. Meggers. Smithsonian Institution Press.

Macalintal, Diana. 2006. "Christian Initiation of Adults: Rites of Acceptance," St. Columba Catholic Parish 2009 pamphlet, macalintal@dsj.org.

Machiavelli, Niccolo. 1940. *The Prince and The Discourses.* Intro., Max Lerner. The Modern Library, Inc., New York, NY: Random House, Inc.

Mails, Thomas E. 1997. *The Hopi Survival Kit.* Welcome Rain Pub.

Mair, Victor H., trans. 1990. Tzu, Lao. 1998. *Tao Te Ching.* Originally by Lao Tzu. Introduction by Huston Smith, 1998. Quality Paperback Book Club 1998 edition, Book-of-the-Month Club, Inc., 1998, New York, NY: Bantam Doubleday Dell Publishing Group, Inc.

"Mansonia," *UrantiaBook.org.* Broomfield, CO: The Urantia Book

Fellowship. http://www.urantiabook.org/newbook/glossary.htm accessed June 4, 2012.

Marciniak, Barbara. 1992. *Bringers of the Dawn: Teachings from the Pleiadians.* Santa Fe, NM: Bear & Co.

Marciniak, Barbara, Karen Marciniak, and Tera Thomas. 1994. *Earth: Pleiadian Keys to the Living Library.* Santa Fe, NM: Bear & Co.

"Marijuana." *Wikipedia.* http://en.wikipedia.org/wiki/Marijuana accessed May 13, 2014).

"Marriage laws." *Wikipedia.* http://en.wikipedia.org/wiki/Marriage_laws accessed May 16, 2014.

Marshall, George N. 1998. "Unitarian Universalism," *How Different Religions View Death and Afterlife.* Christopher Jay Johnson and Marsha G. McGee, eds. 2nd edition, Philadelphia, PA: The Charles Press.

Matt, Daniel C. 1995. *The Essential Kabbalah: The Heart of Jewish Mysticism.* Introduction by Huston Smith, 1998. Quality Paperback Book Club 1998 edition, Book-of-the-Month Club, Inc., 1998, New York, NY: HarperSanFrancisco, a division of HarperCollins Publishers, Inc.

McDannell, Colleen and Bernhard Lang. 1988. *Heaven: A History.* 2nd edition, 2001, New Haven, CT: Yale University Press.

McIntosh, Steve. 2012. *Evolution's Purpose: An Integral Interpretation of the Scientific Story of Our Origins.* New York, NY: Select Books, Inc.

McLeod, Melvin. 2014. "Basic Breath Meditation," *A Beginner's Guide to Meditation: Practical Advice and Inspiration from Contemporary Buddhist Teachers.* Edited by Rod Meade Sperry. Boston, MA: Shambhala Publications, Inc.

McNab, David, and James Younger. 1999. *The Planets.* New Haven, CT: Yale University Press.

McTaggart, Lynn. 2002. *The Field: The Quest for the Secret Force of the Universe.* New York, NY: HarperCollins Pub.

McTaggart, Lynn. 2007. *The Intention Experiment: Using Your Thoughts to Change Your Life and the World.* New York, NY: Free Press.

Measuring the Immeasurable: The Scientific Case for Spirituality. Numerous contributing authors. Boulder, CO: Sounds True, Inc., 2008.

Melton, J. Gordon. 2008. *The Encyclopedia of Religious Phenomena.* Canton, MI: Invisible Ink Press.

Metaphysical Bible Dictionary. 1931. Charles Fillmore Reference Library, 18th printing, 2005, Unity Village, MO: Unity House.

Metzner, Ralph. 2010. *The Unfolding Self: Varieties of Transformative Experience.* Earlier version 1st published by J. P. Tarcher as *Opening to Inner Light* and by Origin Press, 1986. Ross, CA: Pioneer Imprints.

Meurois-Givaudan, Anne and Daniel. 1993. *The Way of the Essenes: Christ's Hidden Life Remembered*. Rochester, VT: Destiny Books.

Meyer, Marvin, ed. 2007. *The Nag Hammadi Scriptures: The Revised and Updated Translation of Sacred Gnostic Texts*. HarperCollins Paperback 2008 edition, New York, NY: HarperCollins Publishers.

McClure, Janet, ed. 1990. *Sanat Kumara: Training a Planetary Logos*. Vywamus, channeled by Janet McClure. Youngtown, AZ: The Tibetan Foundation; Sedona, AZ: Light Technology Pub.

Milanovich, Norma J. and Shirley D. McCune. 1997. *The Light Shall Set You Free*. Albuquerque, NM: Athena Publishing.

Miller, Barbara Stoler, trans. 1998. *The Bhagavad-Gita: Krishna's Counsel in Time of War*. Introduction by Huston Smith, 1998, English trans. Miller, 1986, Quality Paperback Book Club 1998 edition, Book-of-the-Month Club, Inc., 1998, New York, NY: Bantam Doubleday Dell Publishing Group, Inc.

Millman, Dan. 1993. *The Life You Were Born to Live*. Tiburon, CA: H. J. Kramer.

Mindell, Arnold. 1993. *The Shaman's Body: A New Shamanism for Transforming Health, Relationships, and the Community*. San Francisco, CA: HarperSanFrancisco.

"Mindfulness." *Wikipedia*. http://en.wikipedia.org/wiki/Mindfulness accessed May 1, 2014.

Mishlove, Jeffrey. 1997. "Intuition: A Link Between Psi and Spirituality," *Body Mind Spirit: Exploring the Parapsychology of Spirituality*. Charles T. Tart, ed. Charlottesville, VA: Hampton Roads Pub. Co.

Monroe, Robert A. 1971. *Journeys Out of the Body*. New York, NY: Bantam Doubleday Dell Pub. Group.

Moody, Raymond A., Jr. 1975. *Life After Life: The Investigation of a Phenomenon--Survival of Bodily Death*. 2001 edition, HarperSanFrancisco, a Division of HarperCollins Publishers, New York, NY: HarperCollins.

Moody, Raymond A. 1975. *Life After Life*. Covington, Georgia: Mockingbird Books, New York, NY: Guideposts.

Moody, Raymond A. 1977. *Reflections on Life After Life*. Covington, Georgia: Mockingbird Books, New York, NY: Guideposts.

Moody, Raymond A. 1988. *The Light Beyond*. Paperback ed., 1989. New York, NY: Bantam Books.

Moore, Thomas. 2002. *The Soul's Religion: Cultivating a Profoundly Spiritual Way of Life*. New York, NY: HarperCollins Publishers, Inc.

227

Morgan, Marlo. 1991. *Mutant Message, Down Under.* 1st HarperPerennial 1995 edition, New York, NY: HarperPerennial, a Division of HarperCollins Publishers.

Mullins, Larry and Meredith Justin Sprunger. 2000. *A History of the Urantia Papers.* Boulder, CO: Penumbra Press.

Murakami, Kazuo. 2006. *The Divine Code of Life: Awaken your genes & discover hidden talents.* Cathy Hirano, trans. Hillsboro, OR: Beyond Words Publishing, Inc.

Murphet, Howard. 1971. *Sai Baba, Man of Miracles.* 1st American paperback edition, 1990 reprint, York Beach, Maine: Samuel Weiser, Inc.

Murphet, Howard. 1977. *Sai Baba, Avatar: A New Journey Into Power and Glory.* San Diego, CA: Birth Day Publishing Company.

Myss, Caroline. 1996. *Anatomy of the Spirit: The Seven Stages of Power and Healing.* New York: Harmony Books.

Nelson, Martia. 1993. *Coming Home: The Return to True Self.* 2nd edition, 1993, Novato, CA: Nataraj Publishing.

Nelson's NKJV Study Bible. 1997. New King James Version, Nashville, TN: Nelson Bibles, a div. of Thomas Nelson Publishers.

Newton, Michael. 2000. *Destiny of Souls: New Case Studies of Life Between Lives.* St. Paul, MN: Llewellyn Pub.

_____. 2000. *Journey of Souls*: Case Studies of Life between Lives.5th revised edition, 1994, St. Paul, MN: Llewellyn Pub.

Nichoson, Shirley. 1987. *Shamanism: An Expanded View of Reality.* 1st Quest edition, 4th printing, 1993, Wheaton, IL: Theosophical Pub. House.

Nietzsche, Friedrich. 1956. *The Birth of Tragedy* (1872) and *The Genealogy of Morals* (1887). Translated by Francis Golffing. Anchor Books edition, Garden City, NY: Doubleday & Company, Inc.

"Noetic Sciences," Institute of Noetic Sciences (IONS). http://noetic.org/about-what-are-noetic-sciences accessed March 16, 2014.

Null, Gary. 2005. *Mind Power.* New York, NY: New American Library, a division of Penguin Group (USA), Inc.

Osis, Karlis. 1997. "Phenomena Suggestive of Life After Death: A Spiritual Existence," *Body Mind Spirit: Exploring the Parapsychology of Spirituality.* Charles T. Tart, ed. Charlottesville, VA: Hampton Roads Pub. Co.

Pearce, Joseph Chilton. 2002. *The Biology of Transcendence: A Blueprint of the Human Spirit.* Rochester, VT: Park Street Press, division of Inner Traditions.

_____. 2002. *The Crack in the Cosmic Egg: New*

Constructs of Mind and Reality. Rochester, VT: Park Street Press, division of Inner Traditions.

Pearson, Anne Mackenzie. 1998. "Hinduism," *How Different Religions View Death and Afterlife.* Christopher Jay Johnson and Marsha G. McGee, eds. 2nd edition, Philadelphia, PA: The Charles Press, Publishers.

Peirce, Penny. 2009. *Frequency: The Power of Personal Vibration.* New York, NY: Atria Books, a Division of Simon & Schuster, Inc., and Beyond Words.

Penelhum, Terence. 1977. "Christianity," *Life After Death in World Religions.* Harold Coward, ed. Maryknoll, NY: Orbis Books.

Penrose, Roger. 2004 *The Road to Reality: A Complete Guide to the Laws of the Universe.* 1st Vintage Books 2007 edition, New York, NY: Vintage Books, a Division of Random House, Inc.

_____. 2010. *Cycles of Time: An Extraordinary New Vie w of the Universe.* New York, NY: Borzoi Book by Alfred A. Knopf, div. of Random House, Inc.

"Personality." *Wikipedia.* http://en.wikipedia.org/wiki/Personality accessed May 3, 2014).

Phipps, Carter. 2012. *Evolutionaries: Unlocking the Spiritual and Cultural Potential of Science's Greatest Idea.* New York, NY: HarperCollins Pub.

Pinchbeck, Daniel. 2006. *2012: The Return of Quetzalcoatl.* New York, NY: Jeremy P. Tarcher/Penguin Group (USA).

Ponn, Rabbi Alan L. 1998. "Judaism," *How Different Religions View Death and Afterlife.* Christopher Jay Johnson and Marsha G. McGee, eds. 2nd edition, Philadelphia, PA: The Charles Press.

Prophet, Elizabeth Clare. 1986. *Saint Germain on Prophecy: Coming World Changes.* Livingston, MT: Summit Univ. Press.

Prophet, Mark L. and Elizabeth Clare Prophet. 2003. *The Masters and their Retreats.* Corwin Springs, MT: Summit University Press.

Radin, Dean. 1997. *The Conscious Universe: The Scientific Truth of Psychic Phenomena.* New York, NY: HarperOne, HarperCollins Publishers.

Radin, Dean. 2006. *Entangled Minds: Extrasensory Experiences in a Quantum Reality.* New York, NY: Parview Pocket Books, Pocket Books, a Division of Simon & Schuster.

Rao, K. Ramakrishna. 1997. "Some Reflections on Religion and Anomalies of Consciousness." *Body Mind Spirit: Exploring the Parapsychology of Spirituality.* Charles T. Tart, ed. Charlottesville, VA: Hampton Roads Pub. Co.

Rambachan, Anantanand. 1997. "Hinduism," *Life After Death in World Religions.* Harold Coward, ed. Maryknoll, NY: Orbis Books.

Rice, Anne. 2005. *Christ The Lord: Out of Egypt.* New York, NY: Alfred

A. Knopf, Random House, Inc.

Ridley, Matt. 1999. *Genome: The Autobiography of a Species in 23 Chapters.* Perennial 2000 edition, New York, NY: HarperCollins Pub.

Ring, Kenneth and Evelyn Elsaesser Valarino. 1998. *Lessons From the Light: What we can learn from the near-death experience.* First Moment Point Press paperback 2000 edition, Needham, MA: Moment Point Press, Inc.

Rinpoche, Chogyam Trungpa. 2014. "The Four Foundations of Mindfulness, *A Beginner's Guide to Meditation: Practical Advice and Inspiration from Contemporary Buddhist Teachers.* Edited by Rod Meade Sperry. Boston, MA: Shambhala Publications, Inc.

Roberts, Arthur O. 1998. "A Quaker Perspective," *How Different Religions View Death and Afterlife.* Johnson, Christopher Jay Johnson and Marsha G. McGee, eds. 2nd edition, Philadelphia, PA: The Charles Press.

Roerich, Nicholas. 1990. *Shambhala: In Search of the New Era.* Rochester, VT: Inner Traditions Intl.

Roll, William G. 1997. "My Search for the Soul," *Body Mind Spirit: Exploring the Parapsychology of Spirituality.* Charles T. Tart, ed. Charlottesville, VA: Hampton Roads Pub. Co.

Rose, Ben Lacy. 1998. "Presbyterianism," *How Different Religions View Death and Afterlife.* Johnson, Christopher Jay Johnson and Marsha G. McGee, eds. 2nd edition, Philadelphia, PA: The Charles Press.

Rosenblum, Bruce and Fred Kuttner. 2006. *Quantum Enigma: Physics Encounters Consciousness.* Oxford University Press 2008 paperback edition, New York, NY: Oxford University Press.

Roth, Gabrielle and John Loudon. 1989. *Maps to Ecstasy: Teachings of an Urban Shaman.* Novato, CA: Nataraj Pub.

Russell, Jeffrey Burton. 1997. *A History of Heaven: The Singing Silence.* Princeton, NJ: Princeton University Press.

Russell, Peter. 2002. *From Science to God: A Physicist's Journey into the Mystery of Consciousness.* 2005 paperback edition, Novato, CA: New World Library.

Russell, Peter. 2007. *The Global Brain: The Awakening Earth in a New Century.* Floris Books.

Ryan, Charles J. 1937. *H. P. Blavatsky and the Theosophical Movement.* Revised 1975 edition, Pasadena, CA: Theosophical University Press.

Saddhatissa, H. 2013. *An Introduction to Buddhism.* Woodinville, WA: Atammayatarama Buddhist Monastery.

Salomon, Frank and George L. Urioste, trans. 1991. *The Huarochiri*

Manuscript: A Testament of Ancient and Colonial Andean Religion. Austin, TX: University of Texas Press.

Sanderfur, Glenn. 1988. *Lives of the Master: The Rest of the Jesus Story.* 4th printing, 1994, Virginia Beach, VA: A.R.E Press.

Saraydarian, Torkom. 1992. *New Dimensions in Healing and the Future.* Cave Creek, AZ: T.S.G. Publishing Foundation, Inc.

Satinover, Jeffrey. 2001. *The Quantum Brain: The Search for Freedom and the Next Generation of Man.* New York, NY: John Wiley & Sons, Inc.

Schlitz, Marilyn Mandala, Cassandra Vieten and Tina Amorok. 2007. *Living Deeply: The Art & Science of Transformation in Everyday Life.* Oakland, CA: New Harbinger Publications, Inc.

Schultes, Richard Evans and Albert Hofmann. 1992. *Plants of the Gods: Their Sacred, Healing and Hallucinogenic Powers.* Rochester, VT: Healing Arts Press.

Seife, Charles. 2006. *Decoding the Universe: How the New Science of Information is Explaining Everything in the Cosmos, from Our Brains to Black Holes.* New York, NY: Penquin Books, Penquin Group (USA), Inc.

_____. 2008. *Transcending the Speed of Light: Consciousness, Quantum Physics, and the Fifth Dimension.* Rochester, VT: Inner Traditions.

_____. 2011. *Where Does Mind End: A Radical History of Consciousness and the Awakened Self.* Rochester, VT: Park Street Press, a div. of Inner Traditions.

Shapiro, Eddie and Debbie, eds. 1998. *Voices From The Heart: Inspirations For A Compassionate Future.* 1st Trade Paperback 1999 edition, New York, NY: Jeremy P. Tarcher/Putnam, a member of Penguin Putnam, Inc.

Sharamon, Shalila and Bodo J. Baginski. 1991. *The Chakra Handbook.* Wilmot, VT: Lotus Light Pub.

Sharma, Arvind, ed. 1993. *Our Religions.* First HarperCollins Paperback 1995 edition, New York, NY: HarperCollins Publications.

Sharpe, Eric J. 1975. *Comparative Religion, A History.* 2nd edition, 2003, London: Gerald Duckworth & Co. Ltd.

Sheldrake, Rupert. 1981. *Morphic Resonance: The Nature of Formative Causation.* 4th revised 2009 edition, Rochester, VT: Park Street Press.

Sheldrake, Rupert. 1988. *The Presence of the Past: Morphic Resonance & The Habits of Nature.* 1995 edition, Rochester, VT: Park Street Press, div. of Inner Traditions, Inc.

Sherwood, Keith. 1995. *Chakra Therapy For Personal Growth & Healing.* St. Paul, MN: Llewellyn Pub.

Sieczka, Helmut G. 1994. *Chakra Breathing: Pathway to Energy, Harmony and Self-Healing.* Mendocino, CA: Life Rhythm.

Siegfried, Tom. 2002. *Strange Matters: Undiscovered Ideas at the Frontiers of Space and Time.* New York, NY: Berkley Books, The Berkley Publishing Group.

Singh, Kirpal. 1965. *Spirituality--What Is It?* Salt Lake City, UT: Kirpal Singh Memorial Library.

Sitchin, Zecharia. 1976. *The 12th Planet.* 1st Avon 1978 printing, New York, NY: Stein and Day Pub.

Sivananda Yoga Vedanta Center. 1996. *Yoga, Mind & Body.* New York: DK Pub.

Snow, Chet B. 1996. *Mass Dreams of the Future.* 1989; 2nd edition, 1993, 3rd reprint, Sedona, AZ: Deep Forest Press.

Salomon, Frank and George L. Urioste, trans. 1991. *The Huarochiri Manuscript: A Testament of Ancient and Colonial Andean Religion.* TX: University of Texas Press.

Spong, John Shelby. 2009. *Eternal Life: A New Vision Beyond Religion, Beyond Theism, Beyond Heaven and Hell.* 1st HarperCollins paperback 2010 edition, New York, NY: HarperOne of HarperCollins Publishers.

Stokes, Philip. 2002. *Philosophy 100 Essential Thinkers.* 2003 edition, New York, NY: Enchanted Lion Books.

Stone, Joshua David. 1994. *The Complete Ascension Manual: How to Achieve Ascension in this Lifetime.* Sedona, AZ: Light Technology Pub.

Stone, Joshua David. 1995. *Beyond Ascension: How to Complete the Seven Levels of Initiation.* Sedona, AZ: Light Technology Pub.

Subramuniyaswami, Satguru Sivaya. 1973. *Lemurian Scrolls: Angelic Prophecies Revealing Human Origins.* 2nd printing, 1998, Kapaa, Hawaii: Himalaya Academy.

Susskind, Leonard. 2006. *The Cosmic Landscape: String Theory and the Illusion of Intelligent Design.* 1st Back Bay paperback 2006 edition, New York, NY: Back Bay Books/Little, Brown and Company.

Susskind, Leonard and James Lindesay. 2005. *An Introduction to Black Holes, Information and the String Theory Revolution: The Holographic Universe.* Reprint 2006, New Jersey: World Scientific Publishing Co. Pte. Ltd.

Swan, James A. 1990. *Sacred Places: How the Living Earth Seeks Our Friendship* Santa Fe, NM: Bear & Co.

Swanson, Claude. 2003. *The Synchronized Universe: New Science of the Paranormal.* 2nd printing, 2005, Tuscan, AZ: Poseidia Press.

Swedenborg, Emanuel. 1984. *The Universal Human and Soul--Body Interaction.* Translated by George F. Dole, ed. *The Universal Human* extracted from Swedenborg's *Arcana Coelestia*, first published between 1747 and 1753, and *Soul--Body Interaction* in 1769. New York: Paulist Press.

Sykes, Bryan. 2001. *The Seven Daughters of Eve: The Science that Reveals our Genetic Ancestry.* New York, NY: W. W. Norton & Co., Inc.

Szekely, Edmond Bordeaux, trans. 1974. *The Gospel of the Essenes: The Unknown Book of Essenes & Lost Scrolls of the Essene Brotherhood.* 12th impression, 2000, Essex, England: Saffron Walden, C. W. Daniel Co. Ltd.

Talbot, Michael. 1992. *The Holographic Universe.* Hardcover 1991 edition, New York, NY: HarperPerennial, a div. of HarperCollins Publishers.

Tart, Charles T., ed. 1997. *Body Mind Spirit: Exploring the Parapsychology of Spirituality.* Charlottesville, VA: Hampton Roads Publishing Company, Inc.

Tart, Charles T. 1997. "On the Scientific Study of Nonphysical Worlds," *Body Mind Spirit: Exploring the Parapsychology of Spirituality.* Charles T. Tart, ed. Charlottesville, VA: Hampton Roads Pub. Co., 1997.

Tart, Charles T. 1997. "Who or What Might Survive Death," *Body Mind Spirit: Exploring the Parapsychology of Spirituality.* Charles T. Tart, ed. Charlottesville, VA: Hampton Roads Pub. Co., 1997.

Teilhard de Chardin, Pierre. 1959. *The Phenomenon of Man.* First published in French as *Le Phenomene Humain*, Paris, Editions du Seuil: 1955; Eng. trans. Wm. Collins Sons & Co, Ltd., 1959; New York, NY: Harper & Row, Publishers, Inc., 1965; Perennial edition, 2002 reprint, New York, NY: Perennial, an Imprint of HarperCollins Publishers.

Teilhard de Chardin, Pierre. 1999. *Pierre Teilhard de Chardin.* Maryknoll, NY: Orbis Books.

"Ten Commandments." *Wikipedia.* http://en.wikipedia.org/wiki/Ten_Commandments accessed November 24, 2013.

"Ten Commandments in Roman Catholicism." *Wikipedia.* http://en.wikipedia.org/wiki/Ten_Commandments_in_Roman_Catholicism accessed November 24, 2013.

The Book of Mormon. 1830. Intellectual Reserves, Inc. 1981 edition, Salt Lake City, UT: The Church of Jesus Christ of Latter-day Saints (Publishers).

The Concise Oxford Dictionary. 1999. Judy Pearsall, ed., 10th edition, New York, NY: Oxford University Press.

The Fatima Prophecy: Days of Darkness, Promise of Light. 1972. Austin, TX:

Association of the Understanding of Man.

The Holy Bible, New International Version (The NIV Study Bible). 1995, 10th ed., Grand Rapids, MI: Zondervan, 1973.

The Mystery of 2012: Predictions, Prophecies & Possibilities. 2007. Boulder, CO: Sounds True, Inc.

The Oxford Dictionary of World Religions. 1997. John Bowker, ed. New York, NY: Oxford University Press.

The Shambhala Dictionary of Buddhism and Zen. 1991. Translation by Michael Kohn. Boston, MA: Shambhala.

The Urantia Book. 1955. Leather edition, 2nd printing, 2001, and CD (electronic) version, Folio Bound Views, Version 3.1, Folio Corps, 1994, Chicago, IL: Urantia Foundation.

"The Urantia Book." *Wikipedia.* http://en.wikipedia.org/wiki/The_Urantia_Book accessed August 1, 2013.

Thoreau, Henry David. 1966. *Walden.* C. Merton Babcock, ed. White Plains, NY: Peter Pauper Press, Inc.

Thurman, Robert A. F., trans. 1998. *The Tibetan Book of the Dead.* Composed by Padma Sambhava. Intro. by Huston Smith, 1998, translation by Thurman, 1994. Quality Paperback Book Club 1998 edition, Book-of-the-Month Club, Inc., 1998, New York, NY: Bantam Doubleday Dell Publishing Group, Inc.

Tiller, William A. 2007. *Psychoenergetic Science: A Second Copernican-Scale Revolution.* Walnut Creek, CA: Pavior Publishing.

_____. 1997. *Science and Human Transformation: Subtle Energies, Intentionality and Consciousness.* Walnut Creek, CA: Pavior Publishing.

_____. Walter E. Dibble, Jr. and Michael J. Kohane. 2001. *Conscious Acts of Creation: The Emergence of a New Physics.* Walnut Creek, CA: Pavior Publishing.

Todeschi, Kevin J. 1998. *Edgar Cayce on the Akashic Records: The Book of Life.*4th reprint, 1999, Virginia Beach, VA: A.R.E. Press.

Torkelson, Jean. 2001. *Colorado's Sanctuaries, Retreats, and Sacred Places.* Englewood, CO: Westcliff Publishing, Inc.

Vallee, Martine, ed. 2009. *The Great Shift: Co-Creating a New World for 2012 and Beyond.* San Francisco, CA: Red Wheel/Weiser, LLC.

Villoldo, Alberto. 2000. *Shaman, Healer, Sage: How to Heal Yourself and Others with the Energy Medicine of the Americas.* New York, NY: Harmony Books.

_____. *Mending the Past and Healing the Future with Soul Retrieval.* Carlsbad, CA: Hay House, Inc.

_____. 2006. *The Four Insights: Wisdom, Power, and Grace of the Earthkeepers.* Carlsbad, CA: Hay House, Inc.

234

_____. 2007. *Yoga, Power, and Spirit: Patanjali the Shaman*. Carlsbad, CA: Hay House, Inc.

Villoldo, Alberto and Erik Jendresen. 1992. *Journey to the Island of the Sun: The Return to the Lost City of Gold*. San Francisco, CA: HarperSanFrancisco, 1992.

_____. 1995. *Dance of the Four Winds: Secrets of the Inca Medicine Wheel*. Rochester, VT: Destiny Books.

Villoldo, Alberto and Stanley Krippner. 1987. *Healing States: A Journey into the World of Spiritual Healing and Shamanism*. New York, NY: Fireside Book.

Walker, Evan Harris. 2000. *The Physics of Consciousness: Quantum Minds and the Meaning of Life*. Cambridge, MA: Perseus Pub.

Walker, Thomas. 2009. *The Force is with Us: The Higher Consciousness That Science Refuses to Accept*. Wheaton, IL: Quest Books, Theosophical Publishing House.

Walsch, Neale Donald. 1995. *Conversations with God: an uncommon dialogue; book 1*. Originally published by Hampton Roads Publishing Company, Inc., 1995. 1st Hardcover 1996 edition, New York, NY: G. P. Putnam's Sons.

_____. 1997. *Conversations with God: an uncommon dialogue; book 2*. Charlottesville, VA: Hampton Roads Publishing Company, Inc..

"Wat Buddhamongkolnimit." http://www.facebook.com/watbuddhamongkolnimit accessed March 17 2013.

Waters, Frank. 1963. *Book of the Hopi: The First Revelation of the Hopi's Historical and Religious Worldview of Life*. Reprint, 1977, New York, NY: Penguin Books.

Weber, Max. 1922. *The Sociology of Religion*. 1st pub. in Germany in 1922 by J. C. B. Mohr (Paul Siebeck) under the title "Religionssoziologie," from *Wirtschaft und Gesellschaft*; 4th ed., revised by Johannes Winckelmann, 1956 by J. C. B. Mohr (Paul Siebeck); Eng. trans. (from 4th ed.) by Ephraim Fischoff; 1963, 1991 by Beacon Press, Beacon Paperback 1964, Boston, MA: Beacon Press.

Weiss, Brian L. 1988. *Many Lives, Many Masters*. New York, NY: Simon & Schuster.

_____. 2000. *Messages from the Masters: Tapping into the Power of Love*, New York, NY: Warner Books, Inc.

_____. 2004. *Same Soul, Many Bodies*. New York, NY: Free Press.

Wexler, Alice. 1995. *Mapping Fate: A Memoir Of Family, Risk, And Genetic Research*. New York, NY: Times Books, a division of Random

House, Inc.

Whitaker, Kay Cordell. 1991. *The Reluctant Shaman: A Woman's First Encounters with the Unseen Spirits of the Earth.* New York, NY: HarperSanFrancisco.

White, Rhea A. 1997. "Exceptional Human Experiences and the Experiential Paradigm," *Body Mind Spirit: Exploring the Parapsychology of Spirituality.* Charles T. Tart, ed. Charlottesville, VA: Hampton Roads Pub. Co.

Wilcox, David. 2011. *The Source Field Investigations: The Hidden Science and Lost Civilizations behind the 2012 Prophecies.* New York, NY: Dutton, a div. of Penguin Group (USA) Inc.

Wilber, Ken. 1996. *The Atman Project: A Transpersonal View of Human Development,* 2nd Quest Books edition, Wheaton, IL: Theosophical Pub. House.

Wilkinson, Richard H. 2003. *The Complete Gods and Goddesses of Ancient Egypt.* London, England: Thames & Hudson, Ltd.

Wilson, Carl L., Walter E. Loomis, Taylor A. Steeves. 1971. *Botany,* 5th edition. New York, NY: Holt, Rinehart and Wilson.

Wise, Michael, Martin Abegg, Jr., and Edward Cook, trans. 1996. *The Dead Sea Scrolls: A New Translation.* New York, NY: HarperSanFrancisco, an Imprint of HarperCollins Pub., Inc.

Wolf, Fred Alan. 1991. *The Eagle's Quest: A Physicist's Search for Truth in the Heart of the Shamanic World.* New York: Touchstone.

_____. 1998. *Parallel Universes: The Search for Other Worlds.* New York, NY: Simon & Schuster Paperbacks.

_____. 1999. *The Spiritual Universe: One Physicist's Vision of Spirit, Soul, Matter, and Self.* Originally published in hardcover as *The Spiritual Universe: How Quantum Physics Proves the Existence of the Soul,* Simon & Schuster, 1996, Needham, MA: Moment Point Press, Inc.

_____. 2001 *Mind into Matter: A New Alchemy of Science and Spirit.* Needham, MA: Moment Point Press, Inc.

Wright, Machaelle Small. 1990. *MAP: The Co-Creative White Brotherhood Medical Assistance Program.* Warrenton, VA: Perelandra.

Yau, Shing-Tung and Steve Nadis. 2010. *The Shape of Inner Space: String Theory and The Geometry of the Universe's Hidden Dimensions.* New York, NY: Basic Books, a member of the Perseus Books Group.

Yogananda, Paramahansa. 1946. *Autobiography of a Yogi.* 12th edition, 12th paper-bound printing, 1993, Los Angeles, CA: Self-Realization Fellowship.

_____. 1975. *Man's Eternal Quest.* 2nd edition, 1982; 5th paperback printing, 1996, Los Angeles, CA: Self-Realization Fellowship.

Young, Jacqueline. 2001. *The Healing Path: The Practical Guide to the Holistic Traditions of China, India, Tibet, and Japan.* London, England: Duncan Baird Pub, (USA, Thorsons Pub).

Ywahoo, Dhyani. 1987. *Voices of Our Ancestors: Cherokee Teaching from the Wisdom Fire.* Boston: Shambhala.

Zukav, Gary. 1989. *The Seat of the Soul.* New York: Simon & Schuster.

About the Author

Craig Kelley has studied at numerous colleges and universities doing undergraduate work, most notably Northeastern University in Boston, and Florida International University (FIU) in Miami, Florida, where he was awarded a Bachelor of Business Administration (BBA) degree in 1985. He has done graduate studies at FIU in the MBA program, and many other diverse areas centered around theology: comparative religions; revelations; the esoteric, mysteries and mysticism; cosmology, astrology and astronomy; psychology, parapsychology, and transpersonal psychology; parallel worlds, multi-universes and superuniverses; physics, quantum theories, energy, and metaphysics; geology; physiology, anatomy, creation and evolution of *Homo sapiens.*

He has experienced some paranormal occurrences: out-of-body experiences; shamanically journeying out of body; experienced Kundalini rising; energetically healing others; experienced previous incarnations and deaths; done some past life regressions to previous lives (incarnations); worked with Peruvian shamans learning about our luminous body (energetic and soul), and the medicinal plants of the Amazon jungle of Peru.

And he has traveled around the globe seeking enlightenment (Mexico, Columbia, Peru, Australia, Singapore, Bali, Thailand) and may have found it.

Other published works include the following:

Messages from Jesus and the Transpersonal Realms: Journals of Out-of-Body Experiences, Akashic Record Readings, Past Life Regressions and Apparitions (2013).

How to Go to Heaven: An Esoteric Dictionary of Theology (2014).

How to Go to Heaven 2: According to Various Religions (2014).

***

www.ingramcontent.com/pod-product-compliance
Lightning Source LLC
Chambersburg PA
CBHW060244290526
45789CB00001B/183